WHAT THE BUTLER SAW

WHAT
THE BUTLER SAW

*Two hundred and fifty years
of the servant problem*

by E. S. TURNER

ST MARTIN'S PRESS
NEW YORK

CONTENTS

ILLUSTRATIONS

INTRODUCTION

THIS book deals with the last two-and-a-half centuries of a problem which has been with us since the human race began: the servant problem. There is no reason why the account should start with the eighteenth century and no reason why it should not.

Today only one British family in one hundred has a resident servant and in America the proportion is more like one in 250. A traditional servants' hall is an oddity to be sought out by television cameras. The question, 'Would you let your servants read this book?', asked by prosecuting counsel in the *Lady Chatterley* trial, aroused incontinent mirth. From which, it might seem that the servant problem has all but solved itself. In fact, it still greatly exercises that bloodied but unbowed world, that world of self-described gentlemen and gentlewomen, in which 'Venetia, aged four, and Christopher, six months, require services of kind-hearted, capable Nanny' or 'lady of refined tastes seeks chauffeuse-companion willing to work in house' or 'peer has vacancy for young footman willing travel between London and country house.' Equally, the servant problem continues to agitate the homes of professional men and women, the old, the invalid and the fertile. The rest of us do our own chores. In the process we try not to worry about the deterioration in our domestic habits which a sociologist has observed: 'The absence of resident domestic servants may partly account for the decline of formal behaviour in the middle-class home. The need to demonstrate social difference to inferiors in all matters of domestic life no longer exists.'[1]

The heyday of domestic service—though nobody at the time thought of it as a heyday—is an eye-opening time to look back upon; when a gentleman with £2000 a year was betraying

[1] Dennis Chapman: *The Home and Social Status.*

his class if he employed fewer than six women servants and five menservants; when middle-class ladies in their nineties could boast that they had never made a pot of tea in their lives; when a wealthy Englishman had a Frenchman to stir his soup, another Frenchman to comb his hair, an Italian to make his pastry and half a dozen Englishmen to iron his *Times*, and his wife had a Frenchwoman to powder her back and an Englishman to carry her prayer-book; and when the very proud could threaten instant dismissal to any housemaid who showed her face after midday.

Domestic service, society has always claimed, is an honourable estate. To be sure, some who took it up were cared for all their lives, honoured and even cosseted, and finally laid to rest in the family plot—possibly with a carved tribute 'Rare character in these degenerate days.' Others, the sad and often damp-souled majority, were exploited, snubbed, hectored and humiliated; and so, whenever a choice of occupation presented itself, they took it.

Sir Max Beerbohm said he would like to think that the improvement in servants' conditions came about through our sense of justice, but he could not claim that this was so. 'Somehow, our sense of justice never turns in its sleep till long after the sense of injustice in others has been thoroughly aroused. . . for the improvement in their lot, servants must, I am afraid, be allowed to thank themselves rather than their employers.'[1] He wrote that in 1918, since when servants have buried a good many more injustices. At no time was there a Florence Nightingale to fight their battles and raise their prestige.

In the hope of getting good and tractable servants, society tapped every source. It took labourers' daughters into service at nine, it raided the workhouses and orphanages, it bought black boys, it set up schools (reading and writing barred), it recruited distressed gentlewomen, it formed a Guild of Household Dames, it beckoned to demobilised soldiers, it opened training centres in distressed areas, it clutched at refugees from totalitarian states. Today society is importing girls, often on ambiguous terms, from Germany, Italy, France

[1] Quoted by S. N. Behrmann in *Conversation With Max*.

and Scandinavia; and there is even a periodical draft from
St Helena.

The word 'servant,' long in disgrace in America, is now little
used outside the Brigade of Guards. Those of us who employ
daily labour must do so on a basis of equality and beware of
seeming to give orders. Counsellors in such matters advise the
housewife not to say 'Clean out the dining-room' or even
'Please clean out the dining-room' but 'Let's clean out the
dining-room.' One of them says: 'If you can contrive to make
a little joke when pointing out something badly done, even the
most sensitive of "chars" will usually take it without offence.'
An example offered is: 'Notice how thin I've got since Thurs-
day? I suppose you thought I was putting on weight, and
that's why you hid the sugar where I couldn't find it.'[1] It is,
as everyone must agree, a grievous day when a mistress must
make jests like this.

Will the clock ever turn back? According to Dr Michael
Young, in that provocative book *The Rise of the Meritocracy*,
domestic service will be re-established by the century's end.
By then, roughly a third of all adults will be unemployable in
the ordinary economy, the complexities of civilisation having
become too much for them. For these waste products of the
secondary modern schools there will be no other outlet than
personal service in the homes of the more gifted, whose
energies will be released for higher things. This backward third
will be enrolled in a Home Helps Corps with fixed wages,
hours and conditions. Dr Young's vision supposes that the
'conditions fostering egalitarianism' will have passed away
by about AD 2000 and Jack will no longer consider himself as
good as his master. All this may, indeed, come to pass; but at
the moment the spirit of egalitarianism shows no sign of
withering.

How a similar spirit sharpened the servant problem in
America is told in these pages. If an American wanted help he
struck a bargain with another man who was prepared to offer
him work, but not servility, respect or affection; and no
question arose of putting this man into fancy breeches. Then
the age of millionaires came to America and English butlers

[1] Agnes M. Miall: *Modern Etiquette.*

were imported by the score, along with sets of footmen, and livery-spotting became a recreation on Fifth Avenue. Today our butlers still stream over the Atlantic, but they are younger men, often slim-waisted, only a shadow of those splendid figures, half-ambassador and half-tomcat, of fifty years ago; in Mr P. G. Wodehouse's words, 'butlers who weighed two hundred and fifty pounds on the hoof, butlers with three chins and bulging abdomens, butlers with large gooseberry eyes and that austere butlerine manner which has passed so completely away. . . .'[1] In the popular mind the manservant is degenerating into a mildly ludicrous figure who is occasionally seen feeding his master's parking meter and whose ultimate function is to write newspaper articles (if not legally restrained from doing so) about the shortcomings of his employers. In prestige he fights a losing battle with the British Nanny, who is an international status symbol, scrambled for by television comedians, property dealers, oil sheikhs and monarchs, ruling or deposed.

This book deals with all the members of the domestic hierarchy, but more especially with butlers, valets, footmen, coachmen, housekeepers, ladies' maids, cooks, nurses and housemaids. It does not include the governess, who may have been treated as a servant but was not one; in any event, a great deal has been written about her. Nor is it concerned with royal servants, a subject which the writer has already covered in *The Court of St James's*.

No one appears to have written a definitive history of domestic service, but D. M. Stuart's *The English Abigail* (1946) is an excellent study of maidservants and Lucy Maynard Salmon's *Domestic Service* (1901) traces the American background admirably.

[1] *Ring for Jeeves.*

I

INSUBORDINATION

O good old man! how well in thee appears
The constant service of the antique world,
When service sweat for duty, not for meed!
Thou art not for the fashion of these times,
Where none will sweat but for promotion ...
WILLIAM SHAKESPEARE: *As You Like It*

'Subordination tends greatly to human happiness.'
DR SAMUEL JOHNSON (Boswell)

AN ancient proverb said that England was 'the hell of horses, the purgatory of servants and the paradise of women.'

When the eighteenth century came in, England was still the hell of horses, but there were loud complaints that it had become the paradise of servants and the purgatory of women.

In almost any period of history, back to Confucius and beyond, it is possible to find the well-to-do sighing for 'the constant service of the antique world,' but in eighteenth-century England indignation against the new breed of servants was unusually shrill; and this was only in part due to the fact that there were now periodicals and newspapers in which anger could be ventilated.

What had gone wrong? For masses of men and women there was no work but domestic service. They sold their time to more fortunate masters, and these masters gave them food, shelter and pocket money. The system had descended, little changed, from feudal times and it suited an age which had not heard of egalitarianism. Master class and servant class were interdependent, linked by self-interest; in Alexis de

Tocqueville's words, they were 'two communities . . . super-posed one above the other, always distinct, but regulated by analogous principles,' each class hereditary, each reverencing formality and precedent in its own ranks, each with a disdain for inferiors.[1] The system had always existed and there was no reason to suppose that it would ever die out. It was all that saved men from starvation and women from prostitution.

Why, then, must servants defy the Great Law of Subordi-nation? Why were the erring so resentful of being caned and cuffed? Why must maids be for ever changing their places? Why should apprentices to shopkeepers and warehousemen refuse point-blank to wait on their masters at table? Why must servants object even to looking like servants and footmen grumble because the Earl Marshal of England would not let them wear swords?[2] Was there no way to stop housemaids conspiring to force up their wages to £8 a year and beyond? Why must they demand gratuities for every extra service? Why did they clamour for expensive tea and sugar when small beer was so much better for them?

It is possible to see it all now as a restless, transitional stage on the way from a rural to an industrial society, or even as a stage on the way from a feudal tyranny to the tyranny of the Victorian bourgeoisie. On all sides the old 'natural' relation-ships between master and man were snapping. At the time, the reasons for the insubordination of servants were difficult to assess, but it was possible to blame the trouble on any or all of these causes: the Civil War, which had broken up great households and scattered masters and servants alike; the wicked example of the Stuarts, who had debauched their own and everybody else's servants, infiltrating French pages and ladies' maids into Britain and spreading a love of extravagance, finery and liquor at all levels; the callousness of those masters and mistresses who had fled from London, abandoning their servants, in the Great Plague, leaving a legacy of bitterness; the folly of county families who went gadding up to London where they tried to maintain false standards of splendour instead of looking after their estates; the grasping spirit which

² This practice was banned in 1701, in the interest of public safety.

infused the new commercialism; the wastage of good servants
who set sail for America hoping to become their own masters
in the New World; and the habit of paying town servants board
wages, thus enabling them to frequent clubs and taverns where,
in Steele's words, 'they are but in a lower degree what their
masters are; and you have in liveries beaux, fops and coxcombs,
in as high perfection, as among people that keep equipages.'[1]

Lecky, one of the few historians to trouble himself with the
servant problem, blames 'the natural consequences of luxurious
and ostentatious habits upon a national character by no means
peculiarly adapted to domestic service.'[2] He points, also, to the
attendance by servants on their mistresses at scenes of fashionable dissipation, the system of vails (tips) which rendered
servants independent of their masters and the law which gave
servants of peers and Members of Parliament the same
immunity from debt enjoyed by their masters.

The new-found passion for speculation, as indulged on the
stock market, was also censured as a cause of England's servant
trouble. It was not only masters and mistresses who put their
hope in 'bubbles'; so did the footmen who stood behind their
chairs and listened to their talk.[3] The more ambitious of these
footmen were setting themselves up in business and a few, if
Swift is right, were buying commissions in the Army, having
learned by drawing-room observation how to behave like gentlemen.

It was chiefly in the cities, notably London, that the insolence
of servants was felt to be insufferable. The young men and
girls of the Metropolis had never shown much desire to enter
domestic service, regarding this as an occupation for simpletons
from the countryside. Such was the lure of the city that it
drew an inexhaustible supply, not only of simpletons, but of
the malcontent and the seduced from villages which had
become too hot for them. In London they were able to come
together in cabals for the oppression of their masters. At Bath,
where society jostled for accommodation, the servants also
held the whip hand.

[1] *Spectator*, No. 88 (1711).
[2] W. E. H. Lecky: *A History of England in the Eighteenth Century*.
[3] *Letters on the English Nation* (1755).

Although urban influences were beginning to taint the countryside, the servant problem in the villages was not nearly as acute as in the towns. The squire's house still drew a willing supply of labour from the near-by cottages and so did the rectory; without these sources of employment there would have been severe hardship in humble homes. Nor was it too difficult to find tractable staffs for the graceful manor-houses which had been springing up since Englishmen had ceased to break each other's skulls, though from time to time there were domestic difficulties which had not vexed earlier generations.

At the topmost level, that of the great families who lit beacons to announce births and laid their dead in mausoleums, the behaviour of servants was often intolerable; usually, because there were far too many of them with too little to do. Slowly, the dukes were cutting away some of their more parasitic retainers and scaling down the feudal style of living, but the more ostentatious of them continued to pattern their households on that of the Court. In his seat at Petworth, the Duke of Somerset treated his servants more royally than did the new Hanoverian kings. He allowed none to speak to him, communicating only by signs. When he set out in his carriage outriders scoured the roads to protect him from the gaze of common people. His dinner was announced ceremonially by an upper servant holding what resembled a bishop's crozier: (*forte*) 'MY LORD DUKE OF SOMERSET (*piano*) My Lord Duke of Somerset (*pianissimo*) My Lord Duke of Somerset—Your Grace's dinner is on the table.'[1] The elderly Duchess of Buckingham, described by Horace Walpole as 'more mad with pride than any mercer's wife in Bedlam,' exacted Court etiquette not only from her servants but from her friends; and on her deathbed she made her women promise that, though she lay senseless, they would not sit down until she was pronounced dead. At Dalkeith, in Scotland, the greatest heiress in the three kingdoms, the Duchess of Monmouth and Buccleuch, also lived in near-royal state. She, too, kept everyone standing in her presence, and when receiving guests she sat under a canopy. No letters were passed direct by inferiors to the Duchess; they had to go through the hands of the gentlewoman

[1] Philip Thicknesse: *Memoirs and Anecdotes*.

in waiting.[1] It was an adequate scale of living, some may have
thought, for one whose first husband, the Duke of Monmouth,
had been executed for treason.

Those noblemen who judged it prudent to abate a little of
their pomp sometimes began by dismissing the chaplain, an
economy which Bishop Burnet regretted because it meant that
the religious instruction of servants was thereby neglected;
he had to admit, however, that too many private chaplains had
been idle, insolent and pedantic.[2] When the century began
very few noblemen still accepted young men of good birth as
pages, to educate along with their own sons. The intimate
personal tasks once performed by sulky young gentlemen were
now carried out, more efficiently, by valets. Great ladies still
had gentlewomen about them, but increasingly their choice
was limited to those whose menfolk had lost their ships or
gambled away their birthrights; and these gentlewomen, while
sometimes willing to fill the office of housekeeper, objected to
doing work which came within the province of a lady's maid.

In all but the most overweening households, the high-
sounding offices copied from the Court were being abolished.
Chamberlains had been responsible for pomp and punctilio,
but their duties were now being discharged by the house
steward (sometimes, but not always, a man of good birth) and
the butler. The clerk of the kitchen vanished, his duties being
divided between the steward, the butler, a woman housekeeper
and the cook. Gentlemen ushers and all the other well-born
floor-walkers gave way to footmen. Unless the stables were of
exceptional size, there was no need of a master of the horse;
a head coachman sufficed.

The new hierarchy of servants took time to establish and it
was subject to endless permutations, but roughly the system
was this: in large houses, almost all servants, male and female,
were hired, disciplined and dismissed by the house steward,
who was less a servant than an agent, a factor or a secretary. He
had his own room in which the upper servants took their meals.
If there was no steward, hiring of menservants fell to the butler
and of women servants to the housekeeper, and it was in the

[1] Violet Biddulph: *Kitty, Duchess of Queensberry.*
[2] *History of His Own Time.*

housekeeper's room that the upper servants met. Personal
servants, like valets and ladies' maids, were engaged direct by
their masters and mistresses and were answerable only to them;
usually, too, a master engaged his own coachman and the
mistress chose her own nurse. In a big house, the servants fell
into five main groups: room, hall, kitchen, nursery and stables,
and each group tended to become a jealous community of its
own.

In small households, without steward, butler or housekeeper,
the master himself would engage a couple of menservants to do
the work of footmen, valets, gardeners and handymen, and
the mistress would engage the maids, who would be required
to cook, wash, clean the house, sew, spin and even milk cows.
Bachelors and maiden ladies might get along with a single
servant of all work, but a married couple who could afford only
one servant were low indeed in the social scale. Even country
parsons, like James Woodforde, often kept three or four
servants.

The duties and privileges of the various ranks are best
considered at a later stage, when a more clear-cut structure
has been established.

It is time to examine more closely the charges which were
being levelled against servants. Daniel Defoe, writing as
Andrew Moreton, Esq., with his tongue half-way to his cheek,
published in 1725 a pamphlet entitled *Everybody's Business Is
Nobody's Business, Or Private Abuses, Publick Grievances:
Exemplified In The Pride, Indolence, And Exorbitant Wages Of
Our Women Servants, Footmen etc.* This caught the public
fancy and ran through five editions in a few weeks. Much of the
pamphleteer's pique seems to have sprung from the fact that
he had the misfortune, when saluting the ladies at a house he
was visiting, to kiss the 'chamber-jade' by mistake, her dress
being so extravagant that she appeared to be one of the guests.
'I was soon undeceived by a general titter which gave me the
utmost confusion,' he laments. It was thanks to the enterprise of
'pert sluts' like this that the wages of women servants had been
forced up from 30s. or 40s. a year to £7 or £8, with the result
that an ordinary tradesman could scarcely afford to keep a

maid. A country girl might be engaged by a mistress for an agreed wage of £3. 'The girl has scarce been a week, nay a day, in her service but a committee of servant wenches are appointed to examine her, who advise her to raise her wages or give warning'; and in no time her leather shoes become 'laced with high heels,' her yarn stockings become worsted with silk clocks, her dress is stuck out with a hoop like that of her mistress, and she is rounding off the performance by drinking tea and taking snuff. In resorting to finery, she forces the wives and daughters of the family into extravagance, since it is a point of honour with them to 'go finer than the maid.'

The pamphleteer describes another error he committed, this time in the house of his sister, where he lavished a certain amount of politeness on a lady visitor only to find that she was a maid in search of a place. She demanded £8 a year with no washing, scouring, sewing or dressing of dinners. Her explanation was: 'If you wash at home, you should have a laundry-maid; if you give entertainment, you must have a cook-maid; if you have any needlework you should have a chambermaid; and such a house as this is enough for a housemaid in all conscience.' Laments Defoe: 'It is very hard that I must keep four servants or none.' Other grievances in his indictment include these: servants pillage their masters' possessions; they exact commissions from shopkeepers; they help themselves to tea, sugar, wine and meat; they entertain at their masters' expense; they treasure up the family's sayings to amuse others; they spoil children by their pert ways; and they employ idle, wicked boys to clean the boots and shoes, paying them in victuals 'which they carry to their trulls.'

Defoe proposes that wages should be fixed at from 40s. or 50s. a year to £4 or £5 according to service and skill; and that fixed-period contracts, instead of monthly engagements, should be drawn up before a justice of the peace. If the servant leaves through the employer's fault, then the master is to be reprimanded or fined. After a certain period a servant will be given a certificate of proficiency as is the custom in the woolcombing trade, and any servant not possessing one will be deemed a vagrant.

Also in 1725 Defoe published an anonymous pamphlet, *The*

Behaviour Of Servants Inquir'd Into, which advocates much sterner measures against offenders. He seems greatly exercised about the inability of servants to endure blows and curses without attempting to retaliate and tells of a man who demanded that he should be dismissed in order that he might sue a gentleman who had cursed him. His master pointed out: 'Your being an Englishman and having the right to the liberty of an Englishman does not make you equal to a gentleman.' Defoe proposes: 'If any menial servant should swear at or curse to his face their master or mistress, from whom they receive wages, or strike or offer to strike or threaten their said masters or mistresses they should upon legal conviction be transported for twenty-one years, not to be in the master's power to remit the sentence and the master not prosecuting to forfeit £500.' Merely to put a servant in the stocks, he says, is no use; all his footman friends from the alehouse will bring up chairs and ale, commiserate with him, curse their masters, and go away leaving their captive comrade too drunk to appreciate his shame.

If Defoe let his bad temper run away with him, Dean Swift probably allowed his sense of satire to do the same. His *Directions To Servants,* compiled over a long period of years, is a painstaking exercise in malice. Among the 'rules' he lays down are that a servant should do only the work for which he is hired; thus, if a groom is absent, a butler will decline to shut the stable door on the ground that he does not understand horses, and a footman, if asked to tack up a corner of the hanging, will refer his master to an upholsterer. Servants must cover up each other's absences, unless the absentee is the master's favourite, when he should be blamed for everything. No servant should answer the bell until it has been rung three or four times, 'for none but dogs will come at the first whistle.'

Swift's heaviest artillery is directed at the footman, 'the fine gentleman of the family with whom all the maids are in love.' Out of doors, he must be careful never to be seen carrying a basket or a bundle and do his utmost to avoid the indignity of lighting through the streets a master too mean to engage a lantern boy. 'If your master or mistress happens to walk the streets, keep on one side, and as much on the level with them

The pleasures of service

as you can, which people observing, will either think you do
not belong to them, or that you are one of their companions;
but, if either of them happen to turn back and speak to you,
so that you are under the necessity to take off your hat, use but
your thumb and one finger, and scratch your head with the rest.'

A footman sent on a message may stay out 'somewhat longer
than the message requires, perhaps, two, four, six or eight
hours or some such trifle.' It is therefore necessary to have a
good set of excuses. Suggested ones are: your uncle came four
score miles to town on purpose to see you; you heard that a
brother servant who borrowed money was running away to
Ireland; you were taking leave of an old fellow-servant going to
Barbados; your father sent you a cow to sell; you wrenched
your foot and had to spend three hours in a shop before you
could move; some nastiness was thrown on you from a window
and you were ashamed to come home until the smell had worn
off; you were pressed for the Navy and carried before a justice
of the peace and had trouble in getting away; a bailiff seized you
by mistake for a debtor; you were told your master had come
to mischance in a tavern so you called to look for him in a
hundred taverns between Pall Mall and Temple Bar.

The footman, says Swift, is the best judge of what acquaintance his lady ought to have; 'therefore, if she sends you on a
message of employment or business to a family you do not like,
deliver the answer in such a manner as may breed a quarrel
with them not to be reconciled; or, if a footman comes from
that same family on a like errand, turn the answers she orders
you to deliver in such a manner as the other family may take
it as an affront.'

If leaving the house only for a short period, 'to tattle with a
wench, or take a running pot of ale, or to see a brother footman
going to be hanged,' the considerate footman will leave the
street door open, to save the trouble of knocking to gain re-
admission, which would gain him the reputation of 'an idle,
rambling fellow.'

At table, the footman wears no socks, 'because as most
ladies like the smell of young men's toes, so it is a sovereign
remedy against the vapours'; he holds spare plates under his
armpit or tucks them between his waistcoat and his shirt; he

takes the chairs from behind the company during grace so that they fall on the floor, 'which will make them all merry'; and breaks lobster claws in the hinges of the dining-room door.

The footman will try not to grow old in his office, which is the highest of all indignities. 'Therefore when you find years coming on without hopes of a place at Court, a command in the Army, a succession to the stewardship, an employment in the revenue . . . or running away with your master's niece or daughter, I directly advise you to go upon the road [i.e. become a highwayman] which is the only post of honour left you: there you will meet many of your old comrades, and live a short life and a merry one, and make a figure at your exit . . .'

None of the other servants receives anything like as much advice as the footman. The butler is urged to notice whether his master pays scant attention at his board to a chaplain, tutor or dependent cousin, and if so to follow his example. The groom is urged to hire out one of his master's horses now and then to give it exercise. The chambermaid is told to empty the necessary vessels out of the window, as 'it is highly improper for menservants to know that fine ladies have occasion for such utensils.' The tutoress should 'make the misses read French and English novels, and French romances, and all the comedies writ in King Charles II's and King William's reigns, to soften their nature and make them tender-hearted . . .' And so on.

Swift's opportunities to study the foibles of servants had been extensive. His first employment, with Sir William Temple, was that of a waiting gentleman, or companion-amanuensis, and he dined at the upper servants' table. His own servants in later life included the drunken Patrick, whose hand shook so much that he was unable to shave his master's head, and who was always vanishing with the keys of the house, and the faithful Alexander McGee. The former he cursed and cuffed and shook as occasion required; the latter he honoured with a cathedral tablet and had to be dissuaded from describing him as a friend, since it would have been improper for a dean to condescend so far.[1] Swift never had another

[1] J. M. Murry: *Jonathan Swift.*

servant like McGee and in his later years he became, outwardly
at all events, a bearish and browbeating master.

It is a pity there was no Swift in the ranks of footmen,
someone who could have scourged the selfishness, the callousness, the ill-temper and the arrogance of so many masters and
mistresses. In a coarse and drunken day, the chances of a servant
receiving a civil word from his master on 'the morning after'
were slight; he was lucky to escape blows and kicks. The
Society for the Reformation of Manners could tackle public
swearing and public drunkenness, but its writ did not run in
my lady's bedroom, where ranting mistresses and pettish
daughters stamped, swore and threw unwanted clothes in the
faces of their maids until some acceptable garment was brought.
Nor did the society's writ run in the nursery, where the ungrateful children of gentlefolk kicked and punched the nurses who
taught them such delightfully coarse songs.

Sir Richard Steele expressed the view in *The Spectator* that
'the general corruption of manners in servants is owing to the
conduct of masters.' As an example of what a master should
be, he created (with Addison's aid) Sir Roger de Coverley,
Baronet: a man who called his servants by their own names,
whose approach did not put the household to flight, whose
worst tyranny was to count heads in church and let no one
sleep there but himself. There were too many masters, said
Steele, who took offence at a cheerful countenance, thinking
that 'a servant is broke loose from them if he does not preserve
the utmost awe in their presence.' It saddened Steele to think
that a man could secretly fret 'to see any appearance of content
in one that lives upon the hundredth part of his income.' But
if a servant wore a sour expression he was liable to be greeted
with: 'Hark ye, sirrah, are not you paid your wages?'

In the household of Sir Roger it was different. 'Respect and
love go together; and a certain cheerfulness in performance of
their duty is the particular distinction of the lower part of
this family.' If a servant was sent for by Sir Roger, he knew
it was not so that the master could threaten to strip him (that
is, turn him out of his livery), but so that he might enquire,
wholly without sarcasm, how he had been able to return so
quickly from his errand, or whether he had paused to ask after

an old man's health. 'A man who preserves a respect founded
on his benevolence to his dependants, lives rather like a
prince than a master in his family; his orders are received as
favours rather than duties; and the distinction of approaching
him is part of the reward for executing what is commanded by
him.'

Sir Roger was a one-man welfare state, awarding pensions,
subsidies and legacies at his discretion. Though he had a
grey-haired groom and a coachman with the looks of a Privy
Councillor, he had no wish to keep his servants in celibate
dependence for their natural lives, but did his best to set them
up in independent livelihoods. His benefactions extended to
his servants' children's children, as when he would send a
coachman's grandson to be apprenticed. But he saw it as no
part of his duty to give cast-off clothes to valets, thereby
giving them a silly air of superiority. Nothing was more
foolish, he thought, than the sight of a young gentleman abusing
a servant in the coat he himself had but lately worn, or for a
lady to distribute rewards and punishments by giving becoming
or unbecoming dresses to her maids.

In great establishments most servants were underworked,
and experience shows that those who are underworked are
quickest to resent being asked to do anything and will complain
bitterly about being imposed upon. Servants of the nobility
were so busy sub-dividing their duties and so anxious not to
do anybody else's work that, in the end, no one did anybody's
work. As a writer in *The World* pointed out, 'were it not for the
friendly assistance of chair-women, porters, chairmen and
shoe-blacks, procured by a generous distribution of coals,
candles and provisions, the common offices of life could never
be executed.' In such households, the writer continued, 'I
have sometimes been shut up in a cold room and interdicted
from the use of fire and water for half a day; and though during
my imprisonment I have seen numberless servants continually
passing by, the utmost I could procure of them was that they
would send somebody to relieve my necessities, which they
never performed.' If a dog was sick on the carpet no one could
be found humble enough to remove the mess and it lay there

'smoking under the noses of the illustrious company during the whole dinner.' This writer claimed that 'the parson or the tradesman who keeps but two maids and a boy not exceeding twelve years old is usually very well waited on; the private gentleman infinitely worse; but persons of great fortunes or quality, afraid of the idols of their own setting up, are neglected, abused and impoverished by their dependants.'[1]

These dependants, it is fair to say, often did no more than copy the example of self-interest and arrogance set by their superiors. Yet there were noblemen who had the knack of creating discipline even in vast and pompous households. Augustus Hervey, who was a guest of Lord Temple at Stowe in 1765, reported:

'How well he is served, with all the magnificence of a palace, all the elegance of a real nobleman and all the ease of a private gentleman. I never saw so large a house so well conducted, servants that have no *embarras*, no noise, but all attention and respect; 'tis a miracle how they have formed them so, and rubbed off the dirt and familiarity from the foreigners and inattention and ill-breeding from the English ones; I wish the master of a certain great family had the art of conducting his as well, then should we see order restored instead of confusion, respect instead of flattery and efficiency in the place of inability.'[2]

The foreigners referred to were probably French and Swiss. In the public prints there was frequently criticism of the vogue for French body-servants, whose qualification, according to a writer in *The Champion* in 1743, was that they could 'fawn, flatter, pimp, lie, swear or carry on any dirty intrigue.' The French defended themselves on the grounds that their heightened sensitivity of nerves, ear and palate especially recommended them for personal service. Once a French valet was hired, said the critic in *The Champion*, the whole household became a den of foreigners. 'The porter is turned away to make room for a Swiss, the cook gives place to a Gascoigne; and ten to one but a negro is introduced instead of a footman; then my lady must have a French maid and the young ladies are to be under a French governess and little master is sent abroad under a Swiss bear leader (for so these gentlemen are

[1] No. 157 (1756).   [2] W. J. Smith (ed.): *The Grenville Papers.*

properly termed abroad) who by infusing his own humours brings back the little spark as much a brute as himself.'

The state of affairs deplored by these critics looked idyllic enough to the next generation. In Smollett's novel *Humphrey Clinker* (1771), Squire Bramble is appalled by the mushrooming of London ('if this infatuation continues for half a century I suppose the whole county of Middlesex will be covered with brick'). Twenty-five years earlier, says the Squire, only the most opulent London citizens kept an equipage with liveried servants. The generality of citizens were content with plain boiled or roasted meat, and a bottle of port or a tankard of beer. Now every broker and attorney maintains a couple of footmen, a coachman and a postillion, with a town house, a country house, a coach and a post-chaise. Their wives and daughters are constantly dressing up, holding assemblies and drinking the most expensive wines. 'The gayest places of public entertainment are filled with fashionable figures; which, upon inquiry, will be found to be journeymen tailors, serving men and abigails, disguised like their betters.' In short, all ranks are 'actuated by the demons of profligacy and licentious-ness, they are seen everywhere, rambling, riding, rolling, rushing, justling, mixing, bouncing, cracking and crashing, in one vile ferment of stupidity and corruption.'

The eighteenth century had its 'rat race' too.

II

A MAN'S JOB?

THE higher a man rose socially, the more essential was it that he should be waited on by menservants, preferably in livery. In great households the number of male dependants always exceeded the number of female, and it was well understood that they were hired for ostentation rather than for use. To have a long file of tall, matched footmen, in silver and lace, preceding one's chair—the Countess of Northumberland had nine—was a gratifying testimony to one's importance, however great an inconvenience it might be to other road users (indeed, a fashionable first night, attended by the nobility in chairs and carriages, must have presented a singular traffic problem). Because these fine footmen were overfed and often tipsy, they got into mischief and demoralised the distaff side of the establishment; but, as no one liked to break a set of footmen, it was always the female party to an intrigue who was dismissed. This was almost as unfair as the disproportion between the wages paid to male and female servants. Boswell says that Dr Johnson was quite unable to answer the question: 'What is the reason that women servants, though obliged to be at the expense of purchasing their own clothes, have much lower wages than menservants to whom a great proportion of that article is furnished and when in fact our female house servants work much harder than the male?'

In the eighteenth century, the duties of butler, valet and footman were not so sharply differentiated as they became in Victorian times. The 'gentleman's gentleman' (the phrase occurs in Sheridan's *The Rivals*) flourished as a combination of all three. Steele provided Sir Roger de Coverley with a

butler who shaved him daily; and when the squire went up to
London to see a play his butler and footmen armed themselves
with cudgels and marched in procession behind his carriage
to beat off Mohocks. A manservant, whatever his nominal
title, had to be ready for all sorts of informal duties which
could not well be defined in a handbook: guarding his master's
clothes when he went swimming; bleeding his master; holding
him down for the surgeon; dragging him from under the
dinner table and putting him to bed; depriving him of the
means of suicide during attacks of hypochondria; lifting gouty
guests into, and out of, carriages; and so on. At election times,
if filled full of liquor, he would be ready to bay at any candidate
who held views in conflict with those of his master.

Menservants ranged from the dullest of clods, whose highest
skill was wood-chopping, to the gayest of sparks, the sort of
man who (as Steele tells) would masquerade in his master's
military uniform, the better to impress his trollops, and with
enough impudence to jolly the colonel of the regiment, if
accidentally encountered; or the sort of confidential servant
who (as Hickey tells) could be sent to prevaricate and bluster
before a Parliamentary Committee on behalf of a purse-proud,
arrogant nabob.

In great houses a footman, while rarely overworked, spent
a substantial part of the day on his feet, his heaviest labour
being the carrying of coals. There were abbeys and castles in
which smoke rose from upwards of sixty hearths. Many a
mansion burned more than a ton of coal a day and at Compton
Wynyates a daily ton was consumed in the kitchen alone.[1]
Sometimes bands of coal-carriers assisted in this task. There
were lamps and candle-holders to be cleaned (unfinished
candles were sometimes the footman's perquisite) and numerous
articles of plate to be polished. Once the dirty work was over,
the footman exchanged his fustian for a suit of his master's
livery and stalked about corridors and public rooms, or stood
outside doors, listening for the sound of handbells or, as at
Horace Walpole's Strawberry Hill, the sound of whistles from
silver owls. He carried up and served the dinner; and in the
evening he trimmed the lamps and candles.

[1] Richard Greville Verney: *The Passing Years.*

One footman—preferably the best-mannered, the most obliging and the most discreet—was at the exclusive call of the mistress of the house. In a wealthy family, each child might have a personal man in livery to stand behind his or her chair at meals and otherwise dance attendance. Another footman would be at the service of the nursery; an unpopular assignment.

When the family went out in their carriage the footman perched on the back with one of his comrades and scowled coldly on the passing scene. His duties were not wholly ornamental, for he was expected to be of some assistance in fending off footpads and highwaymen, or in browbeating turnpike men, beggars, idlers and all who sought to hinder his master's progress. If the carriage reached a bad patch of road he might have to carry the ladies in his arms; a service which, on occasions, seems to have afforded pleasure to both parties.

When his master and mistress paid a social call, the footman presented himself at the servants' hall, was given free beer, exchanged gossip and flirted with the housemaids. Outside balls or assemblies he killed time as best he could, drinking, boasting and chaffing prostitutes, and contriving to remain sober enough not to fall from his perch on the way home.

Frequently he would be sent on foot to enquire after the health of his master's friends. If he served a gentleman with a disposition to gallantry, he would find himself carrying notes to courtesans, whose own footmen would receive him with the degree of condescension merited by the status of their employers. He would then return to his master with a note of invitation or refusal.

More strenuous, much more strenuous, was the lot of the running footman, who had two roles: one, as a messenger with urgent dispatches; two, as a species of herald in front of his master's carriage. This fleet-footed servant took enormous pride in his calling, but it was a dying one, rendered superfluous by steady improvements in highways and communications; and by the end of the century only old-fashioned noblemen retained servants of this type. The sort of emergency in which the running footman excelled is illustrated in a story of the Duke of Lauderdale (the 'l' in Cabal). In his castle at Thirlstane, near Lauder, the Duke was informed, as his table was being laid for dinner, that there was a shortage of plate. He therefore sent a running footman over the Lammermuir Hills to his other castle at Lethington, near Haddington, fifteen miles away to fetch some additional articles, and the mission was completed in time for dinner.[1]

An Earl of Home one evening ordered a running footman to set off at once from his Berwickshire castle to Edinburgh on important business. On going downstairs next morning the Earl found the man asleep in the hall and was about to chastise him for disobedience when the man explained that he had already been there and back, a matter of thirty-five miles each way.[2]

The writer John O'Keeffe says of a running footman he saw in his youth in Ireland:

'He looked so agile, and seemed all air like a Mercury; he never minded roads but took the short cut and, by the help of his pole, absolutely seemed to fly over hedge, ditch and small river. His use was to carry a message, letter or dispatch; or on a journey to run before and prepare the inn, or baiting-place, for his family or master who came the regular road in coach-and-two, or coach-and-four or coach-and-six; his qualifications were fidelity, strength and agility.'[3]

The running footman who preceded his master's carriage did so primarily to let people know that a great man was coming, though in theory his function was to assist the equipage over rough or muddy ground. Usually he wore a jockey-style parti-coloured livery with white linen trousers and carried a long ornamental staff, in the head of which might be housed a hard-boiled egg and a small quantity of wine. If he needed a respite he would signal with his staff to the coachman, but this was rarely necessary. The running footman on carriage duty was prepared to cover sixty miles and more in a day, at an average of six to seven miles an hour.

In London the fourth Duke of Queensberry ('Old Q') continued to employ running footmen until his death in 1810. He would try out applicants in Piccadilly, lending them his livery for the occasion, and then stand watch in hand on his

---

[1] Chambers' *Book of Days*.   [2] *Ibid.*
[3] *Recollections* (1826).

balcony to time their performance. There is a story that he said to one candidate: 'You will do very well for me.' The reply was, 'And your livery will do very well for me,' with which the runner bolted.[1]

Only one footman in the eighteenth century appears to have published full-length memoirs.[2] He was young John Macdonald, sometimes called 'Beau' Macdonald, and his career is of more than passing interest. A cadet of the family of Keppoch, in Inverness-shire, he had fled to Edinburgh as a child after his father was killed at Culloden and the family beggared. One of his first employments was as guide to a blind fiddler. Then, at the age of nine, he became a postillion in a livery stable in Edinburgh and soon afterwards went in the same capacity to serve the Hamilton family at Bargeny, Ayrshire, changing his jacket for one of scarlet and silver. The post had its peculiar perils; once, when not strapped to his mount, the boy fell among the horses' heels. Lady Anne Hamilton, who much admired her boy postillion, was a daughter of the Earl of Wemyss and her husband, John Hamilton, 'had £10,000 by her.' She was a daughter, as she boasted, of the family that slew Macbeth and her intentions were not easily thwarted. In 1755 she decided to set out in mid-winter by coach-and-six to Edinburgh, first taking the precaution of ordering a chair and six men to carry it. The company set out in deep snows with the butler, the first cook and two footmen on horseback and a horse in hand for the master. When the going was heavy Lady Anne took to her chair, her husband rode alongside and two ladies in the company sat astride the horses behind the servants, as did the ladies' maids.

The Bargeny establishment of servants, according to Macdonald, was eight upper or ladies' maids, four chamber-maids, two laundry maids, a butler, two footmen, a coachman and various stablemen. Indoors, there were more women servants than was usual in a noble family, but the residents included a 'Lady Polly' and a 'Lady Nelly.' The servants taught the young postillion to read and he took his spelling

[1] *Notes and Queries* ii.
[2] *The Life and Travels of John Macdonald* (1790).

book with him everywhere. 'I thought that if once I could
read the Bible I should not go to hell,' he explains. Then
Lady Anne sent him to school, as there was little for him to
do when the coach-and-six was not required. Soon he was in
the grip of a morbid piety. The coachman damned him because
he disturbed the horses by his praying. 'If any person died
within a mile or two I went to sit up with the dead; and there
we all told stories and talked on religious matters. I was always
to be found at those wakes.' The youth had a great desire to
meet the Devil and often turned round suddenly in the hope
of seeing him, in order to rebuke him.

All too soon young John shook off the Devil, thanks to the
influence of pretty maids and the excitements of the family's
social distractions. These included 'kettles of fish' beside
the Tweed, when marquees were set up and fishermen whipped
the salmon out of the river, sliced them up and threw the pieces
into boiling water. Lady Anne had intended John to be her
personal footman and was angry when she learned that he had
been found a place as coachman to the Earl of Crauford, more
especially as she had been to the trouble of schooling him; but,
having got one of the Earl's chambermaids with child, he
returned as manservant to John Hamilton. 'Now,' he says, 'I
set out on life, without conduct, or this world's cunning. I
was a greater plague to my master and benefactor than one
would think. I did not know the value of good law nor of
money. Coming into two such plentiful families I thought
the whole world was my Garden of Eden. My master knew
what was good for me, but I had not the sense to take his
advice . . . I was put out of my latitude by contrary winds; I
mean women.'

Macdonald's wild oats are more conveniently dealt with in
a later chapter; here, we are concerned with him chiefly in his
capacity as manservant to various single gentlemen of position.
Rarely were his duties closely defined. Of one appointment
under two gentlemen, he says: 'I was part of everything there.
I marketed, kept the book, and had the keys of everything in
the house. I was steward, butler, housekeeper, head cook and
footman. I taught the maid to dress the Scotch dishes.' His
wages in this place were twenty guineas a year, with two suits

of clothes. In other posts his duties might consist of little more than dressing his master in the morning, and then he would be left to his own diversions for the day. Masters varied much in condescension. Of an Army major, 'a polite man,' Macdonald says: 'If he met me in the streets of Dublin and I lifted my hat he returned it; but no more.' Evidently it was more usual for masters to ignore their servants in the street. Sometimes Macdonald wore livery, sometimes ordinary clothes; sometimes he would be allowed to travel in a chaise with his master, sometimes not. On the whole he got along best with single military gentlemen. One of his employers was a brother of the Earl of Galloway, the Hon. Keith Stewart, whose hours of coming home were from two to seven in the morning. 'I have had the chaise at the door many a time by six in the morning to go to a hunt before he had come home. When he came at last he walked upstairs, took off his bag, and changed his dress clothes to go into the chaise. Wherever the hunt was he went sometimes four score miles.' Mostly, Macdonald resigned from his places of his own will, as when he grew tired of waiting on a colonel's lady or was jealous of a valet being preferred over him, but sometimes he was dismissed. He lost one post for failing to provide a pack of cards on a Sunday afternoon. On another occasion he and his master returned from dining out, both being merry. 'When I put his hair in papers and undressed him I took up his shoes in my left hand and put his coat over the same arm; and seeing me do so, he said, "You take up my clothes as if you had never seen anp clothes before." "Sir, I have handled better than yours many times." He turned me out of the room and next morning he discharged me: so I lost a good place in speaking one foolish word and I was very sorry for it.'

Spells of unemployment rarely troubled Macdonald, even though at any given time there were two thousand footmen in search of places in London. He walked the streets in good clothes with rich vests and laced ruffles, but when applying for a place he dressed, as a rule, in more sober clothes. Sometimes he lost a place by appearing too grand, at other times he failed by not appearing grand enough. Undoubtedly he had accomplishments which many others lacked. James Coutts,

the banker, had been trying for a month to find a servant to
dress his hair and had rejected the services of twenty. The
difficulty was that he wore a wig over his hair. But when
Macdonald had gone to work on him 'there was no person
could tell there was anything but his own hair, and he had the
handsomest head and face I ever saw in my life.' Not the least
of Macdonald's recommendations was his skill in making
'Queen of Scots soup,' liberally concocted of eggs and chickens.

His wages ranged from fifteen or sixteen guineas a year to as
much as forty guineas, plus various extras including tea money
at the rate of perhaps two guineas a year. The higher wages
were payable usually for foreign travel, as when he accepted
forty guineas a year to accompany a Colonel Dow to India. It
was part of Macdonald's usefulness that he was ready at three
hours' notice to go anywhere in the world. In Spain and
Portugal he found it easier for himself and all concerned if he
went through the motions of being a Roman Catholic. 'I had
seen many different religions and found it was best to pay
respect to the people and form of their religion.' So, while
shooting game from the coach for his masters, he did not
neglect to cross himself at roadside crucifixes; it was little
enough for a good servant to do. In Cadiz his master had a
severe fever. 'I never pulled off my clothes for sixteen nights.
I had a fire burning all night and a lamp to warm everything
he wanted.'

At an inn in Holland Macdonald gained an unfavourable
impression of the ways of Dutch footmen. He and other
servants were dining in the kitchen, but a Dutch footman in
coarse livery declined to eat there, calling in only to pick up a
slice of bread and meat and then going into the parlour to eat
it, continually talking to his master and ladies about the state
of the roads and such matters. Macdonald laughed much to
think that his own master was dining in the same room as a
footman, for this master was 'so proud he would not let a
servant ride in the chaise with him but would rather be at the
expense of a horse.' The Dutch family, however, 'seemed as
much pleased with their footman's behaviour as if he had been
a prince.'

When in a prosperous post, Macdonald would give a ball

for his friends in a public-house, regaling perhaps forty persons with baked ham, turkeys, punch, wine, negus and much else. His guests were mostly gentlemen's servants. The cost of one such meal, including music and tips to two menservants, was £5 10s., rather more than a year's wages of a country housemaid. There were, he notes with satisfaction, no breakages, since everybody behaved well. He mentions another ball-supper given by a gentleman's servant to sixty-two guests in a Knightsbridge public-house, with country dancing and minuets.

In the history books Macdonald enjoys two brief mentions. In London one of his masters sent him to enquire after the health of Lawrence Sterne, then seriously ill in his lodgings. Sterne's servant invited him into the bedroom and he was in time to see poor Yorick die. 'Now it is come,' exclaimed Sterne. He put up his hand 'as if to stop a blow and died in a minute.' Macdonald's other claim to note is one he shares with Jonas Hanway: he did much to popularise the umbrella. The mob accused him of being a Frenchman and coachmen used to shout after him to take a carriage.

John Macdonald's life was that of the eighteenth-century manservant at his freest. Whether the functions he performed were worth the attention of a man of vigour and talent is another matter. That writer in *The Champion* who has already been quoted felt that all such menservants were encumbrances on a trading society. 'It is really a shame to see a strong, able, lusty fellow spending the prime of his life in curling his own hair and that of his master; that they may appear like puppies of the same litter. . . . When occupations like these will furnish a man with better bread than following the plough or any other honest way of getting a livelihood it is a plain sign that luxury is at the utmost height and the nation in a fair way of being ruined.'[1] The fact remains that Macdonald, parasitic though his employments may have been, was a man with an independent spirit. There was nothing lickspittle about him and at no time does he suggest that he was ashamed of his calling. He had a variety of useful accomplishments at his command and he exacted their market price. If his employers did not like him or he did not like them, then either party was free to end the

[1] No. 62 (1743).

The running footman—from an inn sign

contract. Thousands of other menservants worked for a fraction of the money that Macdonald enjoyed and saw nothing of the great world, having fewer skills and less assurance. In rural Buckinghamshire, Elizabeth Purefoy's idea of a good footman was a man who, besides laying the cloth and waiting at table, would work in the garden or 'go to cart when ordered' or perform any other business, and who was not too heavy to sit on a horse.[1] Under a good master, the rural manservant's life was dull but tolerable. When a master treated his servant's honest efforts with contumely the servant made no further efforts to please; it was all too easy to find solace in drink. What pride could be felt in the service of a boor who showed affection only to his dogs? Or in the employment of such a master as Steele saw one hot day in the fields near Chelsea—a fat fellow puffing along in open waistcoat, followed by a boy of fourteen in livery carrying his cloak, upper coat, hat, wig and sword, almost ready to sink, while his master kept turning round impatiently to see what made him lag?

[1] G. Eland (ed.): *Purefoy Letters, 1735–53.*

Standards of literacy among menservants varied enormously. A private gentleman might be fortunate enough to have a footman who could read to him; a nobleman, like the Duke of Bedford, might have half a dozen menservants who could only sign their names with a cross. The Hon. Edward Wortley by accident opened a letter written by his footman, James Hirst, to his sweetheart. When the footman claimed it his master said: 'No, James, you shall be a great man. This letter shall appear in *The Spectator*.' And so it did. Whether the footman appreciated Steele's comments we do not know—'the style . . . seems to be confused with scraps he had got in hearing and reading what he did not understand.'[1] But with all its faults it showed a level of literacy which many a squire could not have emulated.

The century produced at least one footman poet in Robert Dodsley, of whom the *Dictionary of National Biography* says that 'his early condition lent a factitious importance to some immature verse.' While in the employ of the Hon. Mrs Lowther he wrote a rhymed reply to Defoe's 'opprobrious railings,' high-mindedly defending his brethren of the livery; but he also wrote verses mocking the footman's calling. His early poems were described on the title-page as 'By R. Dodsley, a Footman to a Person of Quality in Whitehall.' His mistress and her friends secured for Dodsley a large number of subscribers, among whom were three duchesses and a duke. Even Pope condescended to receive the footman author. Later Dodsley turned bookseller and dramatist; in the former capacity he published poems by Akenside and Johnson.

Devotees of Smollett will recall the dismay felt by Squire Bramble on finding his footman, Humphrey Clinker, addressing a Methodist meeting attended by the Squire's own womenfolk. The Squire at once orders him from his pulpit and berates him: 'Since you are called upon by the spirit to preach and to teach, it is high time to lay aside the livery of an earthly master; and, for my part, I am unworthy to have an apostle in my service.' In real life, a distinguished footman-preacher was David Taylor, who was sent periodically on tour by his mistress, Selina, Countess of Huntingdon. He was 'a man of ability,

[1] *Spectator*, No. 71.

knowledge and wisdom,' with 'a tolerable education.'[1] Taylor
tried first to convert his fellow-servants at Donnington Park,
Leicestershire, to Methodism. His mistress, a leading pro-
tagonist of the movement, considered his talents deserved a
wider sphere than the servants' hall and encouraged him to
visit the nearby hamlets 'to speak to lost sinners of their
dreadful state.' Then, after a spell of polishing silver and
carrying coals, he would be sent out on ever-widening tours,
into Cheshire, Derbyshire and elsewhere. Eventually, Taylor
seems to have incurred the displeasure of his mistress, possibly
on account of an unfortunate marriage.

Not all the nobly born were fascinated by the idea of a
footman-preacher. Among those who regarded the doctrines of
Methodism as subversive was the Duchess of Buckingham who,
in the early days of the movement, wrote to Taylor's mistress
as follows:

'I thank your ladyship for the information concerning the
Methodist preachers; their doctrines are most repulsive, and
strongly tinctured with impertinence and disrespect to their
superiors, in perpetually endeavouring to level all ranks, and
do away with all distinctions. It is monstrous to be told that
you have a heart as sinful as the common wretches that
crawl on the earth. This is highly offensive and insulting; and
I cannot but wonder that your ladyship should relish any
sentiments so much at variance with high rank and good
breeding.'[2]

At his best, the English footman was poised, majestical,
discreet, courteous. He committed none of the solecisms
observed by Dr Johnson on his visit to France where, in the
house of a literary lady, a footman put the sugar in the tea with
his fingers and then, at his mistress's order, blew down the spout
of the teapot to free it of an obstruction.[3] He would not have
committed the *gaffe* of Horace Walpole's Swiss footman at
Strawberry Hill who twice told the Duke of Württemberg to
call again, as his master was not yet out of bed. 'Good God,'
said Walpole, 'tell him to call again! Don't you know he is a

[1] *Life and Letters of Selina, Countess of Huntingdon.*
[2] *Ibid.*
[3] James Boswell: *Life of Samuel Johnson.*

sovereign prince?' The answer was: 'No, I did think he was only a common Duke.'[1]

There were English footmen, too, who far outshone their masters in polite behaviour; at least, in the opinion of house-maids. In Henry Fielding's *The Virgin Unmask'd* Lucy is upbraided for falling in love with a footman and exclaims:

'A footman! He looks a thousand times more like a gentleman than either Squire Foxchase or Squire Tankard and talks more like one, ay, and smells more like one too. His head is so prettily dressed too, done all down upon the top with sugar, like a frosted cake, with three little curls on each side, that you may see his ears as plain! and then his hair is done up behind just like a fine lady's with a small neat hat, and a pair of charm-ing white stockings too, as neat and as fine as any white-legged fowl; and he always carries a great swinging stick in his hand as big as himself that he would knock any dog down with, who was to offer to bite me.'

In places where many idle menservants congregated there was often disorder. In London the areas of turbulence were to be found near Parliament, the law courts, the parks and the pleasure-grounds. The footmen of Members of Parliament are said to have set up a species of third chamber, in which affairs of the day were debated; but those who lacked a talent for polemics made themselves a nuisance in the surrounding taverns. It was the humour of great men's lackeys to address each other in the style of their masters; thus, Steele tells how, in a victual-house near Parliament, he heard a maid come down to tell the landlady at the bar that 'my Lord Bishop would throw her out of the window if she did not bring up more mild beer and that my Lord Duke would have a double mug of purle.'[2] This usage was also employed, more decor-ously, among upper servants in the housekeeper's room, when visiting valets and ladies' maids were entertained.

To lazy yokels from the country the footman's life at West-minster appeared a wholly idyllic one; what better than to be paid to drink all day in fine clothes and to be addressed as

[1] Peter Cunningham (ed.): *Letters of Horace Walpole.*
[2] *Spectator*, No. 88.

'My Lord Archbishop'? But there were never enough places
for the multitudes of would-be footmen and the more unprincipled of them often became petty criminals. Not a few
gravitated, in the earlier years of the century, to the service of
Jonathan Wild, the thief-taker who employed more thieves
than he arrested. Wild was prepared to train menservants for
his own nefarious ends. He employed a band of 'spruce prigs'
who wore fine clothes and were attended in places of fashion
by confederates in livery. In fact, these flunkeys served to
receive the goods picked by the prigs from the pockets of the
unsuspecting. Sometimes, for a change, prigs and their lackeys
played confidence tricks on tradesmen. No footman was
promoted to the role of prig until he had acquired the graces
of a gentleman about town, and Wild is said to have hired a
dancing master to smarten them up. It was the duty of these
footmen, also, to extract information from servants in wealthy
households. If necessary they would make love to maids over a
period of weeks in order to obtain ready access to the house,
a door being left open for the convenience of a confederate.
Servants who knowingly collaborated in these plots were
blackmailed into committing further crimes. For the well-to-do
it was a harassing period: was the demure young woman who
applied for a post all that she seemed, or was she the tool of a
highwayman? Was the deferential young lackey with the
seemingly excellent references interested in polishing the silver—
or stealing it? The system of robbing houses by planting corrupt
maids, did not, of course, die out with the execution of Jonathan
Wild, in 1725: but Wild's death did at least remove a powerful
source of temptation to the servants of the Metropolis.

Swift, it will be recalled, pointed to the gallows as the
footman's predestined end, and not a few menservants were
'turned off' or 'launched into eternity' at Tyburn. One of them
was Daniel Blake, footman to Lord Dacre in Hill Street. When
he climbed out of bed one February night in 1763 and crept
to the butler's pantry to murder the occupant, he left a fellow
footman asleep in his bed, and found him still asleep when he
climbed in again. A few days later Blake's bedfellow had the
couch to himself and Blake was dangling in chains.

There were times when a master held his servant's life in

his hands, for to denounce a man for theft might well send him to the gallows. George Selwyn's gossiping friend Gilly Williams wrote to him in 1764: 'Lady Townshend is going to have an execution of her own. Draper, the butler . . . has turned out the d——est thief in the world . . . her ladyship not being very compassionate, he must go to the gallows.'[1] But Draper fled to Ireland. In 1765 Lord Harrington's porter, John Wisket, who helped thieves to rob his master's house, went to the gallows with a white cockade in his hat, as a profession of innocence. George Selwyn, who hated to miss an execution, missed this one, but his friends told him the details. Wisket wore his blue and gold, ate several oranges on the way to the gallows and enquired whether his hearse was ready. At the start of this unfortunate decade, a nobleman's servants had the privilege of driving their master in his coach-and-six to the scaffold. This was Lord Ferrers, executed at Tyburn for the murder of his steward. In the procession was a hearse-and-six to carrry his body to Surgeons' Hall.

Footmen earned themselves a good deal of ill-will by their behaviour in theatres. It was a custom among playgoers to send livery servants to keep their places until they saw fit to arrive, perhaps half-way through the show. The footmen would then move upstairs to the gallery, where they would claim free or half-price admission, while reserving the right to make noisy criticism of the play. Increasingly, managements resisted the right of free admission to the gallery, and tension mounted. Angry footmen were behind at least two of the big riots which chequered the history of Drury Lane during this century. In 1737 a periodical reported: 'This night a great number of footmen assembled together with sticks, staves and other offensive weapons in a tumultuous and riotous manner, and broke open the doors of Drury Lane Playhouse for not being let in to what they call *their gallery*; and fought their way in so desperate a manner to the stage door (which they forced open) that twenty-five or twenty-six persons were wounded in a very dangerous manner in the fray. Colonel de Veil tried to read a proclamation but such was the violence and number of footmen that notwithstanding the presence of

[1] J. H. Jesse: *George Selwyn and His Contemporaries.*

their Royal Highnesses the Prince and Princess of Wales and others of the royal family it was impossible to appease their fury without going to such extremities as he thought improper.'[1]

A play which caused high indignation among the occupants of the gallery was James Townley's famous farce *High Life Below Stairs*, first produced at Drury Lane in 1759. The theme is that of a young gentleman of fortune who decides to find out for himself what his servants get up to when his back is turned. This he does by disguising himself as a simple yokel and obtaining a place in his own house. Almost all the servants betray themselves as scallywags, intent only on self-indulgence and stealing, while aping the follies of their betters. The disguised master is initiated in his duties with the aid of a work entitled *The Servant's Guide To Self*, by Timothy Shoulderknot, containing maxims like:

> Let it for ever be your plan
> To be the master, not the man,
> And do as little as you can.

High Life Below Stairs, in George Selwyn's view, was a welcome change from low life above stairs. Stalls and pit agreed with him, but the gallery objected loudly:

'The whole race of the domestic gentry, on the first night of this excellent little piece, were in a ferment of rage at what they conceived would be their ruin; and from the upper gallery to which they were admitted gratis came hisses and groans, and even many a handful of halfpence was flung on the stage. . . . This tumult went on for a few nights but ultimately was a good thing for all theatres as it gave Garrick, then manager, a fair occasion to shut the gallery from the servants and ever after make it a pay place . . .'[2]

In Edinburgh, when the play was staged there, the servants in the gallery also made a loud disturbance and lost their privileges.

---

[1] Quoted in *The Autobiography and Correspondence of Mrs Delany* (ed. Lady Llanover).
[2] John O'Keeffe: *Recollections*.

In a hot-tempered age, gentlemen were sometimes involved in duels by the rash behaviour of their menservants. In 1790 a servant of Sir George Ramsay waited with a chair at the door of an Edinburgh theatre. A Captain Macrae ordered him to move it, but he refused to do so. High words were exchanged, then the Captain chastised the servant severely. Next day, his feathers still ruffled, the Captain called on the Baronet and demanded the dismissal of the offender, which Sir George refused on the grounds that the man had already been heavily punished. Captain Macrae, regarding this as a slight on his honour, issued a challenge; and on Musselburgh Links the master who stood by his servant died in much agony.[1]

Footmen, as we have seen, often performed the duties of valet, but the valet proper was an upper servant who did not wear livery, and who was distinguishable from his master, the wags said, only by being better dressed. The more epicene among them appear to have acted as ladies' maids. Addison says: 'I remember the time when some of our well-bred country women kept their *valet de chambre*, because, forsooth, a man was much more handy about them than one of their own sex. I myself have seen one of these male abigails tripping about the room with a looking-glass in his hand, and combing his lady's hair the whole morning together.' But he believes that such practices are now extinct.[2]

An anonymous valet who published his life story,[3] in 1752, 'as a caution to others,' tells a tale of backstairs intrigue in diplomatic circles in London. 'To know one of the foreigners in England,' he says, 'is to know them all, and to be the valet of one of them is, I find in general, to be the pimp of them all.' The masters, he says, spent their time trying to capture each other's mistresses. 'While each [valet] was paid for watching the honour of the mistress of his patron, each was paid also for procuring that of the other. The valets under these circumstances almost universally had both mistresses alternately for their own amusement.' These revelations need not be taken too seriously but they offer a glimpse of the ways in which

---

[1] *Annual Register*, 1790.   [2] *Spectator* No. 45.
[3] *The Adventures of a Valet, Written by Himself.*

menservants and women servants of no principle could make easy money. A gentleman setting up a mistress clandestinely (many, of course, were set up openly) could not simply instal her in an apartment and leave her to do her own cooking and cleaning; it was necessary to provide her with a footman, a personal maid and a coachman at the least. All three had to be paid highly enough to overcome their moral scruples, if any, and to discourage them from talking about their master and his affairs. The philanderer not only had to worry whether his mistress was faithful but whether her servants were faithful too. It was impossible for anyone, man or women, to carry on an illicit liaison without being exposed to the risks of tale-telling and blackmail by servants, either in his own house or in those of other people. At every turn of the affair mouths had to be stopped with money. Even money bought no assurance of loyalty if the servants took a dislike to the man who paid them. William Hickey became visibly interested in Charlotte Barry, mistress of the eccentric, vile-tempered Captain Henry Mordaunt. One night, in Mordaunt's absence, his staff delicately suggested to Hickey, who was a guest in the house, that if he had any enterprise in mind they would give him ample warning of their master's return, and delay him as much as possible. 'Thus secured against accident,' says Hickey, 'I with confidence usurped the tyrant's place.'[1]

If a master sought a catamite for a valet, it was not difficult to recruit one. Notorious among dubious households was that of William Beckford who, behind the twelve-foot barrier encircling his Gothic abbey at Fonthill, surrounded himself with comely menservants with names like Madame Bion (his valet), the Doll and the Calf. What really went on in the Abbey the county never knew, but they ostracised Beckford for what they suspected.[2]

If there were wicked masters, there were also exceedingly innocent ones. The historian of Cobham Hall, in Kent, tells how John Bligh, later fourth Earl of Darnley, was sent to Eton in the 1770s with a French valet. The boy was then aged nine. 'I walk out with my man every fine day,' he reported in his

[1] William Hickey: *Memoirs.*
[2] Boyd Alexander (ed.): *Life at Fonthill.*

letters home; and in return he was counselled to treat his servant with every politeness. Of the exact relations between the two we learn little. For an ambitious manservant it was probably as good an entry into a noble household as any.[1]

[1] Esme Wingfield-Stratford: *The Lords of Cobham Hall.*

III

THE OPEN PALM

THROUGHOUT Europe, the servants of Britain were notorious for their exaction of vails, or tips, from their masters' guests. If a British government had proposed putting a tax on hospitality, it would have been kicked out of office; yet society allowed its servants to impose just such a levy and to collect it, as often as not, with an air of chilly insolence.

The system was a corruption of the old institution of *largesse*, when princes were expected to shower gifts on the servants of those whom they visited. 'Now,' said Jonas Hanway, the philanthropist, 'we are all princes.'[1] Defoe complained that vails-giving was 'unknown to our forefathers, who only gave gifts to servants at Christmastide.'[2]

As the eighteenth century progressed, the abuse was intensified. Servants saw no reason, perhaps, why they should not indulge in the general greed and corruption of the times. In operating the system they traded successfully on the pride, indifference or pusillanimity of their masters.

Swift, writing to Stella in 1710, said: 'Lord Halifax is always teasing me to go to his country house, which will cost me a guinea to his servants and 12s. coach hire; and he shall be hanged first.' Similar complaints were being voiced with varying degrees of bitterness over the next fifty years. An impoverished Irish peer told the Duke of Ormonde he would dine with him 'if your Grace will give me a guinea each time to pay your servants—I am too poor else.' Thereafter His

---

[1] *Eight Letters to His Grace the Duke of* ——.
[2] *Everybody's Business Is Nobody's Business.*

Grace was kind enough to send a guinea with each invitation. On a similar plea Alexander Pope used to wring five guineas a time from the Duke of Montagu.

The satirical Dr John Shebbeare, writing as Battista Angeloni, 'a Jesuit,' said the vails system gave English noblemen the meanest of reputations; 'my lord looks on whilst his guest discharges the house by paying the servants; and no servants are in any comparison so insolent and inattentive in their service, because they know that it is not his lordship's hands from which they receive their money.'[1] Sometimes, according to a writer in *The World*, a host who was obliged to be a witness of the rapacity of his servants would assume 'the silly look of an innocent man who has unfortunately broke in upon the retirement of two lovers and is ready to affect with great simplicity that he has seen nothing.'[2] The attitude of hosts varied. Jonas Hanway said that 'the master of the house, with all the adroitness he can exert, shuns the sight of his guests when they leave his doors that he may not be a spectator of a practice of which he is equally ashamed and scandalised notwithstanding the universality of it.' He also thought 'it must excite the highest indignation in a generous mind to see a gentleman anxious to get change for his gold that he may be provided with the moneys to pay for his dinner at the house of his friend.' An eccentric Irish nobleman, Lord Taafe, is supposed to have said to his guests, as they made to distribute money, 'If you do give, give it to me, for it was I that did buy the dinner.'[3]

According to Hanway, there were houses in which servants expostulated with their masters for allowing guests to slip away quietly without paying tribute. It was the master's duty, they argued, to ring the bell to call the servants up in time to receive their due.

The custom bore heavily on those officers of the Army or Navy who had no private incomes, and also on poor clergymen who, on dining with their prelates, were milked of enough to support their families for a week. A colonel in a ducal home begged his host for the names of the servants. When asked for

[1] *Letters on the English Nation.*   [2] February 21, 1754 (No. 10).
[3] John Timbs: *A Century of Anecdote.*

what purpose, he replied: 'Why, my Lord Duke, in plain truth I cannot afford to pay for such good dinners as your Grace gives me and at the same time support my equipage, without which I cannot come here; therefore I intend to remember these gentlemen in the codicil of my will.'

It was customary for the servants to line up in the hall in a double row, like musketeers, and to extend their palms quite openly. The guest would be expected to disburse sums from left to right alternately as he headed for the door. With luck, in a not unduly pretentious house, he might get away with 2s. 6d. each for servants out of livery and 1s. 3d. for servants in livery. A visitor from overseas with ambassadorial or high ecclesiastical rank would be expected to do very much better than this; by the time he had run the gauntlet of English hospitality he would be the poorer by £10 or more. The degree of generosity shown by a guest was reflected in the vocal inflection of the man who afterwards called his carriage. A liberal visitor might find himself upgraded from captain to colonel, or from apothecary to physician.

From time to time, guests rebelled. There is a tale of a diner who bought back his hat, sword, cane and cloak, each from a different footman, but declined to accept his gloves, on the grounds that they were too old to be worth repurchasing. An acquaintance of Hanway's would shake each extended hand and enquire after the owner's health; another gave each servant an apple. An Army officer cut the silver buttons from his coat and distributed them. In one ducal home a storm arose in the servants' hall because a departing guest, in the course of a handshake, was thought to have transferred twenty guineas to the palm of the steward, who denied that he had received any money. To clear his steward's name, the host had to ask his guest whether he had handed over any money. 'When the greatest personages in a kingdom are thus obliged to become actors in such scenes, 'exclaimed Hanway, 'is it not a most wretched farce indeed?'

Guests who were known to be opposed to paying vails would be neglected or insulted in various ways. That writer in *The World* said: 'If I am bold enough to call for wine, after a delay which would take away its relish were it good, I receive a mixture of the whole sideboard in a greasy glass. If I hold up my plate, nobody sees me; so that I am forced to eat mutton with fish sauce and pickles with my apple pie.' When they left the house, non-paying guests would find unpleasant objects in their pockets or discover that their carriage harness had been slashed. In the servants' hall of one house the occupants wrote in large letters on the wall: 'Mr —— is a scoundrel for he was here six weeks and gave us but five guineas.'[1]

Vails were exacted not only from diners but from all callers wishing to see the master of the house. A non-contributor might be told that the master was not at home. Thus, a man's servants regulated his business and discriminated between his friends and acquaintances. A variation of the system was the levy of card money, which meant that guests were expected to leave two or three times the value of a pack of cards for the servant whose duty it was to provide them.

When hiring servants, masters and mistresses sometimes found themselves being questioned as to their standards of hospitality: how many times a week did they have guests to dinner? how often did they play cards? If a family did not entertain twice a week they might have difficulty in obtaining servants (to this extent the custom of vails may be said to have encouraged hospitality). One lady was asked whether there was a reasonable expectation of a lying-in each year, for births were a splendid excuse for mulcting visitors. If the hoped-for rate of vails was not forthcoming the more unprincipled servants held themselves justified in appropriating items of their masters' property, blandly explaining the reason if detected.

In the servants' hall, the sharing out of vails gave rise to many jealousies and injustices. John Macdonald as a boy postillion at Bargeny was flogged by the coachman for holding back vails given to him for performing various duties. Once, after searching him, the coachman offered to give Macdonald his daughter when he grew up, so that he would receive back his money in the form of dowry. Prudently, the boy continued to hide his money in holes in the ground, but he did not always succeed in finding it again.

[1] *The Sentiments And Advice of Thomas Trueman, A Virtuous And Understanding Footman* (1760).

What could be said in defence of giving vails? In a house where much entertaining was done, it was reasonable that the servants should receive something by way of compensation, but difficult to show that such compensation ought to be paid by the guests. A manservant wrote to *The World* to say: 'A good servant, and one who knows his business, will endeavour all he can to keep low people from intruding at his master's table.' This may have been written partly in jest, but there seems to have been a feeling, among the more precious men-servants, that the vails system performed a useful service in keeping away what would now be called 'free loaders,' in other words, indigent poets and philosophers who were glad enough of a free dinner. Such exclusion, in the lackeys' eyes, was a contribution towards decorum and dignity; meaning that wealth alone was to be regarded as a passport to the dinner table. A more difficult argument to rebut was that gentlemen in high office were not above accepting 'fees' for doing their duty. Why, then, should mere servants show more com-punction?

By 1760 there were belated signs of rebellion among the nobility and gentry. In Edinburgh the Clerks to the Signet and the Faculty of Advocates declared that the vails system was destroying the morals of servants and was a tax on the domestic intercourse of friends. They pledged themselves not only to stop paying vails but to prevent their own servants accepting them. Similar resolutions were drawn up by the nobility and gentry in Aberdeen. When James Boswell, defending Scotland against Dr Johnson's onslaughts, claimed that the Scots had been the first to take steps against the tyranny of vails, the Doctor retorted: 'Sir, you abolished vails because you were too poor to be able to give them.' Be that as it may, the Grand Jury of Northumberland took similar action, and so did the members of the Opera Club in London. In that year, too, Jonas Hanway published his *Eight Letters to His Grace the Duke of ―― on the Custom of Vails Giving in England*. The Duke was the Duke of Newcastle, and the dedi-cation was thought to have been prompted by an incident which occurred in the ducal mansion. Sir Timothy Waldo, on the way to his carriage after dinner, put a crown in the hand of the Duke's cook, who returned it saying, 'Sir, I do not take silver.' Sir Timothy replied: 'Don't you, indeed? Then I do not give gold.'[1] Addressing the Duke, Hanway points out that a person of low rank 'entertains your Grace with his discourse and pays honour to your rank and condition, but he demands nothing for it. Your Grace entertains him to a dinner and your servants make him pay for it ten times as much as it is worth to him. Can you enjoy the advantages of your high station, your great fortune and nobleness of mind with such an incumbrance? Can the pleasures of friendship in all their native simplicity and charms be enjoyed under those disguises and constraints which are the appendages of this custom?'

Hanway says that the vails system is hardly ever encountered abroad. Britain is derided on this count even by the Russians and the Portuguese, who are 'some centuries behind us.' Is it surprising that a visitor from overseas, on leaving the house of a man of prime quality, regards us as 'the meanest, the most mercenary and at the same time the most prodigal people upon earth?' He might have added, for good measure, an anecdote about the Duke of Ormonde who, after staying with a French nobleman at St Germain-en-Laye, left ten pistoles for the servants. His host, learning of the commotion caused by this act, set off in furious pursuit and, having caught up with his late guest, asked coldly whether he had any complaint to make. The Duke replied that he had never spent such an agreeable time in his life. To this the nobleman retorted that to leave ten pistoles for his servants was to treat his house as an inn and the greatest affront that could be offered. Faced with taking back his pistoles or fighting a duel, the Duke accepted his money; of which, as it happened, he had urgent need.[2]

Although he set his face against vails, Hanway occasionally gave a shilling to a pretty maidservant, not without a qualm that the handing over of such sums might well be a cause of debauching female servants and filling the Magdalene House. It was customary for maids to accept money with a smile and a curtsey, which made the benefaction more pleasurable, whereas the powdered footman accepted his vail with 'the lofty look of a tax gatherer.'

[1] John Timbs: *A Century of Anecdote*.   [2] *The World*, No. 69.

The Duke of Newcastle did not deny the justice of Hanway's arguments. He showed the letters to the new sovereign, George III, aware no doubt that the royal servants were as rapacious as any. As an example to the nation the young king banned the acceptance of vails within his own household, which caused angry mutterings both above and below the royal stairs. The next time he visited the theatre he was booed and hissed by his own servants, from the anonymity of the gallery, but he sat through the performance with 'the greatest composure.'[1]

Slowly, more and more of the fashionable world screwed up courage to defy their servants. Cumberland and Westmorland joined with Northumberland; the gentlemen of Wiltshire, meeting at Salisbury, preached rebellion but got cold feet. It was a campaign which could best be fought by collective action, so the way was pioneered by faculties, associations and even by infirmary boards, outsiders being invited to sign the pledge of abstinence. Many gentlemen who might have taken individual action had been deterred by the fear of appearing mean or Methodist, or by the risk of losing all their servants. Aware that they had been paying more to other men's servants than to their own, they now proposed, as a compensation for banning vails, to make a modest increase in wages. But a modest increase was no satisfaction to the more rapacious servants, whose vails had amounted to three or four times the value of their wages. There were butlers who pocketed from £60 to £100 a year from this source, often with the help of guineas from gentlemen worth but £50 a year. Many of them earned far more than did the lesser clergy or the clerks of the revenue.

In Northumberland a number of servants were dismissed for refusing to forswear vails and they migrated from the county. If their references explained why they were out of a place, they found masters and mistresses in no hurry to engage them. Among the early victims of the struggle were fifty English servants who had accompanied their masters to Germany. There their demands for higher wages and perquisites led to their dismissal. News of the affair got abroad,

[1] Robert Huish: *Memoirs of George III.*

and when the returning servants reached Sheerness the captain of the *Princess Royal* man-of-war sent his long boat in pursuit and pressed them into the Navy.[1]

In London, feeling ran high. A baronet, Sir William Blackett, who announced that he would pay no more vails, received a letter threatening to kill him and a reward of £100 was offered for information identifying the sender. Ranelagh became the scene of disturbances, notably in 1764 when coachmen and footmen hissed their masters, broke lamps and windows, extinguished torches and pelted the fashionable company with anything that came to hand. The result was that swords were drawn and several of the obstreperous servants were pinked.[2]

In that same year the leaders of Stamford society went a step farther than their neighbours and resolved to pay no vails to waiters in taverns and coffee-houses, 'as their masters can afford to give sufficient wages for the genteelest attendance.'[3] This move would hardly have commended itself to Dr Johnson, who preferred dining in taverns rather than in private houses because 'no servants will attend you with the alacrity that waiters do, who are incited by the prospect of an immediate reward in proportion as they please.'[4] Dr Johnson liked to have the waiters running briskly at his commands and he has his modern imitators who try to monopolise the service by the promise of high vails.

Smollett's novel *Humphrey Clinker* suggests that the servants of Bath did not lightly give up their right to vails. Squire Bramble's rustic maidservant, Winifred Jenkins, after describing the servants of Bath as 'devils incarnate,' says:

'They won't suffer the squire and mistress to stay any longer; because they have been already above three weeks in the house; and they look for a couple of ginny's a-piece at our going away; and this is a parquisite they expect every month in the season; being as how no family has a right to stay longer than four weeks in the same lodgings; and so the cuck swears, she will pin the dish-clout to mistress's tail; and the housemaid vows, she'll put cow-itch in master's bed, if so be he don't discamp without further ado.'

[1] *Annual Register*, 1760.   [2] *Annual Register*, 1764.
[3] *Notes and Queries*, IX.   [4] J. W. Krutch: *Samuel Johnson*.

Winifred Jenkins does not blame the servants for making the most of their opportunities. She tells of an argument with a grumbling manservant who objects to his master giving away an old coat to a poor man. 'I told him, by his agreement, he was to receive no vails; but he says as how there's a difference between vails and parquisites; and so there is for certain.'

The gentlemen of England gradually put down the worst of the abuses, but it was a long-drawn fight. Not for the first time, or the last time, a body of workers who had found the secret of easy money over-reached themselves through avarice. The luckier ones had made enough to buy themselves boarding-houses at spas or lodging-houses in London. As members of the petty bourgeoisie they probably found themselves giving modest vails at houses where they were entertained, for the system spread right down to one-servant houses. Parson Woodforde repeatedly records in his diary disbursements of a sixpence or a shilling to his friends' maids.[1] To this day the etiquette books are careful to set out the tariff of tips payable to the servants of one's host.

[1] *The Diary of a Country Parson, 1758–1802.*

IV

VIRTUE IN DANGER

Now Betty from her master's bed has flown
And softly stole to discompose her own.
SWIFT: *A Description of the Morning*

IT is difficult, at this distance, to see how a domestic system which called for the immuring, by day and night, of strapping young men and vigorous wenches, with little or no time off but a great deal of unorganised leisure on their hands, with plenty of meat and drink and scores of rooms and corners in which to wander, could have been expected to conduce towards the maintenance of chastity. What is surprising, perhaps, is that chastity was so often preserved. Is it cynical to suppose that, if the youth of the nineteen-sixties were suddenly to be conscripted into this way of life, the results might be more than a little scandalous?

Handbooks for serving maids warned that even brave gallants were liable to 'fall foul on the wench in the scullery.' These brave gallants included the master and the young master, but it is probable that, on balance, most servant girls who were undone were undone by their fellow-servants or by the local handyman.

To lessen the risks of seduction, girls were constantly urged to discount the flatteries of gentlemen, to beware of idleness, wanton looks and gestures, to wear no bright ribbons, feathers or other incitements to lust. The less a girl went gadding abroad, it was thought, the less likely was she to be ruined; but there were respectable homes in which a maid's virtue was in as much danger as it would have been in a thieves' kitchen.

In Pepys's day society expected pretty young women to put

old gentlemen to bed and could hardly complain if the morals of pretty young women suffered in the process. What passed between the Clerk to the Acts and little Deb Willett is familiar knowledge; but a couple of generations later maids were no longer expected to help undress their masters, comb their hair, wash their feet and sleep in the marital chamber. Nevertheless, Defoe thought very little indeed of the morals of female servants. In his *Everybody's Business Is Nobody's Business* he says: 'Many good families are impoverished and disgraced by these pert sluts who, taking the advantage of a young man's simplicity and unruly desires, draw many heedless youths, nay, some of good estates, into their snares; and of this we have but too many instances. Some, more artful, shall conceal their condition and palm themselves off on young fellows for gentlewomen of great fortune; how many families have been ruined by these ladies?' How many, indeed? Defoe does not venture an estimate. He goes on to deplore that even the master of a family may prefer 'the flirting airs of a young prinkt-up strumpet' to the 'artless sincerity of a plain, grave and good wife,' thus destroying his soul, body, family and estate.

Defoe is in no doubt where these saucy maids acquire their arts. 'Many of 'em rove from place to place, from bawdy-house to service and from service to bawdy-house again, ever unsettled and never easy, nothing being more common than to find these creatures one week in a good family and the next in a brothel. This amphibious life makes 'em fit for neither, for if the bawd use them ill away they trip to service and if their mistress gives 'em a wry word, whip they're at a bawdy-house again, so that in effect they neither make good whores nor good servants.'

Regrettably, says Defoe, there are gentlemen in the town who 'kiss and slop' their hosts' maids as a matter of course, and with an air of gallantry. 'Nay, some gentlemen are so silly that they shall carry on an underhand affair with their friend's servant maid, to their own disgrace and the wrong of many a young creature. Nothing is more base and ungenerous, yet nothing more common and withal so little taken notice of. D—— me, *Jack*, says one friend to another, *this maid of yours is*

a pretty girl. You do so-and-so to her, by G–d! This makes the
creature pert, vain and impudent and spoils many a good
servant. What gentleman will descend to this low way of
intrigue when he shall consider that he has a foot-boy or an
apprentice for his rival, and that he is seldom or never admitted
but when they have been his tasters! And the fool of Fortune,
though he comes at the latter end of the feast, yet pays the
whole reckoning: And so, indeed, would I have all such silly
cullies serv'd . . .'

To show that he is not striking too severe a moral attitude,
Defoe then says: 'If I must have an intrigue let it be with a
woman that shall not shame me. I would never go into the
kitchen when the parlour door was open.'

In his other pamphlet, *The Behaviour Of Servants Inquir'd
Into*, Defoe says that the moral rot begins when country
wenches go into the factories to spin. Having earned some
easy money, they turn vagrant and idle, 'getting big bellies,'
are turned out, leave their bastards in the parish and then go
up to London to become servants. 'Who would come away to
London to go into service if things were all well at home?'

Swift, in his *Directions To Servants*, does not overlook the
theme of female frailty. To the waiting maid in a nobleman's
household, he says:

'Never allow [my lord] the smallest liberty, not the squeezing
of your hand, unless he puts a guinea into it; so by degrees
make him pay accordingly for every new attempt, doubling
upon him in proportion to the concession you allow, and always
struggling, and threatening to cry out, or tell your lady,
although you receive his money; five guineas for handling
your breasts is a cheap pennyworth, although you seem to
resist with all your might; but never allow him the last favour
under a hundred guineas or a settlement of twenty pounds a
year for life.'

In such a household, says Swift, a handsome girl will normally
have the choice of three lovers: the chaplain, the steward and
my lady's gentleman. 'I would advise you to choose the
steward; but if you happen to be big with child by my lord,
you must take up with the chaplain.'

He continues: 'I must caution you particularly against my

lord's eldest son: if you are dextrous enough, it is odds that
you may draw him in to marry with you, and make you a lady:
if he be a common rake (and he must be one or t'other) avoid
him like Satan . . . after ten thousand promises you will get
nothing from him, but a big belly or a clap, and probably both
together.'

Swift is well aware that, just as the master may lust after
his maid, so may the mistress lust after her manservant. To the
waiting maid, he says: 'If your lady should happen to cast an
eye upon a handsome footman, you should be generous enough
to bear with her humour, which is no singularity, but a very
natural appetite; it is still the safest of all home intrigues, and
was formerly the least suspected, until of late years it hath
grown more common.'

All of which helps to set the stage for *Pamela* and the furore
which the publication, in 1740, of that immensely popular
novel inspired. Samuel Richardson, a vain and portly printer,
had been accustomed to put his pen at the disposal of servant
maids who wished help with their love letters. Then he con-
ceived the idea of publishing a book of 'familiar letters' suited
to all occasions and emergencies. It did not appear until after
Pamela was published, but two of the letters may appropriately
be quoted first. One is entitled: *A Father To A Daughter In
Service On Hearing Of Her Master's Attempting Her Virtue:*

My dear Daughter,

    I understand with great grief of heart that your master
has made some attempts on your virtue and yet that you
stay with him. God grant that you have not already yielded
to his base desires! For when once a person has so far forgotten what belongs to himself or to his character as to make
such an attempt, the very continuance with him and in his
power and under the same roof is an encouragement to him
to prosecute his business. And if he carries it better and
more civil at present it is only the more certainly to undo
you when he attacks you next. Consider, my dear child,
your reputation is all you have to trust to. And if you have
not already, which God forbid! yielded to him, leave it not
to the hazard of another temptation; but come away directly

(as you ought to have done on your own motion) at the command of
Your grieved and indulgent Father.

The prescribed form of reply from the daughter is as follows:

Honour'd Father,
  I received your letter yesterday and am sorry I stayed a moment in my master's house after his vile attempt. But he was so full of his promises of never offering the like again that I hoped I might believe him; nor have I yet seen anything to the contrary: But am so much convinced that I ought to have done as you say that I have this day left the house; and hope to be with you soon after you have received this letter.
Your dutiful Daughter.

If the heroine of *Pamela* had taken this sensible course there would have been no novel. The plot need be summarised only briefly. Pamela, an unusually literate girl of fifteen, is in service when her mistress dies, and Mr B., the young master, at once begins to show her attentions. Besides giving her a great many of her former mistress's clothes, in accordance with custom, he presses four guineas into her hand, possibly by way of recompense for her late arduous duties, and possibly not. This gift, when reported to Pamela's parents, fills them with not unjustified alarm. Mr B. corners and kisses Pamela in the summer-house and incurs from her the rebuke: 'You have taught me to forget myself and what belongs to me; and have lessened the distance that Fortune has made between us, by demeaning yourself to be so free with a poor servant.' But Mr B. continues to press gold in her hand, calling her a foolish slut when she spurns it, and soon afterwards begins putting his hand in her bosom. Instead of demanding Swift's tariff of five guineas, Pamela faints outright, and does so whenever the audacity is repeated. She is sent to Mr B.'s Lincolnshire estate, where a rascally housekeeper does her utmost to further her master's desires, even to the point of holding the girl down in bed for him; but again Pamela faints. In her conscious moments

The country maid is intercepted by a procuress
From Hogarth's 'The Harlot's Progress'

she begins to wonder whether she is, as her master says, a
'sauce-box' in presuming to resist him. She knows that such
goings-on occur daily—'there is Squire Martin in the Grove
has had three lyings-in, it seems, in the house in three months
past; one by himself and one by his coachman and one by his
woodman; and yet he has turned none of them away.' Among
Mr B.'s hunting companions are many others no better than
Squire Martin. But Pamela's virtue is invincible, and Mr B.,
driven desperate by her refusals, finally risks social ruin and
offers her his hand in marriage. Pamela has always cherished
an admiration for him, save only in the role of Tarquin, and
she accepts with much pleasure.

The moral is a highly ambiguous one. A number of clergymen
were so convinced that the work was all that was claimed for
it on the title page, namely a story designed 'to cultivate the
principles of religion and virtue in the minds of the youth of
both sexes,' that they preached sermons extolling it. Richardson
was hailed as 'a salutary angel in Sodom.' Pope thought the
novel was of more value than any number of sermons, which

is not very high praise. Less indulgent critics described Pamela as a minx, a young politician and a hard bargainer, resolved only to sell a valuable commodity for a just price. Her example, they said, would encourage servant maids to unheard-of audacities in the presence of their masters, and the result could only be a weakening of the natural order of society. Sir Walter Scott moderately summed up the views of the critics when he said of *Pamela:* 'It may be questioned whether the example is not as well calculated to encourage a spirit of rash enterprise as of virtuous resistance . . . it may occur to a humble maiden that to merit Pamela's reward she must go through Pamela's trials; and that there can be no great harm in affording some encouragement to the assailant. We need not add how dangerous this experiment must be for both parties.'[1]

Richardson protested that his heroine had reached a legitimate goal without the aid of art, coquetry, prudery or affectation. 'The moral meaning of Pamela's good fortune, far from tempting young gentlemen to marry such maids as are found in their families, is, by teaching maids *to deserve to be mistresses* and to stir up *mistresses to support their distinction.*'

While the excitement over *Pamela* was still high, there appeared a coarse deflating work entitled *An Apology For The Life Of Mrs Shamela Andrews*, by 'Conny Keyber.' Very probably Henry Fielding wrote it. Shamela is made to say: 'I thought once of making a little fortune by my person. I now intend to make a great one by my virtue.' Soon afterwards Fielding set out openly to deride *Pamela* in his novel *The History of Joseph Andrews*. In this he describes the temptations of Pamela's virtuous brother Joseph, a footman who resists not only the advances of a crude housekeeper, Mrs Slipslop, but those of his lickerish mistress, Lady Booby. In the park Joseph's mistress leans on his arm too frequently and grips his hand hard for fear of stumbling. In the house she encourages him to bring messages to her bedside, leers at him at table and indulges 'in all those innocent freedoms which women of figure may permit without the least sully of their virtue.' But all in vain; and Lady Booby faces the intolerable humiliation of being rejected by the lackey who carries her prayer-book.

[1] *Lives of the Novelists.*

Fielding appears to have had no objection, in principle or in practice, to a union between master and maid, for on his first wife's death he married Mary Daniel, the servant who had worked for her and shared his grief. She was a good wife and he treated her with all honour. Nor did this marriage prevent his being appointed justice of the peace in Westminster.

It would be as difficult to show that *Pamela* put ideas into servant girls' heads as to show that it did not. In the eighteenth century, as in any other century, even the highest families occasionally married into the servants' hall. Usually, such unions put a severe strain on social life, but the price might be worth paying. Boswell mentions an attorney in the Exchequer who married his cookmaid because she 'dressed a lovely bit of collop.' This gentleman may well have considered that a lovely bit of collop was worth more than a string of fashionable carriages at his door, and who shall blame him? Boswell was against the match for a different reason. 'There is something, I think, particularly indelicate and disgusting in the idea of a cookmaid. Imagination can easily cherish a fondness for a pretty chambermaid or a dairymaid, but one is revolted by the greasiness and scorching connected with the wench who toils in the kitchen.'[1]

In 1785 the fifth Earl of Berkeley tricked an eighteen-year-old lady's maid, Mary Cole, into what she believed to be a form of marriage and did not make an honest Countess of her until she had borne him seven children—and even then he did so only under duress. As 'Miss Tudor,' ostracised by society, she ran his household with extreme competence. Regrettably, her eldest son, deprived of the title, lived such a dissolute life —he was said to have thirty-three bastards within ten miles of Berkeley Castle—that no mothers would let their daughters enter his service.[2]

Occasionally, high-born ladies married their menservants, to the great delight of the gossips. In 1764 Horace Walpole helped to disseminate the news that Lord Rockingham's sister, Lady Henrietta Wentworth, had 'stooped even lower than a theatric swain' and married her footman, John William

[1] 'On Cookery,' 1779; quoted in *Boswell's Column*.
[2] H. Costley-White: *Mary Cole, Countess of Berkeley*.

Sturgeon. She proposed to live with his family in Ireland, as plain Mrs Sturgeon, and had given away all her fine clothes, saying that linen gowns were best suited to a footman's wife. It was the terms of her settlement on her husband that chiefly excited Walpole. The lady had 'mixed a wonderful degree of prudence with her potion,' declining to sweeten the draught too much for her lover. She settled £100 a year on him for life, entailing her whole fortune on her children, if any. A deed incorporating these arrangements was sent to Lord Mansfield, the Lord Chief Justice, as trustee, and he considered it to be 'as binding as any lawyer could make it.' Exclaims Walpole: 'Did one ever hear of more reflection in a delirium?'[1] Gilly Williams, a member of Walpole's circle, told George Selwyn: 'It is supposed she is with child by him, for they used to pass many hours together, which she called teaching John the mathematics.' Later Williams reported a *gaffe* made by a member of White's who pressed the Marquis of Rockingham to help himself to sturgeon.[2]

The career of 'Beau' Macdonald gives some idea of the havoc a handsome footman could cause in fashionable households. Macdonald lacked the iron resistance of Joseph Andrews. In his autobiography he is both proud of, and reticent about, his affairs, reporting merely the rumours about himself and the measures taken to remove temptations from his path. When a chambermaid at Bargeny told Lady Anne Hamilton that there was an intrigue between him and the housekeeper, the housekeeper was dismissed, lest Macdonald 'ruin his soul with her,' and replaced by an elderly woman. Then rumours were spread about Macdonald and the chambermaid, 'so the housekeeper always locked the rooms as she thought thereby to keep us from meeting.' Next, Lady Anne sent packing one of her guests, a widow of good family, on hearing that the good-looking footman had been in her room three times in a week to shave her head (she wore a wig). When the widow expressed surprise to the chambermaid at the summary manner of her dismissal, the servant said that Lady Anne had already turned off a housekeeper, a chambermaid and her own

[1] Peter Cunningham (ed.): *Letters of Horace Walpole.*
[2] J. H. Jesse: *George Selwyn and His Contemporaries.*

god-daughter on 'Jack's' account, 'and you know, Madam, the Earl and Countess of Crauford have been parted almost a twelvemonth, and I dare say you know for what.' The widow then left, consoled by the knowledge that she was not alone in being expelled for her indiscretion, but regretting perhaps the custom, not confined to Bargeny, of invariably dismissing the female partner to a domestic intrigue. It is hard to discover from the narrative just how many women were ordered from Bargeny for failing to rebuff 'Jack,' but a French governess and possibly another housekeeper seem also to have fallen from grace. Macdonald does not deign to say whether the rumours were true. It seems unlikely that he was the main cause of a breach between the Earl and Countess of Crauford, though quarrels over his conduct may have contributed to it.

Meanwhile John Hamilton, Lady Anne's husband, was growing irritated by Macdonald, who was so plainly getting above himself, and one night, in drink, he set about the footman with a golf club. Perhaps he, too, had begun to wonder why his wife retained this troublemaker. Macdonald is careful to mention an occasion when Lady Anne's coach reached a difficult patch of road and she would permit no servant but 'Jack' to carry her.

It could not last. For the second time Macdonald left Lady Anne's service and sought employment in Edinburgh. The city, he says, was so full of rumours about him that a Colonel Skeene advised him to go to London to look for a place, 'for no family here will hire you for fear of their women.' To test the truth of this he applied for a post with a Mr Campbell, 'who, being newly married, refused me.' The ladies of Edinburgh had now reached the stage of nudging each other when they saw 'Beau' Macdonald in the street, asking, 'Is that him?'

Macdonald thought his trouble was that he was too polite and obliging to women. A Major Joass, who hired him, said: 'I shall take you for my servant, for you must live with a single gentleman: no family will admit you into their house. I like a man that is given to women—that is gentleman-like— but to drink and swear is to be a blackguard.' Macdonald's reputation still accompanied him. On a visit to Tullibodie he was dining in the servants' hall when one of the housemaids said: 'Ever since the Major came here our ladies lock themselves in their rooms; is it for fear of the Major or his man?' This, says the ever-discreet Macdonald, 'went round the table as a joke.'

When his major, 'the best of masters,' became engaged to marry, Macdonald was wise enough to bow out, saying, 'Sir, servants that live with single gentlemen are not good family servants; so, sir, if you please to get a servant by the fifteenth of May and I shall go a little further.' The Major was sorry to have to heed this warning, 'but reason bore the sway.' Clearly, here were two men who thoroughly understood each other.

'Beau' Macdonald did not always yield to temptation. He mentions that he stayed in an apartment where a maid used to sit in bed with a lighted candle and leave the door open. 'I spoke to her and told her the danger of leaving a candle burning and falling asleep; so I put it out and came away.' For revenge, this girl locked him out early one morning when he had gone for a drink, hoping to disgrace him with his master. Another maid began to throw fainting fits and had to be carried to bed and undressed. 'I was proof against her,' says Macdonald, but 'from this day she became my enemy. What a terrible thing is lust! How terrible, when disappointed!'

The 'Beau' passes on another rumour that he was the cause of a separation between Lady Anne Hamilton and her husband. It does not seem to have caused him any distress. He obtained a new post with a married man, a powder merchant for the Army, who 'kept the best house in England,' but gave notice when his mistress began to send for him to receive instructions in her bedroom. 'I would rather have suffered death than to have been the cause of disturbance,' he explains. After his departure he heard a rumour that his late mistress was so desolated that she did not dress herself for three weeks.

Macdonald's story ends, respectably enough, after he gets a girl with child while travelling with his master in Spain. He finishes his tour of service and then returns to Spain to marry the girl, obtaining a post in a hotel. For all we know he lived happily ever after.

In modest establishments, like that of Parson Woodforde, there was no threat from Lotharios in livery, but the maids fell

The harlot and her maid
From Hogarth's 'The Harlot's Progress'

from grace just the same. The Parson had an alert eye for a
'big belly' and his diary contains entries like this: 'I told my
maid Betty that the other maid Nanny looked so big about the
waist that I was afraid she was with child, but· Betty told me
she thought not, but would soon inform me if it is so.'
The Parson was usually right. His maid Molly, after many
denials, admitted to being 'more than half gone,' thanks to Sam
Cudble, the carpenter. She was 'a very poor weak girl, but I
believe honest . . . for my own part I have long thought her
breeding.'[1]

Another entry records how 'Dr Clark's maid, Mary, was
this morning found out in concealing a dead child in her box
of which she had delivered herself yesterday morning, whether
she murdered it or not is not yet known.' That a maid in a
doctor's house should be able to give birth to a child without
anyone being aware of it may seem odd; but the annals of
infanticide do not lack instances of maids who disposed of
their infants, set the bodies temporarily on one side, and went

[1] *The Diary of a Country Parson, 1758–1802.*

on with the day's work, admitting only to being a little off colour.

The letters of Elizabeth Purefoy, of Shalstone, Buckinghamshire, also harp on the lapses of housemaids. Henry Purefoy had the painful task of writing a letter to the father of one maid saying: 'I am very sorry to tell you that she is very forward with child' and inviting him to take such measures as he thought proper (this was one letter for which there was no model in Samuel Richardson's collection). Mrs Purefoy notes how one of her servants falsely accused himself of having got a girl into trouble: 'My coachman John is gone from me, pretending a wench followed him with a great belly, but he was drunk when he ran away and they say there was no wench followed him.'[1]

Housemaids of doubtful virtue were a difficult enough problem, but wicked nursemaids were a worse one. The dissolute William Hickey claims, possibly with truth, that his morals were corrupted in childhood by his nurse. Nanny Harris, 'a pretty, smart little girl,' arrived in the Hickey household with strong recommendations from the Duchess of Manchester, her situation in the family being half-companion, half-servant. Hickey at that time was about seven years old and the girl's chief responsibility was towards his twin sisters; but, he says, 'Nanny Harris at once became my delight and I was no less hers.' Each night, when the servant had removed the candles from the nursery, the girl used to lift young Hickey out of his bed, take him into hers 'and there fondle and lay me upon her bosom.' She was 'as wanton a little baggage as ever existed,' and, according to Hickey, her ways strongly influenced him through several years of his life. Long after the Hickey family had turned her away, for indulging in too many amours, it was discovered that the Duchess of Manchester had dismissed her 'for debauching Master Montague (her only son) when thirteen years old, which circumstance Her Grace most improperly omitted to mention when recommending the girl as a confidential servant in a private family.'[2] Families who entrusted the upbringing of their children to servants ran a constant risk of dangers such as these, no matter what

[1] G. Eland (ed.): *Purefoy Letters, 1735–53.*
[2] William Hickey: *Memoirs.*

precautions they took to employ only nursemaids of impeccable morals and unexampled piety.

A heavy load of responsibility for girls 'going wrong' lay on a society which did its best to keep servants celibate and frequently dismissed them when they married. 'Few people,' said Jonas Hanway, 'have humanity and patriotism sufficient to entertain married servants . . . I see no reason why this class of people should be prohibited marriage more than any other.'[1] The ban had the same effect that it had on soldiers and sailors: it contributed to immorality. Society was culpable on another count: callous or quick-tempered masters and mistresses often turned servants adrift, without references or resources, after disputes in which at least 50 per cent of the blame, and perhaps 90 per cent, lay with the employer. Without a character, it was difficult to find respectable employment again. The outcast went for shelter where the rents were lowest, and where the rents were lowest so were the morals. The mistress who had turned the girl away for a perhaps trivial reason thought nothing more of her; if she later heard that the girl had exchanged hunger for prostitution, it was easy to assume that she had a natural disposition to vice. Even virtuous servant girls were sometimes waylaid by harpies and decoyed into brothels, where strenuous efforts were made to debauch them.

On the whole, maids in households faced fewer temptations than those who worked in inns. In *Joseph Andrews* Fielding tells of twenty-one-year-old Betty: 'Her constitution was composed of those warm ingredients which, though the purity of courts or nunneries might have happily controlled them, were by no means able to endure the ticklish situation of chambermaid at an inn; who is daily liable to the solicitations of lovers of all complexions; to the dangerous addresses of fine gentlemen in the Army, who sometimes are obliged to reside with them a whole year together; and, above all, are exposed to the caresses of footmen, stage coachmen and drawers; all of whom employ the whole artillery of kissing, flattering, bribing and every other weapon which is to be found in the whole armoury of love, against them.'

[1] *Eight Letters to His Grace The Duke of* ——.

To take a girl who had worked at an inn into private employment was thought to be asking for trouble. Even if her morals were unimpaired, her ways were likely to be too free for a gentleman's household; though not necessarily too free for that same gentleman when staying at an inn.

V

CONDITIONS OF SERVICE

IN the eighteenth century, the State cared little or nothing for the welfare of domestic servants. Masters had a personal responsibility towards those who had served them long. As the cynics said, they were expected to leave to their servants what little their servants had left to them. Footmen and maids who flitted from place to place were expected to make their own arrangements for their old age; if they failed to do so, and if they had no claim on private philanthropy, they ended up in the parish workhouse—if the parish would accept them.

It was an unwritten rule, though a much-broken one, that a master should maintain his servant in sickness. He might call in the family physician, but more often he would summon the apothecary, who presented himself respectfully at the back door. It did not follow that the servant was any the worse treated in consequence, for neither physician nor apothecary could offer any cure, save for the simplest ailment.

Masters tended to grudge the upkeep of ailing servants whose misfortunes were avoidable. Horace Walpole, writing to the Countess of Ossory in 1783, said:

'You may laugh at my distress, Madam, but it is a very serious thing to have taken an old cook as yellow as a dishclout and have her seduced by a jolly dog of a coachman and have her miscarry of a child and go on with a dropsy. All my servants think that the moment they are useless I must not part with them and so I have an infirmary instead of a *ménage*: and those that are good for anything do nothing but get children so that my house is a mixture of a county and a foundling hospital.'[1]

[1] Peter Cunningham (ed.): *Letters of Horace Walpole.*

At Strawberry Hill there was space to maintain a casualty or two. In lesser households, shortage of room meant that a seriously sick servant must be sent home, or to the workhouse; and the sooner the better unless the master wanted to find himself saddled with a bill for the funeral. Parson Woodforde had a maid who suffered from severe fits; with regrets, he returned her to her parents. A sick maidservant with no home would pawn her clothes and go to lie in a garret, where she could expect to receive overtures from pimps and harpies if she recovered. She was liable to receive similar approaches in hospital; right into the nineteenth century the wards were infested by miscreants hoping 'to make merchandise of the innocence of deserted and ignorant females.'[1]

In many households, the fear that servants would bring in smallpox was a very live one. The more enlightened masters, notably the fourth Duke of Bedford, had their servants inoculated, whether they liked it or not. The Duke also subsidised heavily the first smallpox hospital opened in 1746. This institution, according to the historian of the Russells, was particularly intended for servants of great houses.[2] Less affluent masters, in their advertisements for servants, often stipulated 'must have had the smallpox.' Any servants who applied for posts with the Purefoy family, at Shalstone, were required to sign a document saying that if they fell ill of this disease the hire was immediately at an end. What happened to them thereafter was their own concern, or that of their parents.

If a servant received a pension, it was—in Army language— a privilege and not an entitlement. Many who should have been pensioned were allowed to dodder out their lives in minor capacities. There was often the chance of a small legacy, provided the master did not live on obstinately long. The fourth Earl of Chesterfield's will, more magnanimous than many, said: 'I give to all my menial or household servants that shall have lived with me five years or upwards at the time of my death, whom I consider as unfortunate friends, my equals in Nature, and my inferiors only by the difference of our positions,

[1] Rev. H. G. Watkins: *Hints and Observations Seriously Addressed to Heads of Families* (1816).
[2] Gladys Scott Thomson: *The Russells in Bloomsbury.*

two years wages above what is due to them at my death, and
mourning; and to all my other menial servants one year's
wages and mourning.' His old groom for forty years was to
receive forty guineas if still in service.[1] As a rule servants
were not to know what was in the master's will, though sometimes a hint—occasionally a misleading one—was dropped by
the master while alive. In 1769 a Mr Bristow who had promised
to remember in his will an aged servant of forty years' service
died leaving £21,000 to three charity schools and £5 to the
servant. The trustees of the schools agreed to pay the woman
£30 a year, 'an act truly generous and equitable,' in the view
of the *Annual Register*. Occasionally, a servant might pick up a
minor windfall through the operation of such a bequest as
that which operated in the parish of St Clement's Dane, where
a sum of £10 (equal to about two years' wages) was payable to
any servant who spent seven years in the service of one master.

What is astonishing is that so many servants were able to
achieve a modest independence in their last years. Facilities
for saving were hardly encouraging (the penny banks did not
come until the nineteenth century) and money deposited under
the hearthstone yielded no interest. Sometimes masters and
mistresses were willing to act as banks. In 1756 Parson
Woodforde writes: 'I received this morning of Elizabeth
Clothier, my mother's maid, the sum of ten pounds, to keep
for her, and I shall give her ten shillings per annum, which is
at the rate of five per centum for the use of it; I do it purely to
encourage her to be careful and to make her saving . . .' Ten
years later Elizabeth Clothier gives him another sum of £10
and Elizabeth Crich £20. He stipulates that he is to have six
months' notice before repayment of principal.[2] Arrangements
of this kind helped, perhaps, to deter servants from seeking
other situations; a roving servant would hesitate to tie up his
or her capital with a master who required six months' notice of
withdrawal, and who might, if crossed, make difficulties about
repayment. There was also the risk that a master might lose
his servant's money in an unfortunate investment, or go
bankrupt. Against this, banking with an employer helped to

---

[1] W. H. Craig: *Life of Lord Chesterfield*.
[2] *The Diary of a Country Parson, 1758–1802*.

preserve a servant's savings from greedy parents, who sometimes called a daughter home and claimed her money as
theirs.

Ordinarily, only upper servants contrived to save enough
money to change their way of life. Their usual ambition was
to buy a tavern or a lodging-house, or to keep apartments for
gentlefolk at spas or seaside resorts; and their chances of
success were enhanced if they married housekeepers or steady
maidservants. William Brummell, valet to Charles Monson,
Member of Parliament for Lincoln, bought a house in St
James's and let the upper rooms to gentlemen seeking more
refined accommodation than they were likely to find at an inn.
His grandson was George Bryan Brummell, otherwise 'the
Beau.' Illiteracy was the usual stumbling-block to advancement
in an ambitious lower servant. Sometimes a likely lad might be
taught the three Rs by the upper servants, or by a governess,
with or without the master's approval (many masters believed
that education merely bred discontent). For the unlettered
servant there was no other career, according to Jonas Hanway,
but 'to stand at a turnpike or sell beer, which if I mistake not
are the principal promotions of domestics who marry, though
some become farmers.'

The parishes were naturally concerned that the cost of
looking after aged or decrepit servants should not fall on them.
Under the rules, if a man spent twelve months in service in a
parish he was entitled to relief in sickness and old age. In
order to spare the pockets of themselves and their neighbours,
masters used to make a point of discharging their servants
before the year was up and then re-engaging them after a
lapse of two or three days. The servants well understood the
purpose of this manœuvre, which was practised by citizens of
the utmost respectability.

The notion that, somehow, women might be *trained* as
servants did not go untried. Ladies of the manor sometimes
set up, and equipped, schools for this purpose and undertook
to find places for those who studied diligently; and the charitable
helped by providing maids with their first outfits. Luxuries
like reading and writing rarely found a place in the curriculum;
it was sufficient if the graduates could sew, mend, wash, iron

One of Hogarth's servants

and cook. Hannah More started schools in the Cheddar area to teach girls sewing, knitting and spinning, her avowed purpose being 'to train up the lower classes in habits of industry and piety.' She was not concerned with raising philosophers; 'I allow of no writing for the poor.' At times the objects of such schools were imperfectly understood by the county families. A squire looked in during classes in a Somerset village and said to the instructor: 'Well, madam, what good are you doing here? What are the girls learning and earning? Where are your manufactures? Where is your spinning and carding?'[1] But the Hannah Mores were not worried about the export drive; they were only, in their foolish, limited way, attempting to produce good and pious servants. Hannah More

[1] M. Phillips and W. S. Tomkinson: *English Women in Life and Letters.*

had her own bone to pick with the squirearchy, who in the latter half of the century became addicted to Sunday card-playing and concert-going. 'I am persuaded,' wrote Miss More, 'that the Hallelujahs to Heaven would make no moral music to the ear of a conscientious person while he reflected that multitudes of servants are waiting in the streets exposed to every temptation; engaged perhaps in profane swearing and idle, if not dissolute, conversation. . . . Your servants have been accustomed to consider a concert as a secular diversion; if you, therefore, continue it on a Sunday will not they also expect to be indulged on that day with their common amusements?'[1]

Very few good servants were recruited from the ranks of pauper children. The Act of 1722 which enabled parishes to set up workhouses has been described as an Act for the Corruption of Youth. It enabled the overseers to pile all human refuse, in the shape of criminals, prostitutes, tramps, idiots, orphans and bastards, in a common heap. By the time workhouse children had reached the age of seven or eight—and many of them never reached it—they were usually depraved and dishonest. At the first opportunity they were taken from their gin-drenched nurses and farmed out to such overworked sluttish housewives as could find no other domestic help. Their fate was no less dismal than that of the orphans who, later in the century, were transported to the mills to work a twelve- or fifteen-hour day.

It was possible, according to Defoe, for a justice of the peace to order idle young people into service, if they were demonstrably a load on their parents, but not if they had already found themselves semi-parasitic jobs as 'self-employed.'[2] A conscripted servant, in any event, would have been singularly useless.

A proposal to set up offices for recruiting servants was made by Henry Fielding.[3] His Universal Register Office was opened, in 1749, opposite Cecil Street in the Strand. A pamphlet expounding its aims, published in 1751, said that it was ready

---

[1] *Thoughts on the Importance of the Manners of the Great in General Society* (1788).

[2] *The Behaviour of Servants.*

[3] In 1671 an 'intelligence office' for servants in London was established under patent of Charles II.

to introduce not only masters to servants, but borrowers to
lenders, landlords to tenants, rectors to curates and travellers
to travelling companions. For a while the Universal Register
Office was prosperous enough to encourage several dubious
imitations. These in turn inspired a ribald farce at Drury Lane,
The Register Office, by Joseph Reed, featuring the establishment
of one Gulwell, in whose hands 'the good old trade of pimping
is carried on with great success and decency.' The clients
include Mrs Snarewell, seeking virgins for her bagnio; simple
Margery from Yorkshire, who complains 'The Squire wad not
let me be — By my truly, Sir, he was after me Mworn, noon
and neeght'; Harwood, a widower, who wants to marry a
housekeeper but cannot lower himself to wed one without a
fortune; Lord Brilliant, who requires a housekeeper to marry
to his chaplain; and a simple Celt or two who are welcomed by
Gulwell as fodder for the American plantations. Another
caller, Lady Wrinkle, who complains that her last footman had
the audacity to make love to her, specifies her needs thus: 'None
of your snipper-snapper, whey-faced jacks, but as proper a
man as one would wish to see at a review of the Guards—
nothing adds more to the dignity of an equipage than the size
and stateliness of one's domestics.' This did not mean that
she required a man of breeding. 'Don't you know, sir, that we
quality always make it a point never to admit into our service
any creature that has the least pretence to birth? With the
mushroom part of mankind we can do as we please; treat them
with all the contempt, state, insolence and superiority that
characterise the woman of quality . . . there is no enduring
the insolence of a decay'd gentleman.'

The references presented by servants were often of scant
value. Some were forged, but it was rarely necessary for a
servant to go to such lengths. Most mistresses, as Steele
complained, were perfectly willing to give a sacked servant 'a
very good word to anybody else.' Thus it was that people saw
'in a year and a half's time, the same face a domestick in all
parts of the town.' The true meaning of the usual testimonial
was:

'The bearer hereof is so uneasy to me, that it will be an act
of charity in you to take him off my hands; whether you prefer

him or not is all one, for I have no manner of kindness for him, or obligation to him or his; and do what you please as to that.'[1]

The editor of *The World* complained that the granting of misleading references made employers accessories to crime. 'A servant after he has committed the most palpable robbery, for which you are turning him out of doors and which would go near to hang him at the Old Bailey, looks composedly in your face and very modestly hopes that you will not refuse him a character, for you are too worthy a gentleman to be the ruin of a poor servant, who has nothing but his character to depend upon for bread.'[2] This blackmail usually worked only too well and the miscreant was duly certified sober, honest and diligent.

Yet sometimes an employer found time to compose an honest, helpful reference. The following was written by Charles Berkeley, a son of the fourth Lord Berkeley:

'Catherine York is the best cook I have had in twenty years or more that I have kept house. She may have lived here about ten months. I believe her honest, not extravagant in the kitchen; she is very clean. Her temper is like charcoal, which kindles soon, and sparks to the top of the house. She is passionate and ungovernably wilful in her way. We had many quarrels and bore many faults for the sake of the table. The final quarrel was, my wife, according to custom, sent her maid to see the other maids' candles out. Catherine York bolted her door, and denied her entrance. I do not charge her with drinking but with being as impetuous as if she did drink. I was afraid we might be burnt in our beds.'[3]

In Scotland, conditions of service were harsher than in England. Lecky quotes a saying that 'every master was revered by his family, honoured by his tenants and awful to his domestics.'[4] Certainly, Scottish servants, save those in the employ of great houses, had fewer distractions, fewer victuals and lower wages. They enjoyed, according to one account, 'three days broth and salt meat, the rest meagre, with plenty of bread and small beer.' Men earned £3 or £4 a year, women 30s. or 40s.

[1] *Spectator*, No. 493 (1712).   [2] *The World*, No. 157 (1756).
[3] J. H. Jesse: *George Selwyn and His Contemporaries*.
[4] *A History of England in the Eighteenth Century*.

Few maids knew how to dress or sew linen, their technical accomplishments being limited to mangling. Gentlemen's shirts were got up by the housekeeper, ladies' head-dresses by their personal maids. In Smollett's *Humphrey Clinker* Winifred Jenkins complains that country people in Scotland rarely have meat and that the servants are poor drudges, often without shoes or stockings. She also protests that there is no jakes in the whole kingdom, 'nor anything for poor servants, but a barrel with a pair of tongs thrown across.' And she is shocked by the housemaids' custom of emptying chamber-pots out of the upper windows into the streets, with cries of 'gardy loo' (*gardez l'eau*).

Although the State took no interest in the welfare of domestic servants, it did not overlook the idea of raising revenue from them. Lord North, worried over the cost of the American wars, decided to put a tax of one guinea on menservants, whom he regarded as a luxury to be discouraged. There were households, as he pointed out, which kept thirty or forty lackeys. If the guinea tax pressed heavily on a man who kept two servants, all he had to do was to keep one. Lord North estimated that some 100,000 menservants were retained for purposes of luxury and ostentation and that the revenue would thus benefit by £105,000.

This tax aroused less grumbling than did the operation of a similar tax in the 1930s. Much stronger protests, however, greeted the proposal by Pitt, in 1785, to extend taxation to female servants, at the rate of 2s. 6d. for one servant, 5s. for two and 10s. for three. Charles Fox thought the idea was 'unmanly' and that it would bear heavily on families with a number of children. A Mr Courtenay feared that numbers of women servants would be dismissed and driven to prostitution; was this what Mr Pitt had in mind? In passing, Courtenay pointed out that in Holland the State cared for a servant out of work. 'If the right honourable gentleman was a sportsman,' he said, 'he never would have thought of distressing females, for it was a rule with those who were fond of game never to kill a hen pheasant.'[1] The Earl of Surrey suggested, instead of a tax on females, a levy on persons wearing powdered hair, carrying

[1] *Parliamentary Register*, 1777.

watches and wearing silk stockings. Pitt was sufficient of a sportsman to modify his original proposal. He said that families would be allowed one tax-free servant to two children, and the loss would be made up by making bachelors pay double rate for their female servants and £1 5s. extra for each of their menservants.

A levy on powdered hair, as urged by the Earl of Surrey and others, was not effectively enforced until 1795. At this period, according to John Donaldson's letter to William Pitt, society used as much flour on their heads in a year as would have made thirty million quartern loaves. Henceforth the practice cost a guinea and voices were raised in Parliament complaining about the cost of powdering a retinue of footmen. Pitt's political opponents combed out their hair and ceased to use powder, dubbing those who used it 'guinea pigs.' The guinea pigs regarded themselves as eminently patriotic in paying the levy, and pooh-poohed the notion that they were depriving the poor of bread. This tax lasted until 1869, when it produced only £1000 in revenue, mostly from footmen and coachmen.[1]

[1] Neville Williams: *Powder and Paint.*

VI

BLACK BOYS FOR SALE

THE richly-dressed black boy, all smiles or all sulks, was such a feature—and a problem—of eighteenth century society that he deserves a chapter to himself.

In earlier generations, the rich had been served by Moorish and Asiatic boys, but with the boom in the slave trade fashionable people were on the look-out for young Africans who could be infiltrated into the British Isles or acquired from their colonial masters on visits home. Steele's *Tatler* carried an advertisement which read: 'A black boy, twelve years of age, fit to wait on a gentleman, to be disposed of at Denis's Coffeehouse in Finch Lane, near the Royal Exchange.' Similar announcements appeared in many publications over the first seventy years of the century. Usually the black boy was 'wellmade,' 'good-natured' and 'handy,' and it was a notable recommendation if his colour was 'an excellent fine black.' Even black girls were bought and sold in inns or coffee-houses. The *Public Ledger* in 1767 had a notice: 'For sale, a healthy Negro Girl, aged about 15 years, speaks good English, works well at her needle, does household work and has had the small pox.'

Usually, black servants were disposed of privately, which spared annoyance to those cranks who did not care to see human beings sold like horses. After the forger John Rice was hanged at Tyburn in 1763 his bankrupt effects were auctioned, and among them was his Negro boy, for whom £32 was asked and given. 'A shocking instance in a free country,' exclaimed the *Stamford Mercury*.

In the main, black boys in Britain were indulgently treated.

Some were groomed as domestic pets, dressed in fine clothes and tricked out in jewelled silver collars as a token of their dependence (William III's slave had a padlocked white marble collar). Often they were sent to school, instructed in the Christian religion and baptised. Such cosseting, physical and spiritual, was resented by plantation owners who, on their sojourns in Britain, kicked and beat their black boys as heartily as they did in the West Indies. When the lads fled they were hunted down with all proper rigour, and a black fugitive had not much chance in a white country. Anyone who enticed a slave from his master, or harboured him while the search was on, was liable to be prosecuted for theft of goods.

If black boys were not invariably good-natured and handy, no one can be surprised. Those who were petted responded in the normal way of petted children, by tantrums, impudence and disobedience. The *Gentleman's Magazine*, in 1764, complained that black servants were no more eager to perform menial work than our own people, 'and if put to it are generally sullen, spiteful, treacherous and revengeful.' It was therefore highly impolitic 'to introduce them as servants here where that rigour and severity is impracticable which is absolutely necessary to make them useful.'

Not every black servant mentioned in the memoirs of the time was, in fact, a slave. Dr Johnson's Francis Barber, a Jamaican, had belonged to a Colonel Bathurst who died leaving Francis his freedom. Johnson, who loathed slavery, went out of his way to treat his Negro well, sending him to the Bishop Stortford Grammar School, instructing him in religion and taking his side in domestic brawls. The Doctor himself went to buy oysters for his ailing cat rather than allow Francis to feel humiliated by being sent on such an errand.[1] Twice Francis ran away, the second time enlisting in the Royal Navy, whence Johnson extracted him (though he was happy where he was). The Sage's liberality in proposing a pension of £70 for Francis, plus a large lump sum, shocked his friends and executors. It was more than many a nobleman paid an English upper servant for a lifetime of devotion.

Casanova brought a black boy with him to England and

[1] J. W. Krutch: *Samuel Johnson.*

took him everywhere, save into my lady's chamber. Once, in
financial straits, he offered Jarbe the choice of dismissal with
twenty guineas, or of leave of absence with the right to rejoin
him later. Jarbe said he would rather stay and offered his
master a bag containing sixty guineas, which was refused. But
Jarbe then vanished.[1]

William Hickey was accompanied in Britain by 'my little
pet boy Nabob,' also described as 'my little Bengally.' 'He
was a great pet with all the ladies, being an interesting-looking,
handsome boy. I dressed him, too, very smart as a Hussar. As
a servant he was not of the least use to me.' Hickey's father
took a fancy to Nabob and arranged for the boy to be taught to
read and write, a course which his master had not apparently
contemplated. When the boy expressed a wish to be a Christian,
Hickey had him baptised. But the *protégé* later acted with
'treachery and baseness,' sneaking out to disclose his master's
whereabouts to a man who was dunning him, after the other
servants had refused all information.[2]

Sometimes, the gentlemen of England showed suspicion of
the affection which their womenfolk showered on well-set-up
black servants, who were excluded from few domestic
intimacies. The more intelligent Negroes were encouraged to
take part in general conversation. Horace Walpole says that
Lord Milford's sisters had a favourite black, who was 'remarkably sensible.' To amuse the ailing Lady Phillips, her relatives
read to her an account of the Pelew Islands. When someone
happened to say that a British ship was being sent there, the
black exclaimed: 'Then there is an end of their happiness.'
Walpole's comment is: 'What a satire on Europe!'[3]

The eccentric Duchess of Queensberry adopted 'an uncommonly smart and intelligent little Mongo' called Soubise,
whom she not only educated but, against the advice of her
friends, instructed in the accomplishments of a gentleman. A
young man who fenced and rode could hardly be expected to
bring in the tea to the drawing-room; instead, Soubise drank
champagne, visited the opera, drove in Hyde Park, joined
fashionable clubs and ran up debts. He used so much perfume

[1] Casanova: *Memoirs*.   [2] William Hickey: *Memoirs*.
[3] Peter Cunningham (ed.): *Letters of Horace Walpole*.

that ladies would exclaim 'I scent Soubise' before they saw him. Eventually he became a heavy embarrassment and was persuaded to accept a post as fencing master and horse-breaker in India.[1]

Until the middle years of the century, little protest was voiced at this extension of slavery to the Mother Country. It was easy to make too much fuss about such matters. Negroes were heathens and heathens were a commodity to be bought and sold, like cattle. In 1729 there was some alarm when the notion was advanced that slaves who had been baptised Christians could claim their liberty, but the Law Officers of the Crown expressed the view that a mere sprinkling of holy water did nothing to weaken the law of property. They said:

'We are of opinion that a slave by going from the West Indies to Great Britain or Ireland either with or without his master doth not become free; and that his master's property or right in him is not thereby determined or varied; and that baptism doth not bestow freedom on him nor make any alteration in his temporal condition in this Kingdom: We are also of the opinion that the master may legally compel him to return again to the plantations.'

It was just what the more callous owners needed. In order to hunt down runaways they now employed thief-takers and miscellaneous ruffians to kidnap them and carry them on board ship. Advertisements offering rewards for missing slaves contained assurances like 'the utmost secrecy may be depended on'; meaning that if the runaway was detained by lawless means, no questions would be asked.

Then Granville Sharp, that stubborn eccentric, philanthropist and musical virtuoso, came on the scene. In 1765 he encountered in Mincing Lane the slave boy Jonathan Strong, standing in a queue outside the surgery of Sharp's brother. The boy had been shockingly beaten and half-blinded by his master, a lawyer named David Lisle, of Barbados, and then turned adrift. Granville and William Sharp took charge of the lad, had him admitted to St Bartholomew's Hospital, and after four months apprenticed him to an apothecary. By misfortune, two years later, Lisle met his slave in the street and realised that he had regained not only his appearance but his value.

[1] Violet Biddulph: *Kitty, Duchess of Queensberry*.

A black boy in evil company
From Hogarth's 'The Harlot's Progress'

Lisle thereupon sold his rights in the lad for £30 to a friend, James Kerr, on the understanding that Strong would be shipped to the West Indies, and, as a precaution, the two had him decoyed into prison. Granville Sharp got to hear of the affair and was able to effect the lad's release, since no charge had been made against him. Lisle and Kerr then sued Sharp for £200 damages for depriving them of property. When his lawyers told him that the 1729 ruling had been maintained, more than once, by the Lord Chief Justice, Sharp turned to the law books himself and was able to raise enough legal dust to frustrate the action. He declined a challenge by Lisle to a duel.

In 1769 Sharp published a pamphlet *The Injustice And Dangerous Tendency Of Tolerating Slavery In England*, which was not without its effect on the public conscience. Then came the case of the Negro Hylas and his wife, who had met each other as slaves in Britain. Hylas was freed by his owner, but shortly afterwards his wife was seized by her owner and sent to the West Indies to be sold. Hylas won an action against the kidnappers and his wife was freed on the grounds that she should

enjoy the same privilege as her husband. Next Sharp rescued
a kidnapped slave from a ship in the Downs, before it could
sail, but he had difficulty in working up a clear case which
would force the evasive Lord Chief Justice to declare cate-
gorically that slavery was illegal in Britain. Lord Mansfield
was obsessed with the thought that there were 14,000 slaves
in Britain, and that each of them represented a capital investment of about £50; thus, if he ruled against slavery, the owners
would be involved in a loss of £700,000. His own view was:
'I would have all masters think them free, and all Negroes
think they were not, because then they would behave better.'

Finally, in 1772, came the watertight case that Sharp had
been looking for, that of the Negro Somerset. His master had
consigned him to a Jamaica-bound ship in the Thames, where
he was held in irons until, by Sharp's intervention, he was
removed and brought before the King's Bench. The Lord
Chief Justice tried in vain to wriggle out of giving the humane
decision, hinting to Somerset's owner that he would be doing
a valuable service by setting the slave free and making a formal
judgment unnecessary; but the owner refused. So, making the
best of a bad job, Mansfield delivered the historic judgment
for which he has received rather more credit than he deserves.
'The state of slavery,' he said, 'is so odious that nothing can
be suffered to support it but positive law. Whatever inconvenience, therefore, may fall from the decision I cannot say
this case is allowed or approved by the law of England; and
therefore the black must be discharged.' It was a sad day; not
only had he let down the property owners of Britain but he
had been defeated by a layman.

The 14,000 slaves in Britain were now free. Some of them
at once detached themselves from their masters, but most
continued to work in the same household at a negotiated wage.
Of those who cut loose, a number were reluctant to take up
further work, regarding themselves as having been emancipated
not only from slavery but from work, and parish officers took
strenuous steps to prevent them from lingering long enough
to become a burden on the rates. Sharp, the benefactor, was
beleaguered by those he had freed; gratefully, he clutched at
a proposal to ship them overseas to found a colony of free

black men. In 1787 a transport sailed to Africa with 411 ex-slaves and, thanks to some cynical intrigue, sixty white women from Wapping mostly prostitutes, made drunk for the occasion. Such was the unhappy origin of the colony of Sierra Leone.

VII

BRAVE NEW WORLD

DURING the eighteenth century there were Englishmen who looked enviously on the system of contractual domestic service which had been established in the American colonies. How gratifying to have a servant, man or woman, bound by strict indentures for a fixed term of years, a person who could be compelled to do any and every job indoors or outdoors, who was forbidden to enter taverns, to marry without permission, to stay out at nights, to traffic in goods or to seek another place.

These servants were not black slaves, though the southern colonists had those too, but white men and women, known as 'redemptioners' or *engagés*. They were penniless Europeans who, in effect, sold themselves to ships' captains in return for a sea passage to the New World. The captain, in turn, sold them to settlers as indentured, all-purpose servants. It was a system which had begun in Virginia in the previous century and other colonies had copied it. The prize for a redemptioner who stayed the course might be fifty acres of land or a sum of money.

Notoriously, not all who sailed from Britain as redemptioners in the early years went aboard of their free will. In Stuart days the authorities closed an eye to the activities of crimps and 'spirits' who seduced, drugged, kidnapped or knocked senseless unwary individuals in seaport towns. The Mother Country had too many poor and the new colonies had not enough servants and labourers; thus, it seemed that a little rugged private enterprise could be relied upon to adjust the balance. In one year of Charles II's reign some ten thousand unwilling citizens were carried to America. Among them were convicted criminals who had the option of choosing transportation instead of the gallows, which they did in such numbers that the colony of Massachusetts earnestly begged to be excused entertaining any more of 'His Majesty's Seven-Year Passengers.'

Among the voluntary redemptioners were a fair leavening of honest men and women—artisans, labourers, schoolmasters— who had their own good reasons for starting life all over again. They were prepared to face menial labour and a good deal of hardship if, at the end of it, they could emerge as free individuals owning land. Some of them were stimulated to emigrate by agents of shipowners who toured the country-side—notably in Ireland and Germany—talking as eloquently of the rich prospects in the New World as the recruiting ser-geants talked of prospects in the Army.

How the emigrants fared depended not only on their own resolution but on the honesty of the ships' captains and the humanity of the settlers who engaged them. To ship a servant, equipped with a minimum outfit, and in the minimum of comfort, to America cost the captain between £5 and £10. Once there, the passenger could be disposed of for anything up to £30 (in the early days he would be bartered for flour or wheat). Towards the end of the voyage, a rascally skipper might bully his redemptioners into accepting new, and more onerous terms. By that time morale would be low, for sickness, disease and death often decimated the payload. John Harrower, who made the passage in 1774, tells in his diary how his fellow-servants nearly mutinied when they were put on an allowance of bread and *maté*. Two men who asked for extra food were locked in irons, and a passenger who returned from shore leave drunk and abusive was horse-whipped and given a taste of the thumb-screws.[1]

At the American port, a captain would often insert an advertisement in the local newspaper, inviting offers for 'a parcel of servants,' and listing such special attractions as 'spinsters 14–35 years of age.' Would-be employers would then come down to the ship and scrutinise his livestock. Some-times dealers called 'soul drivers' came aboard, bought a

[1] Quoted in *Diary of America* (ed. Josef and Dorothy Berger).

selection of servants and drove them inland, like cattle, until
they were able to dispose of them. As a rule, the captain had
thirty days in which to sell off his passengers. By the twenty-
ninth day his attitude towards his unclaimed stock was likely
to be a long way from civil.

The colonies made varying efforts to regulate the traffic,
but abuses flourished. An employer was bound to give his
servant board, food, clothing and medical attendance. In
Pennsylvania, towards the close of the century, the rules were
that no servants were to be hired for more than four years or
to be sent beyond the confines of the colony. Wives and
children were to be accepted along with their menfolk, unless
the family agreed otherwise, and the purchaser was bound to
provide schooling for children. If a child's parents died on the
voyage out, he was to be indentured until the age of twenty-one;
a rule which may or may not have served to keep children
dancing attendance on their ailing parents.

For serious offences, the employer had the right to put his
servant in prison for up to thirty days and to punish absentee-
ism by demanding five extra days for every day of truancy.
Normally, he was supposed to exercise only the usual discipline
of the head of the family. In practice some redemptioners
were whipped, even to death. If a redemptioner fled, he was
hunted down by all available methods. It was permissible,
however, for an employer to pass on his servant to another
master.

The system had most of the stigmata of slavery, and indeed
many Negro slaves were treated more humanely than indentured
whites. But, for a man of toughness and resolution, it offered
a road to independence and self-respect. On his fifty acres he
could hold up his head and be on a level with the established
settlers; he could even go down to the ship and hire a servant
for himself. Much play has been made with the fact that in
1663 one-third of the members of the Virginia House of
Burgesses were former indentured servants. Some redemptioners, of their own will, chose to continue working for those
who had hired them, at an agreed wage; but often a servant
who intended to remain in service made a special point of
moving on after the engagement expired, lest it be thought

that he or she was still in a state of bondage. Servants of weak fibre, disheartened by hardships and ill-treatment, became 'poor whites,' a heavy drag on a land of promise.

A woman redemptioner had the right to sue her employer for seduction, but, before the Revolution, all too many women servants from England had already been seduced on their home ground and were experienced profligates. This did not help the morals of the seaboard colonies. Moreau de St-Méry, who travelled in the United States in the last decade of the century, had little good to say of the freed women servants he encountered. 'They are usually libertines,' he said, 'and there are hardly any women servants in Philadelphia who could not be enjoyed for a very small sum.' Usually, they possessed only one chemise, which they washed on Saturdays, but they had the usual passion for 'finery,' walking out in the evenings with ribboned hats on their heads and their feet bare. They had an aversion to waiting on French people, who washed their feet too often, which meant carrying more water than seemed reasonable. They would leave their employment at the slightest whim, in the middle of a meal. All demanded coffee, sugar and *pain tendre*.[1]

Before the Revolution, between one-third and a half of the immigrants to America were indentured servants and labourers. The first wave were mostly English; then, in mid-eighteenth century, the demand was for Germans, notably the loyal and honest Germans from the Palatinate. When the German states began to impose restrictions on emigration, it was the turn of Switzerland and Ireland. St-Méry estimated that Philadelphia in the 1790s received annually some 4000–5000 white *engagés*. He quoted the *Philadelphia Gazette* as saying that in three voyages an Irish vessel had made £10,000 for its operators. Of these national categories, the least tractable, in pre-Revolutionary times, were the English, too many of whom consisted not of honest peasants but of urban scourings.

The indentured servant system was still operating well into the nineteenth century. In his diary for 1817, Samuel Breck of Philadelphia describes a visit he makes to the port on hearing that a shipload of servants has just arrived from Amsterdam.

[1] *Voyages Aux Etats-Unis, 1793–8.*

He buys a German–Swiss woman for $76, a sum which represents her passage money, and promises her $20 more at the end of three years, if she serves him faithfully. Breck also pays $53 60 cents for a boy who has already paid twenty-six guilders towards his passage money. He undertakes to give the boy twenty-six guilders after two years and to give him six weeks schooling every year. 'Whether they will be worth anything is a lottery,' he writes, 'for the choice of strangers in this way is truly a leap in the dark.'[1]

The South already had its well-established system of slavery, of which more will be said later. In their day, the Puritans had tried to make bondsmen of the Indian, but his spirit was not easy to domesticate. James Russell Lowell summed up the difficulty when he said: 'Your cook might give warning by taking your scalp or *chignon*, as the case might be, and make off with it into the woods.'

Of native American servants there was only the merest handful. The tradition in this New World was one of independence; menial tasks were for Negroes and the indentured. This attitude was to provide the United States with a most formidable servant problem as the nineteenth century progressed.

[1] *Recollections of Samuel Breck, 1771–1862.*

VIII

THE WIDENING GULF

DESPITE the dark apprehensions of Defoe, the Great Law of Subordination survived the century without fundamental damage. Sometimes a structure full of holes will withstand a high wind better than one which presents a solid face.

To the ruling classes, the situation seemed grave enough. Twaddle about the rights of man was being mouthed by rogues and radicals, fools and Frenchmen, renegade colonists and ranting Methodists. Yet somehow, while other societies underwent revolution, the British class structure survived. Visitors to these shores were impressed by the scrupulousness with which servants kept, or were kept in, their place, by the sheer width of the gulf between master and man. Elkanah Watson, from Revolutionary America, dined at a 'sumptuous seat' at Blackheath in 1782 and reported:

'The servants attending upon my friend's table were all neatly dressed and extremely active and adroit in performing their offices and glided about the room, silent and attentive. Their silence was in striking contrast with the volubility of the French attendants, who, to my utter astonishment, I have often observed in France intermingling in the conversation of the table. Here the servant, however cherished, is held at an awful distance. The English servant is generally an ignorant and servile being who has no aspiration beyond his present dependent condition. In America our domestic feels the consciousness that he in turn may become himself a master. This feeling may perhaps impair his usefulness as a servant, but cannot be deprecated whilst it adds to his self-respect as a man.'[1]

Other visitors made the point that the exclusion of familiarity between Englishmen and their dependants helped to give the servant class a good deal of external dignity. In middle-class households of the more prosperous kind this external dignity was allied to a high degree of physical comfort. Thomas de Quincey considered that servants at this period were uncommonly well off. He was the son of a prosperous merchant who was engaged in foreign trade, and who employed more servants than similar merchants in Europe. Of his father's household in the closing years of the eighteenth century, de Quincey says: '. . . this same establishment, when measured by the quality and amount of the provision made for its comfort, and even elegant accommodation, would fill [the foreigner] with twofold astonishment, as interpreting equally the social valuation of the English merchant, and also the social valuation of the English servant; for, in the truest sense, England is the paradise of household servants. Liberal housekeeping, in fact, as extending itself to the meanest servants, and the disdain of petty parsimonies, is peculiar to England. And in this respect the families of English merchants, as a class, far outrun the scale of expenditure prevalent, not only amongst the corresponding bodies of continental nations, but even amongst the poorer sections of our own nobility—though confessedly the most splendid in Europe.'[2]

De Quincey is grateful that 'amidst luxuries in all things else, we were trained to a Spartan simplicity of diet—that we fared, in fact, very much less sumptuously than the servants.'

By natural choice, and by the upbringing of her aristocratic father, de Quincey's mother was the sort of woman who held aloof from direct contact with her servants; but she could worry mightily about their spiritual welfare. About the year 1797 she was much embarrassed by the behaviour of a guest whom de Quincey describes as 'the female infidel,' otherwise the young, beautiful and rich Mrs Antonia Dashwood Lee. She was the illegitimate daughter of Sir Francis Dashwood and was separated from her husband. It was her pleasure to

[1] *Men and Times of the Revolution.*   [2] *Autobiographical Sketches.*

ridicule Christianity at the dinner table and her powers of disputation were such that the local clergymen were no match for her; 'every touch from her, every velvety paw, drew blood.' Mrs de Quincey was much alarmed at the thought of the corruption which might be caused among her servants by the knowledge that a person with great gifts might deny Christianity.

'Such a danger was quickened by the character and pretensions of Mrs Lee's footman, who was a daily witness, whilst standing behind his mistress's chair at dinner, to the confusion which she carried into the hostile camp, and might be supposed to renew such discussions in the servants' hall with singular advantages for a favourable attention. For he was a showy and most audacious Londoner, and what is *technically* known, in the language of servants' hiring-offices, as 'a man of figure.' He might, therefore, be considered as one dangerously armed for shaking religious principles, especially among the female servants.'

Although Mrs de Quincey nearly suffered a breakdown through worry, it does not appear that any doubts were spread in the servants' hall by the activities of this 'leopardess' or her lackey. In 1804 Mrs Lee was involved in a resounding scandal with two dissolute brothers.

In the houses of the lesser bourgeoisie, where 'petty parsimonies' were by no means disdained and mistresses had no time to worry about their dependants' life hereafter, the conditions for servants were less paradisal. The word 'slavey' was in use at this period and the maid of all work thus described was already an object of compassion. Philip Thicknesse in his *Memoirs* (1788) says that the veriest slaves he has seen in two hemispheres are the all-work maidservants of London. Many of these maids were country girls driven to the towns, not through bad behaviour on their part, but as a result of the great landowners' policy of merging small farms into bigger ones, with scant regard for those who lived on them. Country mothers, facing a bleak future, were anxious to get their daughters off their hands at the earliest possible age—perhaps nine or ten—if only to ensure them food and shelter, preferably in a home where a girl, to use the phrase of the day, would have 'her morals attended to.' Some of these fledglings were taken into considerate homes and others became 'slaveys' when scarcely in their teens. In unpretentious households the growing tendency was to employ girls instead of menservants. The Rev. Sydney Smith, in his vicarage at Foston, solved his staff problem thus: 'I caught up a little garden girl, made like a milestone, christened her Bunch, put a napkin in her hand and made her my butler. The girls taught her to read, Mrs Sydney to wait and I undertook her morals. Bunch became the best butler in the county.'[1]

In the home of a Sydney Smith or a de Quincey servants might be addressed civilly enough, but there were still plenty of households in which a servant was an object to be bawled at. Scotland, at the close of the eighteenth century, was a curiously quarrelsome land, as the spate of academic feuds testifies. Henry Cockburn (Lord Cockburn) says that 'people had got into a bad style of admonition and dissent. . . . This odious practice was applied with particular offensiveness by those in authority towards their inferiors. In the Army it was universal by officers towards soldiers; and far more frequent than is now credible by masters towards servants.'[2]

Drunkenness still raged above and below stairs, but politer days were not far distant. By the time the last Hanoverian monarch had left the throne the gentlemen of England rarely required to be dragged from under the table by their servants and put to bed. Some of the old guard were incorrigible. The eleventh Duke of Norfolk, 'the dirty duke,' also known as 'the Jockey,' regularly drank himself insensible, which gave his servants their only chance to wash him, for he could not face soap and water when sober. But masters also looked after their drunken servants. Sir Walter Scott, finding his men incapable at the roadside, would solicitously drag them into the shade where they could sleep it off.

A glance at two or three court reports, all in the *Annual Register*, will show the sort of contumacy which high-handed masters were willing to visit on their servants. In 1804 an overseer of the parish of Lidlington, finding that his maid-

---

[1] Hesketh Pearson: *The Smith of Smiths.*
[2] Henry Cockburn: *Memorials of His Life.*

High life below stairs, by Robert Cruikshank

servant was in labour, ordered a workman to walk with her to Ampthill, three miles away, and leave her at the first public-house. This was too much for the Bedford Magistrates who sent him to prison for two months and fined him £20. In 1818 a 'man of property' at Hinckley was convicted of administering laudanum to the governess of his three daughters, 'with the view of rendering her subservient to his passions.' He was imprisoned for twelve months and fined £100. In 1819 a professional man, unable to find two of his spoons, plastered the streets of Plymouth with handbills offering £5 reward for the apprehension of his maidservant who had left his house 'and is supposed to have stolen some of my plate,' the notice ending with 'whoever harbours her shall be prosecuted according to law.' The maid's story was that she left because her master committed adultery in his wife's absence. For an 'inexcusable attempt to ruin a young woman's character' he was ordered to pay £200. That same year a Captain O'Brien was sued by his servant whom he had dismissed and then knocked senseless because the man demanded his clothes and wages. 'Horrible indeed have been the consequences,' said Mr Serjeant Pell. 'A fractured jaw, a concussion of the brain leave this young man a dreadful object, a decrepit burden on society, a creature maimed in body and intellect.' A constable who gave evidence said that the servant cried: 'For God's sake, do let me get up or pull your fingers out of my eyes.' The man was attended night and day at an inn for three weeks and O'Brien refused to settle the bill. He was ordered to pay £200 damages.

The law could bring justice on occasion to ill-used servants, but it could still punish the erring with blind savagery. At Bury the nineteenth century was ushered in with the execution of Sarah Lloyd, a maidservant convicted of robbing her mistress, Mrs Syer. Before the cart was driven from under her a local dignitary climbed on to it and addressed the crowd for fifteen minutes 'in a very impressive strain.' He granted that the culprit had been the tool of a greater villain, but this was not to be regarded as mitigation of her wickedness. Fortunately, she had enjoyed a period of repentance which was a happy prelude to her future bliss; and into this bliss Mrs Syer's Sarah was forthwith launched.

At the turn of the century it was estimated that there were never fewer than ten thousand servants of both sexes out of place in London. Patrick Colquhoun, in his *Treatise On The Police Of London* (1796), classes this out of work army as 'servants, males and female, porters, hostlers, stable boys and post boys etc out of place, principally from ill behaviour and loss of character, whose means of living must excite suspicion at all times.' Colquhoun also lists a lesser battalion of parasites whose function is to prey on, and corrupt, servants in employment: 'Of itinerant Jews, wandering from street to street holding out temptation to pilfer and steal, Jew boys crying bad shillings who purchase articles stolen by servants, stable boys etc generally paying in base money: 2000.'

From the total of ten thousand, all too few qualified for admission into respectable households. Nominally, supply of servants always exceeded demand; but always the demand for good servants vastly exceeded the supply. Long-suffering employers sought the impossible by means of advertisements like this from the *Morning Post* in 1819:   /27709

'Wanted immediately a SERVANT of ALL-WORK: so uniting COOK and HOUSEKEEPER that the utmost excellence in either capacity would not answer, without corresponding perfection in both; accompanied by absolute sobriety and universal honesty. Her age must be from 25 to 40. In regard to her character, that of her last service, unless it has been a long one, will not be sufficient. The Advertiser, being of opinion that all the malefactions of mankind originate in practical falsehood, gives warning, that the first lie shall be the last. There is no possibility of any perquisite nor impunity for the slightest fraud or waste; but liberal wages and the kindest treatment may be confidently counted on by a really deserving woman.'

Meanwhile, the Industrial Revolution was changing the whole social pattern of Britain. The new middle class was largely an urban class contemptuous of the domestic arts and skills which gentlewomen, hitherto, had been expected to have at their finger-tips. In a town house, a woman had no dairy or herb-garden in which to display a personal interest; fashion now bade her stay out of her kitchen and still-room. The arts of baking and preserving, pickling and wine-making were surrendered to housekeeper, cook and butler. Of what use was it to set the maids spinning when there were textile factories all over the northern moors? Why make medicines and corn-salves when there was an apothecary round the corner?

Britain was now entering that long and grievous phase when a lack of occupation in women—always excepting women servants—was regarded as both necessary and virtuous. 'At the end of the eighteenth century,' says Mr James Laver, 'the women of the well-to-do suddenly found that they had no real duties except to "keep up their position." And the best way to keep up their position was to live a life of complete idleness.'[1] If wives or daughters were seen to do household work it was a reflection on their menfolk; a gentleman's success was measured by the number of idle women he could maintain. Obviously, there had to be some economic excuse for this system and one was readily found: a woman who worked when she had no need to do so was depriving a more needy person of employment.

The women thus liberated from household chores still felt the need to do something with their hands, other than turning over the pages of those unsettling novels which their menfolk so freely condemned. They therefore took up 'artistic' pursuits. Scissors which should have cut cloth cut out imbecilities in paper and a score of trumpery crafts were invented. As an occasional refuge from these, women were incited to join literary and philosophical societies.

All this tended to deepen the chasm between a woman and her female servants. So long as a mistress had taken part in household tasks, she could not very well despise the servants who assisted her. Having elevated herself to a higher plane, she could and did. In the nineteenth century the servant's status steadily slumped. Lord Chesterfield had viewed menial servants as his 'equals in Nature . . . inferiors only by the difference of our positions'; but the employers of the nine-teenth century would have none of this. Their problem was to get servants to recognise that their inferior status (or 'humble

[1] James Laver, 'Homes and Habits,' *The Character of England* (ed. Ernest Barker).

station in life') was the clear will of God as laid down in both
Testaments (see Chapter 13); and that He expected them to
put up with inferior food and to sit out of earshot in church.

To express this distinction between the classes in the clearest
possible terms, the new town houses—like those of Belgravia
—were built in such a way that, as Mr Laver says, the 'lower
classes' were literally the lower classes: they were relegated to
basements. There they remained for a century, and the sensitive
observer even in our own days could detect

> . . . the damp souls of housemaids
> Sprouting despondently at area gates.[1]

To this submerged plane the self-respecting mistress did not
dream of descending. Since she would not have known how to
instruct the denizens in their duties, it was better to make a
virtue of aloofness. The servants, for their part, did not want
her down there, and, aware of her ignorance, they were able
to 'blind her with science.' If she wanted to keep up her
position, they would assist her to do so by spending her money
freely and giving away her victuals to the clamorous poor.
The basement was not wholly without its advantages; it was
pleasantly accessible to gossips, relatives, policemen, soldiers,
traffickers in scraps, fortune-tellers and hangers-on of all kinds.

Indeed, it would be a gross error to suppose that all who
worked in basements had 'damp souls' or that they were
unhappy in their work. A good flesh-and-blood picture of a
cheerful maidservant in one of the new town houses was
contributed, unsigned, by Leigh Hunt to William Hone's
Every-Day Book (1820). Hunt sketches the girl, first, by
cataloguing her possessions. In the kitchen drawer she keeps,
among other things, a brass thimble, a pair of scissors, a piece
of wax candle, an old volume of *Pamela*, and a sixpenny play
(e.g. Mrs Behn's *Oroonoko*). In her garret are a good looking-
glass on the table, a Bible, a comb and a piece of soap; but the
most important exhibit is that 'mighty mystery,' the Box—the
padlocked stout receptacle in which every servant girl carried
her belongings from place to place (and which some mistresses
relegated to an outhouse on the grounds that it was probably

[1] T. S. Eliot: 'Morning at the Window,' *Collected Poems*.

full of bugs). It contains, says Hunt, 'her clothes, two or three
song books consisting of nineteen for the penny; sundry
tragedies at a halfpenny the sheet; the *Whole Nature of Dreams
Laid Open*, together with the *Fortune Teller* and the *Account
of the Ghost of Mrs Veal; the Story of the Beautiful Zoa who
was cast away on a desert island, showing how* etc.; some half-
crowns in a purse, including pieces of country money, with the
good Countess of Coventry on one of them riding naked on the
horse; a silver penny wrapped up in cotton by itself; a crooked
sixpence, given her before she came to town, and the giver of
which has either forgotten her or been forgotten by her, she is
not sure which; two little enamel boxes with looking-glass in
the lids, one of them a fairing, the other 'a trifle from Margate';
and lastly various letters, square and ragged, and directed in
all sorts of spelling, chiefly with little letters for capitals. One
of them written by a girl who went to a day school with her is
directed 'Miss.'[1]

Hunt says that in her manner this maidservant sometimes
imitates her young mistress; 'she puts her hair in papers,
cultivates a shape and occasionally contrives to be out of
spirits. But her own character and condition overcome all
sophistications of this sort; her shape, fortified by the mop and
scrubbing brush, will make its way; and exercise keeps her
healthy and cheerful.'

The maid does not like to be seen scrubbing the steps. Sometimes she says 'drat the butcher' but hastily adds 'God forgive
me.' Mostly she is on chaffing terms with the tradesmen, both
with those who call and those on whom she calls. The morning
passes with working, singing, giggling, grumbling and being
flattered, with many a run up steps to hear a new song or see
soldiers go by. From her days off she derives the purest enjoyment—'the maidservant, the sailor and the schoolboy are the
three beings that enjoy a holiday beyond all the rest of the
world.' In Vauxhall she thinks she is in heaven, but she loves
the menagerie, Astley's, the Tower, the Circus. In the theatre,
where she eats apples and gingerbread nuts, she prefers tragedy
to comedy, 'because it is grander and less like what she meets

[1] It was customary for employers when writing to maids to omit the
word 'Miss.'

'Oh you slut, let us hear all about it!'
From a print 'Symptoms' by H. Aiken

in general.' Her favourite play is *Alexander the Great*, or *The Rival Queens*.

This girl is obviously no downtrodden slavey. Hunt makes it clear that she is one of an establishment of servants and he mentions that when the master and mistress hold a ball, it is the custom for the servants to leave the doors open and dance to the music. In houses like these the servants, though despised by milliners, needlewomen and book-folders, were well fed and sheltered from economic winds. When they walked out, they were healthier-looking, and more neatly dressed, than the girls of industry, who worked just as long hours, and probably harder, for their 'independence.'

In the country, there were still to be found households which Sir Roger de Coverley would have commended. When Sir Henry Oxenden, of Broome, near Dover, died in 1838 the years of service of his staff were as follows: butler, 54 years; sawyer, 47; carpenter, 45; nurse, 43; thatcher, 40; gardener, 38; coachman, 37; labourer, 37; groom, 36; bailiff, 36; gardener, 30; labourer, 25; labourer, 25; carpenter, 25; housemaid, 23: dairymaid, 21; labourer, 21; valet, 19; housekeeper, 16;

shepherd, 15; labourer, 15; footman, 12; labourer, 10; labourer, 10. The total number of employees was 24 and their average period of service was just over 28 years.

Good servants were the support and solace of old age, but bad or ungrateful servants were sometimes the scourge of it. The elderly Lord Melbourne knew that the sixteen servants in his house in South Street, Mayfair, were all 'thievish and drunk,' yet his aristocratic indolence was such that he could not bring himself to go through their accounts. To preserve him from similar exploitation in his Hertfordshire home of Brocket Hall, Lady Beauvale took over the direction of his household and acted as his hostess.[1]

Much more odd is the story of the victimisation of the frail and venerable Hannah More by her servants. In 1828, all her sisters having died, she was living alone at Barley Wood, her beautiful home near Wrington, in Somerset. Here she was waited upon, after a fashion, by a housekeeper, lady's maid, housemaid, cook, scullery girl, coachman, gardener and gardener's man. Although their mistress had done much to instil them with religious principles, although each repeated a Scripture text daily in her presence, the servants had formed a conspiracy to rob and defraud her; and this despite the knowledge that each stood to receive a handsome gratuity which was liable to be forfeited through unworthy conduct. 'The most shameless peculation prevailed in the kitchen,' says the Rev. Henry Thompson. 'Orders were issued to the tradesmen in her name of which the servants reaped the benefit. Monies given for charity were appropriated by the servants. Presents of game to Mrs More were intercepted in the like manner. . . . Intoxication was frequent. A person discharged from service for disreputable conduct, a relative of one of the servants, was actually harboured in the house for two months without Mrs More's knowledge.'[2] On top of this the servants held frequent festivities after their mistress had retired for the night, indulging in a continual round of 'high life below stairs' at her expense. At midnight, when Miss More was deemed asleep, the servants from neighbouring houses would converge stealthily on Barley Wood, 'some creeping through hedges,

[1] David Cecil: *Lord Melbourne*.   [2] *Hannah More*.

others descending down laurel walks or emerging from thickets.'
Miss More's servants, 'superbly decorated,' waited on 'their
frilled and furbelowed guests,' and all sat down to 'hot suppers
laid out with parlour-like elegance.'[1] These orgies, as Joseph
Cottle calls them, had to be conducted very quietly, for fear of
waking Miss More or her occasional guests. Perhaps for this
reason the servants began to organise balls in a hall a mile away
belonging to a tradesman who supplied Barley Wood. It was
evidently in his interest to keep in with the two most important
personages in the parish, namely Miss More's coachman and
the housekeeper he drove out in his coach.

A woman guest of Miss More, suspecting that the servants
were up to no good, decided to keep watch, and one night she
was a witness of what she had secretly hoped to see. The eight
servants had all trooped in to Miss More's presence as usual
for family prayers, each repeating his or her verse from the
Bible and all uttering a hearty 'Amen.' Then Miss More
retired, the lights were put out and the woman guest took up
her position at a window. Soon enough she saw the servants,
all dressed up, leave the house, the housekeeper and coachman
arm in arm followed by the others. Only one stayed behind—
the little scullery maid whose function it was to sit up and admit
the revellers in time for morning prayers. She too had wanted
to go to the ball but was assigned the role of Cinderella.

The revelation that her trusted servants were prepared to
let her be robbed and murdered while they pursued their
dissipations elsewhere came as a violent shock to Miss More:

'She preserved silence, while a tear stole down her pallid
cheek. At length with a faltering voice she said: "What, Susan
unfaithful, who has lived with me so many years?" "Yes."
"And Timothy, whose relations I have fed and clothed?" "Yes."
The venerable and afflicted lady continued, "And Teddy and
Rebecca and Jane?" "Yes, all." "What?" she continued, "not
one faithful?" The answer was, "The whole are faithless!"
"Then," said the aged Hannah More, "I will leave it all. Find
me a retreat where my last days may be spent in calmness,
prayer and praise." '[2]

While a new home was being found for her at Clifton, the

---

[1] Joseph Cottle: *Early Recollections.*   [2] *Ibid.*

servants were told nothing, but as her departure neared
ominous rumours circulated below stairs. A dozen gentlemen,
old friends of Miss More, arrived in the house—why? They
were there, says Cottle dramatically, to defend Miss More if
necessary against her servants.

On the last morning the servants guessed that the game was
up and 'tore off the mask of civility.' As a last gesture of insolence, the housemaid laid breakfast for her mistress and a
guest without a cloth. 'Mary, can you breakfast without a
cloth?' asked Miss More of her guest. 'I desire to do what you
do,' was the reply. 'Well, I will at last pluck up the courage to
be mistress in my own house the last morning,' said her hostess
and called for the maid. Surlily, the woman said she 'thought
it would do' for that morning. 'I will thank you for a cloth,'
said Miss More, and a cloth was laid.[1]

This incident, when reported below stairs, can have done
little to allay apprehension, but apprehension had now turned
to mutual recrimination. The suspense was ended by a summons
to the crowded drawing-room, where all eight offenders were
lined up before Miss More. She then addressed them in a
firm tone: 'You are no longer my servants. By deserting me and
my house at midnight to pursue your revels, you all proved
yourselves to be unworthy of my confidence. Your unprincipled
conduct has driven me from my home, forced me to seek a
refuge among strangers.' Then, rising with dignity, she walked
out between a double file of gentlemen, with never a glance at
her servants but a long and lingering look at the portraits of
friends on the walls of her dining-room. She did not trust
Timothy, her coachman, to drive her to her new home but
entered a friend's coach. 'I am driven like Eve from Paradise,'
she said, 'but not by angels.' Once inside the coach, 'she closed
her eyes and thought alone on the better inheritance to which
she was so fast hastening.'

This operation was later described by Miss More as the
exchange of eight 'pampered menials' for four sober servants.
The pampered eight each received a quarter's wages. Probably
a similar degeneration would have occurred in any isolated
household tethered to the will of a rich old woman. That the

[1] Thompson.

servants should have abandoned her was no doubt inexcusable; that they should have sought some relaxation in a dull life is at least understandable.

Happily, the great landowners still kept a tight grip on their servants. When the Reform mobs were marching, in 1832, the Duke of Rutland wrote as follows from Belvoir Castle to Frances, Lady Shelley:

'I am having all my labourers and servants drilled to the use of the great guns here. I have an artillery sergeant residing here for the winter, and we have drills every day. Last week I obtained a large supply of shot and ammunition from Woolwich. I am determined to make a good defence, if attacked.'[1]

To an English duke his servants were still his soldiers. His cause could not be other than their cause. A footman who objected to manning the 'great guns' against his fellow-men was doubtless a man to be stripped and sent packing.

In a happier cause, ducal cannon were fired in 1841— presumably by ducal servants—at Stowe, Blenheim, Alnwick, Inveraray and elsewhere to mark the birth of a Prince of Wales (the future Edward VII).

[1] Richard Edgcumbe (ed.): *The Diary of Frances, Lady Shelley, 1818–73.*

IX

THE DUTY TO EMPLOY

FROM the Regency onwards, there was a steadily rising
output of books purporting to instruct mistresses of
households in their duties and in the treatment of servants.
And, since a good proportion of those below stairs could now
read and write, there was also a proliferation of tracts, pamphlets
and handbooks addressed to servants, especially female servants,
telling them on one page how to preserve their virtue, on the
next how to preserve fruit, and on the next urging them to
refrain from coughing, scratching, whistling and blowing their
noses in the master's presence. Some of these books were
written by ex-servants, some by mistresses, some by clergymen,
some by hacks, and all copied freely from one another. A few
are sensible enough; others are so overlaid by piety, by servility,
by prejudice or by sheer silliness that they are of value only for
the incidental sidelights they shed on the manners of the times.

One of the more readable of this company is Dr William
Kitchiner, an old Etonian with a Glasgow medical degree, who
began to turn out his manuals in 1811. In *The Housekeeper's
Oracle* he says the best way to obtain a good servant is by
recommendation of a friend, or failing that by recommendation
of a baker, butcher, poulterer, greengrocer or milkman. In
extremity a master could advertise, but it was desirable to
direct applicants to a tradesman and let him filter them (if the
tradesman passed on only those who agreed to pay him a
commission, the householder had no one but himself and Dr
Kitchiner to blame). Registry offices were still dubious institutions, an exception being the Free Registry of the London
Society for the Encouragement of Faithful Female Servants,

established in 1813, which charged no fees to servants or subscribers. Dr Kitchiner urged masters to adhere to these rules: *Hire no servant who cannot read or write. Never keep bad servants in the hope of their reformation.* A master's duty was not to reclaim the wicked but to save his household from being polluted; it was Dr Kitchiner's conviction that 'bad servants make bad masters'.

Not that Dr Kitchiner was one to treat servants harshly. As an example of a mild, restrained reproof he told the story of a gentleman who, on receiving his breakfast late, rang for the cook and asked her whether there were any arrangements in the house which were unpleasing to her. 'No, sir,' she replied, 'I am very comfortable, I thank you.' Said her master: 'Then I hope you will be so good as to make me very comfortable and not let me have to wait for my breakfast.'

As an illustration of humane treatment, Dr Kitchiner mentioned that some mistresses now allowed servants a whole holiday every third month, provided they were home by ten o'clock, and a half-holiday in each intervening month. Since a maid cost the householder in board and wages about £40 a year, and a manservant £20 or £30 more, there was obviously a limit to the amount of free time that could be allowed. But a householder ought not to grumble at servants' appetites, remembering that they worked harder than their masters.

Dr Kitchiner quoted with approval the words of a fellow-writer who said: 'Some people seem to expect from their dependants from the sole motive of fear all the good effects which a liberal education, an affluent fortune and every other advantage cannot produce in themselves.' This writer was the Rev. H. G. Watkins, a London vicar who founded and nurtured, at first in his own parsonage, the London Society for the Encouragement of Faithful Female Servants. Its objects were 'to promote mutual tenderness, good will and confidence among the superior and subordinate branches of a family; and to secure the young and unwary but virtuous female from the danger of resorting to *common* registry offices.'

The Rev. H. G. Watkins thought that young servants ought to be very thankful and submissive to those who took the trouble to teach them. There was no better way of showing their gratitude than by staying a long period in their first place. Christian masters had a heavy responsibility towards them, viewing them 'not as stepping stones to their pleasure or profit' but as persons placed under their care by God, who would in due time demand an account of the master's stewardship.

Like other counsellors, the Rev. H. G. Watkins was against allowing servant girls to meet their friends on Sundays; 'Sabbath pleasures put a young woman in the highway of danger—and of ruin.' If a girl wanted to see her friends, a mistress would afford other opportunities; but not, of course, in the evenings, when even mistresses walking alone were subject to insult and molestation. A servant was expected not to make a freakish selection of a church: 'be sure you do not by a determinate choice of some distant favourite place or preacher break in upon the order of the family or lead your employers to suspect that you may be influenced by other motives than religious ones.'[1]

No master or mistress, said the Rev. H. G. Watkins, would fail to provide a kitchen library for his servants. Some basic titles suggested by him were:

The Bible;
Jones's *Scripture Directory;*
Biddulph's *Prayers for the Morning and Evening of Every Day Through the Week;*
The Pilgrim's Progress;
Beveridge's *Private Thoughts;*
Doddridge's *Rise and Progress of Religion in the Soul;*
Tracts of the various societies for promoting Christian knowledge;
Three volumes of 108 tracts by the author;
Scott's *Sermon on the Fatal Consequences of Licentiousness.*[2]

Another busy instructor of masters and servants was the Rev. Dr John Trusler, an erratic divine who frequently passed off as serious advice the satirical directions of Dean Swift (one of his early enterprises was to provide the lazier clergy with a range of 150 sermons in script type at a shilling each). Trusler's

[1] *Friendly Hints to Family Servants* (1814).
[2] *Hints and Observations Seriously Addressed to Heads of Families* (1816).

An easy place, by George Cruikshank

proposals for putting down quarrels among servants seem to
have been inspired less by a spirit of justice than a regard for
self-interest. 'If servants quarrel with each other the cause
should be well investigated: and if it be necessary to part with
one a master is justified in discharging the one he will feel less
the loss of; for surely in such a case the master or mistress may
prefer their own comfort and interest to that of their servant,
who may readily find another place equally desirable.' If two
servants were equally blameable, 'that one would be naturally
discharged that was the cause of the disturbance.'[1]

Dr Trusler found courage to tackle a problem which most
other writers ignored: what should a servant do when master
and mistress gave contradictory orders? Or when a mistress
countermanded the master's orders? 'It is his duty to obey his
master rather than his mistress; such mistress being bound in
duty to honour and obey her husband himself.'

Dr Trusler argued that it was best to hire servants by the
year and not to pay them until the end of that period; then, if
they left before the year was up, their wages were forfeited.
This prudent system, said Dr Trusler, 'purchases respect.'

[1] *Domestic Management* (1819).

Coachmen, grooms and footmen could not, however, be engaged
on these terms. A little wistfully, Dr Trusler cited the ideal
solution of the servant problem as practised by a nabob from
India. This gentleman kept a double set of servants and made
them serve him turn and turn about. If one left, there was
always another to take his place. 'He thought no sacrifice too
great for domestic comfort,' said Dr Trusler.

One of the most informative of the handbooks was *The
Complete Servant* (1825) by Samuel and Sarah Adams. Samuel
had been, successively, groom, footman, valet, butler and
house steward; his wife had been maid of all work, housemaid,
laundry maid, under-cook, lady's maid and housekeeper. They
wrote with the guidance of a lady of position who preferred to
remain anonymous.

The book set out in most specific fashion the scale of servants
suitable to gentlemen of varying incomes. This was the Adams's
advice on 'how to appropriate a large income':

33 per cent for household expenses, including provisions
          and all other articles of household consumption;
25 per cent for servants and equipage, including horses,
          carriages and liveries;
25 per cent for clothes, education of children, medical
          assistance, pocket, private and extra expenses,
          including entertainments, etc.;
12½ per cent for rent, taxes, repairs of house and furniture;
4½ per cent reserve for contingencies.

As an example of how expenditure would work out, the
authors quoted these figures:

Income	Household	Servants	Clothes	Rent	Reserve
£1000	£333	£250	£250	£125	£42
£5000	£1666	£1250	£1250	£625	£210
£10,000	£3333	£2500	£2500	£1250	£420

These budgets would seem to bear out the cynical view
that servants had no interest in encouraging their masters to
save.

Then followed 'The Number and Description of Servants Usually Employed':

£100 a year	a widow or other unmarried lady may keep a young maid at a low salary, say, from five to ten guineas a year;
£150–£180	a gentleman and lady without children may afford to keep a better servant maid at about ten or twelve guineas;
£200	*ditto*, a professed servant maid of all work at from twelve to fourteen guineas;
£300	*ditto*, with one, two or three children, two maidservants;
£400	*ditto, ditto*, three female servants, or two and a boy; viz. a cook, housemaid and nursery maid, or else, instead of the latter, a boy; with gardener occasionally;
£500	*ditto, ditto*, three females and a boy; viz. a cook, housemaid and nursery maid, with a boy as groom and to assist in the house and garden. A gardener occasionally.
£500–£600	a gentleman and lady with children: three females and one man; viz. a cook, housemaid and a nursery maid or other female servant; with a livery servant as groom and footman. A gardener occasionally.
£600–£750	*ditto, ditto*, three females and two men; viz. a cook, housemaid and another female servant; a footman and a groom who may assist in garden; and a gardener occasionally.
£1000–£1500	*ditto, ditto*, four females and three men; viz. a cook, two housemaids, a nursery maid or other female servant; a coachman, footman and a man to assist in the stable and garden;
£1500–£2000	*ditto, ditto*, six females and five men; viz. a cook, housekeeper, two housemaids, kitchen maid and nursery maid or other female servant; with a coachman, groom, footman, gardener and an assistant in the garden and stable;

£2000–£3000	*ditto, ditto,* eight females and eight men; viz. a cook, lady's maid, two housemaids, nurse, nursery maid, kitchen maid and laundry maid; with a butler, valet, coachman, two grooms, a footman and two gardeners;
£3000–£4000	*ditto, ditto,* nine females and eleven men; viz. a housekeeper, cook, lady's maid, nurse, two housemaids, laundry maid, kitchen maid and nursery maid; with a butler, coachman, two grooms, valet, two footmen, two gardeners and a labourer;
£4000–£5000	*ditto, ditto,* eleven females and thirteen men; viz. a housekeeper, cook, lady's maid, nurse, two housemaids, laundry maid, still-room maid, nursery maid, kitchen maid and scullion; with a butler, valet, house steward, coachman, two grooms, one assistant groom, two footmen, three gardeners and a labourer.

Observe that in the above table 'butler' first appears at the £2000–£3000 level, 'housekeeper' at the £3000–£4000 level[1] and 'house steward' at the £4000 level (being placed, rather oddly, after butler and valet). In practice, these establishments were shuffled about a good deal to suit the needs, predilections and pretensions of individual families.

One last table from the Adams is worth quoting. It is entitled: 'Household establishment of a respectable country gentleman with a young family, net income £16,000 to £18,000, and whose expenses do not exceed £7000':

Housekeeper	24 guineas
Female teacher	30
Lady's maid	20
Head nurse	20
Second nurse	10
Nursery maid	7
Upper housemaid	15
Under housemaid	14

[1] The 'housekeeper' listed in the £1500–£2000 range, after cook, is presumably not a housekeeper in the full sense.

Kitchen maid	14 guineas
Upper laundry maid	14
Under laundry maid	10
Dairy maid	8
Second dairy maid	7
Still-room maid	9
Scullion	9
French man-cook	80
Butler	50
Coachman	28
Footman	24
Under footman	20
Groom	liveries and gratuity
Lady's groom	12
Nursery room boy	clothes and gratuity
Head gamekeeper	70 guineas a year, and 13s. a week board wages; a cottage and firing;
Under gamekeeper	one guinea a week
Gardener	40 guineas a year and 13s. a week board wages; a house and firing;
Assistant gardener	12s. a week.

In general, the board wages of servants when the family was absent were 10s. a week for women and 12s. for men. The men had a pot of ale a day and the women a pint, besides table beer.

In addition to the servants listed, noblemen and gentlemen of great fortune employed land stewards, bailiffs, woodwards, park keepers, huntsmen, whippers-in, racing grooms, jockeys, grooms of the chambers, pages, ladies' coachmen, postillions, seamstresses, chambermaids, boys for the steward's room, boys for the hall and so forth.

Mrs William Parkes, whose *Domestic Duties* appeared in the same year as the Adams's guide, quoted a rather higher scale of wages. She gave a double table for women servants, one payable if a tea and sugar allowance was made, a higher one if tea and sugar were not allowed. Thus, a housekeeper with a tea and sugar allowance would receive from £21 to £36 15s.; without tea and sugar, from £26 to £42. The corresponding rates for a cook were £10 10s. to £21 (with) and £14 14s. to £31 10s.

(without). In many households, warned Mrs Parkes, servants were liable to be dismissed if they asked for vails; it was better to pay slightly more on the clear understanding that no vails were solicited. As for beer, Mrs Parkes said: 'A pint of good beer for the men and half that quantity for the women servants at each meal is a very sufficient allowance.'

X

THE FEMALE BRANCH

As the Victorian reign begins, it is time for a closer look at the duties and privileges of the leading figures in the servants' hierarchy. On the female side, those worth especial examination are the housekeeper, the lady's maid, the cook, the nurse and the housemaid.

The information in this chapter and the next comes mainly from instructional books published in the first forty years of the nineteenth century, with occasional references to Mrs Beeton's first (1861) edition and the booklets of Houlston's Industrial Library which appeared in the 1870s. This is a wide span, but duties and methods varied little over this period.

The Housekeeper

The housekeeper discussed here is the head of a female establishment of servants, not to be confused with the type of working housekeeper whose function was to manage the house of a gentleman of modest means, preferably (from her point of view) a bachelor.

Normally, as the table of Samuel and Sarah Adams shows, a housekeeper was appointed only in families of substantial income. At lesser levels, a wife was her own housekeeper; but as soon as she decided that the management of her household was too much trouble, or that it was beneath her personal attention, she would engage a housekeeper, answerable only to her.

The housekeeper was expected to be grave, solid and serious. Ideally, she was of good education, but this was not essential.

According to the team of Adams, a woman reared in useful pursuits, 'with that well-trained ductility of mind which bends its attention to the lesser objects of life and is frequently found to be essential in the management of a family,' was well suited to the post. Mrs William Parkes thought that the housekeeper 'should endeavour to regard everything round her with the keenness and interest of a principal rather than with the indifference of a servant.'

The housekeeper was always 'Mrs,' whether married or not. She wore no uniform, but her great bunch of keys was equivalent to a badge of office. Hers was the responsibility of engaging and dismissing the female staff, with the exception of the ladies' maids and nurse. If the maids were impertinent, it was her duty to correct them; if they were shy or frightened it was her duty to mother them; if they brushed the dirt through slit holes it was her duty to detect them.

The housekeeper had her own well-furnished room, where the still-room maid acted as her personal servant. In this 'Pugs' Parlour,' as it became known to the lower servants, the upper servants (butler, groom of the chambers, valet, lady's maid, cook) joined the housekeeper for breakfast, tea and supper. If there was a house steward, who ranked above the housekeeper, the upper servants would take their meals in his room, but it was still the housekeeper's privilege to entertain them to tea. In all but the most exalted houses, the housekeeper and the upper servants descended to the servants' hall for the first part of their dinner. They entered strictly in order of precedence and the lower servants stood silently and respectfully to greet them. At the table, all sat according to a hallowed plan: the housekeeper at the head of the table; the butler at the lower end; the cook on the right of the housekeeper and the lady's maid on the left; the under-butler on the right of the butler and the coachman on the left; the housemaid next to the cook; the kitchen-maid next to the lady's maid, and so on. Grace was said by the oldest, or the principal, servant. There was considerable formality during the meal and the lower servants knew better than to strike up conversation; they were too busy watching their table manners. The upper servants remained only for the meat course; then, sufficient

The housekeeper—with her keys

condescension having been shown, they withdrew to the house-keeper's room for their pudding or cheese, and conversation. Procedure would vary a little from household to household. Thus, the roast might be ceremonially borne out ahead of the departing 'Pugs,' or it might be left behind so that the lower servants could have second helpings. Sometimes the upper servants would carry their plates and glasses out with them in as dignified a fashion as possible. In spite of all the elaborate-ness of ritual, there was perennial dissension over who should lay the cloth for pudding in the housekeeper's room. The still-room maid, for some reason, objected to this chore and so did the housemaids, the under-housemaids, the kitchen-maids, the steward's boy and the odd job man. Occasionally it became necessary for the mistress to nominate someone specifically for this task. At the end of the century the dispute was still going on.

In theory, if not always in practice, the housekeeper could teach any of the other female servants the niceties of their tasks. She controlled the still-room, the store-rooms and the linen cupboards. No expendables were issued without her knowledge. If there was no house steward, she was responsible for the marketing. She gave orders direct to tradesmen and recorded all her transactions in ledgers. Once a week her books had to be passed by her mistress.

In buying meat, the housekeeper was expected to be exceptionally alert. She would know, and if she did not there was the Adams's guide to tell her, that 'the flesh of cattle of all kinds fatted in confined and filthy places on oil cakes or rank and half-decayed vegetables should be rejected as unfit for use'; how she recognised such meat we do not know, but apparently she did. She was aware that the best meat came from well-exercised cattle grazing on open situations, high lands, extensive downs, dry commons, heaths and large enclosures. Hence the superiority of Welsh and South Down mutton, Scotch and Welsh beef. Samuel and Sarah Adams would have shaken their heads at modern veal houses. So, in her generation, would Mrs Isabella Beeton, who was nothing if not fastidious in her choice of meat: 'No other animal possesses in so remarkable a degree the power of converting pasture into flesh as the Leicestershire sheep; the South Down and the Cheviot, the two next breeds in quality, are in consequence of the greater vivacity of the animals' nature, not equal to it in that respect.'[1]

The housekeeper did not delegate all the preparing of food to the cook. She herself was responsible for fashioning the higher confectionery and pastry, 'devices in sugar' and bonbons. She made all preserves and pickles, eschewing the 'pernicious custom' of using brass utensils to give her pickles a fine colour. When the demand arose she prepared syllabubs of wine and cream. Every day she made the tea for the drawing-room.

A really resourceful housekeeper would brew her own imitation wines, her equipment comprising vats, a vat-staff, fruit bruiser, strainer, hair-bags, canvas bags, wine press,

[1] Mrs Isabella Beeton: *The Book of Household Management* (1861).

bottling machine and thermometer. 'British champagne' was produced by crushing unripe gooseberries and adding brandy; 'imitation of port wine' began with a basis of real port, heavily diluted by large quantities of cider, elderberry juice and some quantity of brandy with a dash of cochineal. More potable, possibly, were honey wine, cowslip mead, raisin wine ('equal to sherry') and sycamore wine, made from the sap. For invalids, the housekeeper might suggest a glass of her scurvy grass wine.[1]

It was also required of a housekeeper that she should have a knowledge of first aid, and that she should be able to distil healing waters and make items like liquorice lozenges. The manuals of an earlier day gave advice on how to make plague waters, poppy waters, 'Dr Stephens' famous water against stone,' cures for melancholy, griping of the guts, mad dog bites and so on. If the housemaids grumbled about their corns, the housekeeper would recommend: 'Take beans and chew them in your mouth and then tie them fast to your corns; and it will help. Do this at night.'

Sometimes the housekeeper was called upon to assist her mistress in dispensing charity among the neighbouring poor, or even to take over this chore entirely. She would organise entertainments for the children of estate workers and ensure that suitable respect was shown by them towards their bene-factors.

In stately, or picturesque, homes a housekeeper could prosper exceedingly. Horace Walpole's *châtelaine*, who guided visitors through the Gothic extravagances of Strawberry Hill, amassed such wealth in gratuities that her master talked of marrying her, 'in order to repay myself for what I have flung away to make my house quite uncomfortable to me.' He thought that Lord Denbigh would certainly have proposed to her if he had known of her riches.[2] It was said that Walpole's house-keeper had 'the best place in England,' but in Regency times that claim could assuredly have been made for the housekeeper at Warwick Castle. Lady Shelley, visiting the Castle in 1819, said 'the old housekeeper is one of the curiosities of the place, and is noted for her devotion to the family.' She had drawn

[1] Samuel and Sarah Adams: *The Complete Servant.*
[2] Peter Cunningham (ed.): *Letters of Horace Walpole.*

up a will leaving her £20,000 fortune, derived from visitors to the Castle, among the younger branches of that family.[1]

A dishonest housekeeper had ample scope for cheating; a greedy one had ample scope for guzzling; a tyrannous one, in league with a tyrannous butler, could make life intolerable for the lower servants; an easy-going one would let all discipline dissolve. But a good housekeeper was worth very much more than her half-guinea a week.

The Lady's Maid

What Swift and Defoe thought of the lady's maid we already know. Dramatists and novelists showed her as a vain, twittering, tongue-poking baggage, with morals hardly any better than those of her mistress. In *The Rivals*, Lucy is made to say: 'Let girls in my station be as fond as they please of appearing expert and knowing in their trusts; commend me to a mask of *silliness* and a pair of sharp eyes for my own interest under it.' Lower servants generally disliked the lady's maid, partly because of her affectations and pertness, partly because she stood too close to her mistress's ear, partly because a housemaid knew her chances of promotion to lady's maid were slim. The governess also disliked the lady's maid and the enmity was returned; each was jealous of the other's standing.

The specifications for a good lady's maid were exacting. Firstly, she had to be willing to perform for another woman those intimate services which nine women out of ten are modest enough to wish to do for themselves.[2] She had to be young, reasonably tall, discreet, cheerful, submissive; healthy enough to withstand long hours; considerate enough not to fall asleep on her mistress in the carriage; virtuous enough to withstand footmen; honest enough to look after jewels; tolerant enough not to resent the master's untidy, time-wasting incursions into feminine territory; educated well enough to read to her mistress and not to go looking for 'a coarse dish

---

[1] Richard Edgcumbe (ed.): *The Diary of Frances, Lady Shelley*, 1818–73.
[2] 'Take the lady's maid, who must attend to her mistress in a way that appears to the unsophisticated to be too personal for the dignity of life. . . .' Lady Bunting in *The Contemporary Review*, 1910.

with a handle' when asked for Corfe's edition of Handel. She
was expected to have a near-expert knowledge of hairdressing
and to be unusually skilled at needlework; and she was even
supposed to have a flair for practical chemistry. In token of
her superior status she usually had her own carpeted room
which the other servants were not suffered to enter, except to
clean the floor and carry away the slops. She took her meals
in the housekeeper's room. A superior lady's maid would
work for one lady only and any request to attend two or more
would precipitate the sort of trouble which occurred in *The
Admirable Crichton*. In a pretentious household, even a child
of seven or eight might have her own maid, but in less wealthy
establishments one lady's maid would be expected to look after
two, or even three, daughters.

The most vivacious ladies' maids were French, but they had
their inbuilt disadvantages, not least at times of international
crisis. In the invasion scare of 1803 Lady Elizabeth Foster,
later Duchess of Devonshire, was called to the Aliens Office to
justify her employment of French maids at Devonshire House
and had to put up quite a spirited fight to retain them.[1] For
the average middle-class mistress, French maids set too fast a
pace. 'A Parisian maid out of her orbit is not a treasure,' wrote
an authority of the later Victorian years.[2] 'In her orbit, as
attendant to an extravagant, wealthy and fashionable mistress,
she suits the post and what is no less important, the post suits
her.' It was impossible to inquire too carefully into the character
of French ladies' maids, according to this writer. Less trouble-
some, more solid, more trustworthy were Swiss maids; but
they lacked vivacity.

In essence the duty of the lady's maid was to dress, undress
and re-dress her mistress as often as the day's commitments
required. Rising early, she ensured that the housemaid had
lit the fire in her mistress's dressing-room. She then called her
mistress, told her the time, laid out her clothes, carried in the
hot water and went for breakfast. When the bell rang she would
attend her mistress in the dressing-room, comb her hair and
wait on her until she was dressed, afterwards tidying up the

[1] D. M. Stuart: *Dearest Bess*.
[2] 'A Member of the Aristocracy': *The Management of Servants* (1880).

bedroom and dressing-room. She then retired to her room or the housekeeper's room to sew or iron, unless she was required to walk out with her mistress, or alone with a pet dog. After lunch she once more attended her mistress, dressing her for her afternoon outing, tidied up again and continued with her sewing or other chores until her employer returned to be undressed and dressed again for dinner. After that she had little or nothing to do until her mistress rang the bell to be undressed for bed, except to see that the maids kept up the bedroom fire and to lay out a nightdress in front of it. If her mistress kept late hours, the lady's maid would not expect to go to bed until three or four in the morning.

Her day would appear to have contained a good deal of sewing, and indeed it did. This left her mind unoccupied, and there was a constant danger that, moving in luxurious surroundings, she would grow to covet her mistress's station. But, as the anonymous author of *The Lady's Maid* in Houlston's Industrial Library explained:

'As long as the rich pay for what they desire to have, they have every right to please themselves. But it is far from being true that they live in luxury for the sake of pleasure . . . they have business to do too, as much as the working man and very serious business indeed. The chief purpose of the many comforts and conveniences that rich people have about them is to set their time and their thoughts free for their serious occupations. A rich nobleman has carriages not because it is a pleasure to him to ride in a coach but because he wants to get from place to place without having to take any trouble about it or any thought except just to give the order to have his carriage ready. A rich lady has a great many servants not because there is any pleasure in ordering a number of people about but because she wants to save her own time and thoughts by hiring other people to do without any care of hers what she likes to have done . . . her mind is free for her children, her friends, her books and all the serious things she has to think of. She has many things to think of and to do that you know nothing about.'

The lady's maid at her sewing would remember this. She would be careful not to sit there rehearsing quarrels and magnifying troubles. A Bible or book of poetry in front of her

The lady's maid tries to read her mistress's letter
From 'The Servants' Magazine'

would help to save her mind from wandering into unprofitable channels. It was possible to learn Goldsmith's *Deserted Village* in five mornings and mend the household's shirts at the same time. 'If your mind is free and your thimble all right you will find many a good thought occur to you over your sewing; some better way of doing your work or of avoiding some fault that you are liable to, or of obliging your mistress or of helping somebody in life. Such a thought will sometimes make you ready to burst out singing.'[1] Not that a well-trained lady's maid would, in practice, sing at her work.

It was for the lady's maid to improve herself without tactlessly imitating the taste and manners of her superiors. ' I trust,' says the writer quoted above, 'you will bear constantly in mind that your elevation into comfort and luxury—your better clothes, your seat in the dressing-room and on your master's carriage

[1] *The Lady's Maid* (Houlston).

are only circumstances in your service and not given to you to last. Your heart should still be where your station is—among the poor; so that if you have to return to your old ways of living when your years of service are over you may not feel hurt or degraded but as if you were returning home.'

This was a clear hint that the lady's maid must not count on living out her years with the family. Mistresses preferred their personal attendants to be young, and the older a lady's maid grew the smaller were the wages offered her. Among middle-aged ladies' maids the unemployment problem was serious. A lucky few became housekeepers, but this was not a form of promotion popular in the servants' hall. If the lady's maid did not marry, her future was bleak. And in the matrimonial market she had two handicaps: she had, almost certainly, ideas above her station and she did not know how to cook.

Any temptation to play the role of Pamela was to be resisted at all costs. 'If you have any personal attractions,' said the author of a book of advice, 'and most young women have something that is agreeable or pleasing, beware of the least familiarity with any of the gentlemen of the family where you live. Anything of the kind must lead to improper consequences, whatever turn it may take. Reflect on the injury which the whole family and their connections would accuse you of having done them should you so far gain the affections of any of the young gentlemen as to induce him to marry you. Such marriages have taken place but they are seldom if ever happy ones and cannot be.

'If you cannot otherwise avoid the evil which will certainly await you by rashly listening to the importunities of passion, leave the situation at once without disclosing to anyone the reason of your conduct; because the least hint of such a circumstance would soon spread and be exaggerated to your disadvantage.'[1]

It was essential that as the lady's maid stood brushing her mistress's hair for half an hour on end she should not yield to the temptation to gossip about the other servants. 'But, if you see any young girl below stairs does not sufficiently respect herself and lets the footman flirt with her so that you think a

[1] *Duties of a Lady's Maid* (Anon.), 1825.

little watchfulness in your lady would do her good and save her from danger and sorrow, this is an occasion in which it is a kindness to speak. In such cases your lady will take care that you do not suffer from doing your duty.' Even if the lady failed to take this precaution, it was for the maid to support her evidence calmly and boldly and take the consequences.[1]

The wise lady's maid forebore from flattering her mistress, by praising her shape or the quality of her teeth. Since vanity was a disease, to feed it was like heating a person in a fever. A cautionary tale was told of a lady who, as she prepared for bed, was reviewing in her mind a long dinner table conversation 'about the affairs of three great nations.' The maid broke into this with, 'What sweet, pretty hair yours is, ma'am! If it were only a little longer!' For this impertinence she was packed off, and the lady put herself to bed.[2]

The author of one manual gave the lady's maid advice in refined speaking. It was as undesirable to say 'La, ma'am!' or 'Goodness me!' as it was to say 'that there house' or to end every question with 'ain't it?' or 'don't it?' Also much to be condemned was this kind of usage: 'She was very kind to me, was Mrs Howard.' Especial scorn was reserved for Scots vulgarities, among them these:

vulgar	*correct*
a bit paper	a bit of paper
a burial	a funeral
close the door	shut the door
below your clothes	under your clothes
I go the day	I go today
a drink of beer	a draught of beer
she is bad or poorly	she is sickly or in bad health
a chapman	a hawker
half-six o'clock	half-past five
come here	come hither
he was lost in the pond	he was drowned in the pond
show me it	show it to me
she was married on him	she was married to him
a milk cow	a milch cow

---

[1] *The Lady's Maid* (Houlston).   [2] *Ibid.*

going to my dinner	going to dinner
she took the pox	she was seized with small-pox
to plenish a house	to furnish a house
give him a clean plate	give him a plate
the child roars	the child cries
a sore head	a headache
butter and bread	bread and butter.

A few Irish vulgarities were also listed, including the notorious inability of that race to say yes and no, as in:

Is your mistress at home?
She is.
Does it rain today?
It does.[1]

When a mistress complained of feeling ill, which was fairly often, it was for her personal maid to offer due solicitude. 'She is in a state of suffering whether her illness be real or imaginary, and you owe her your pity and your help.' The help might consist of reading a chapter or two from a novel or it might be necessary for the maid to 'manage a blister and to apply leeches,' or to scrape her mistress's tongue with a silver tongue-scraper. It was for her to cope as far as possible without exposing the nature of her mistress's malady to the knowledge of the other servants. Never, in her ministrations, would she forget her own good fortune: 'The health of servants is really better on the whole than that of their ladies. It is better . . . than that of any class of people in society. They have none of the hardships of poor people and few or none of the cares which drag down the health of the rich.'[2]

Especial tact had to be used towards a mistress who was still breeding. It was the maid's duty to try to prevent her from tight-lacing her breasts and abdomen. 'Some married ladies, conceiving most erroneously that suckling has a tendency to injure the beauty of their breasts, employ a hireling wet nurse for their children; and in such circumstances have recourse to bandages and plasters to stop the secretion of the milk. In my opinion, however, they are absolutely wrong; for

[1] *Duties of a Lady's Maid.*   [2] *The Lady's Maid* (Houlston).

nothing has a greater tendency to improve the form of the breasts than the performance of the natural office of a mother. You ought to know these facts, though you may not always be able to persuade your mistress to follow the path pointed out by Nature. It is your duty to mention it, but it would be impertinent to press its adoption.'[1]

A mistress might succumb to the craze for sea bathing, in which event it was the maid's duty to attend her with a bundle containing towel and dry clothes. In Scotland, according to Henry Cockburn, the art of changing wet clothes for dry in public was somewhat inexpertly managed. At Ardrossan, for example:

'The maid holds a portion of the dry vestment over the dripping lady's head, and as the soaked gown descends to the heels, the dry is *supposed* to descend over the head as fast, so that the *principle* is that the lady is never seen. I wonder how, when they happen to look at a fellow exhibitor, and observe the interest taken from every window and by all the street, they can avoid discovering that such acts are seldom performed without revelations.'[2]

If one thing was needed to keep a lady's maid conscientious it was the thought that some day she might be called upon to attend her mistress's deathbed. Then, every pettish word, every neglected chore, would rise up accusingly when it was too late to atone. It was an offence before God that any deathbed should be disfigured by the upsurge of such reproaches.

When the tears were over, the virtuous lady's maid could rejoice in a material consolation: she was entitled, as was Pamela, to her mistress's wardrobe, save for a few specified items. In *Humphrey Clinker* a 'worthless drab' becomes the richer by £500 through a happy misfortune of this type.

Whether mistresses, in their lifetime, ought to present their maids with cast-off clothing was a vexed point. According to one school, this merely encouraged a love of finery, which led to a seeking for the sort of low company which relished finery. This in turn led to borrowing clothes from a mistress's wardrobe, which was a long step down the slippery slope; and the maid who was capable of such a step would scarcely halt at

[1] *Duties of a Lady's Maid.*   [2] *Memorials of His Time.*

arranging with her low friends to leave the dressing-room
window unlocked and the jewel case open. According to another
school, a lady's maid would have more incentive to look after
garments properly if she knew she would inherit them.

The lady's maid faced temptation of another sort on her
errands to the linen draper or haberdasher, who would offer
her £2 10s. for herself if her mistress could be induced to
spend £50 in the shop in a year. An honest maid would realise
that this was a direct bribe and a gross insult; the sum would
be added to her mistress's bill in disguised form, and the
result was as much theft as if the £2 10s. were stolen from a
locked chest. Many mistresses closed their eyes to the secret
commissions which they suspected their maids drew. After all,
they did not pay the bills; their husbands did.

Dishonest ladies' maids, if G. W. M. Reynolds is to be
believed, wheedled finery out of their mistresses by voicing
such criticisms as: 'Your ladyship does not look at all well in
the pale satin dress but the dark one becomes you admirably.'
The pale satin dress would then be relegated to the maid.
Another trick was to spill grease or fruit stain on a treasured
garment and 'with wild exclamations of "A thousand pities!"'
show it to the fastidious mistress, who would at once discard it.
In similar fashion, furs were soiled, dresses inked, bonnets
bent and linen torn. The devastated garments were taken to
marine stores and other shops which existed to buy cast-offs
from ladies' maids and valets.[1]

The honest lady's maid, such as is described in Mrs
Beeton's famous volume, was an adept at freeing garments of
ink stains, wax stains and mud stains (mistresses often came
home spattered with candle fat from chandeliers). 'If the
flowers with which the bonnet is decorated have been crushed
or displaced, or the leaves tumbled, they should be raised and
readjusted by means of flower-pliers,' says Mrs Beeton.[2] Dishonest ladies' maids presumably used their flower-pliers to pull
the flowers out.

There is plenty of evidence to suggest that ladies' maids
were adept at snubbing mistresses whose aspirations exceeded

[1] *Mary Price, or Memoirs of a Servant Maid.*
[2] *The Book of Household Management.*

their resources. A maid had standards below which she could not descend. The caption below a *Punch* drawing read:

Lady's maid: Please, ma'am, I wish to resign.
Lady: Why, Parker? You came here only yesterday.
Lady's maid: I have been looking over your drawers, ma'am, and find your things are not up to the mark and would not do me credit.

Although there were cosmetic preparations on the market, including those of Mr Rowland, the skilled lady's maid was expected to know how to make her own washes, balsams and lotions. She was responsible for removing her mistress's pimples, smoothing her wrinkles and purifying her breath. She would know that white paint was to be avoided, on the grounds that it caused swollen eyes, changed the texture of the skin, created eruptions, loosened the teeth, produced rheums, heated the mouth and throat, corrupted the saliva, corroded the lungs and took on the smell of liver and garlic; but if her mistress was prepared to face these inconveniences it was for the maid to apply the paint as ordered. Dangerous, too, was nitrate of silver or lunar caustic, as used in certain hair dyes. It was warranted to make the hair black if carefully applied, but 'you must take care not to burn yourself with it as it will eat through your skin like a piece of red-hot iron' (doing the same, no doubt, to the mistress's scalp). One disadvantage of this treatment was that the hair soon changed from black to purple. A dye like this could be bought, but 'it will be better for you to make it for a few pence than give away shillings and pounds to perfumers and patentees,' said the guide-book.[1]

To make her various concoctions and decoctions, the lady's maid required something very like a laboratory, with alembics, pestles and Bunsen burners. In practice, she used the still-room. When not dissolving steel filings in vinegar she would be pounding musk with amber, counterfeiting Rowlands' Hair Oil with bears' grease, stirring quicklime with yellow litharge and white lead, or making eau-de-Cologne. A recipe for alum water ran: 'Take three calves' feet chopped small, three melons of middling size, three cucumbers, four or five fresh eggs, a slice

[1] *Duties of a Lady's Maid.*

of gourd, two lemons, a pint of skimmed milk, a gallon of rose
water, a quart of juice of water lilies, a pint of juice of plantains
and wild tansy and half an ounce of borax. Distil the whole in
a *balnea mariae.* . . .' To make Italian pomatum: 'Take 25
pounds of hog's lard, eight pounds of mutton suet, six ounces
of oil of bergamot, four ounces of essential oil of lemons, half
an ounce of oil of lavender and a quarter of an ounce of oil of
rosemary.' The result was to be stored in gallipots.

For black spots and freckles on her mistress's complexion
the maid would apply bullock's gall, which housemaids used
no less effectively to clean dirty marble. Sunburn could be
counteracted 'with asses' or even women's milk,' no indication
being given as to how the latter commodity should be obtained.
It was not to be confused with virgin milk, which the
maid would manufacture herself by precipitating tincture of
benzoin in water. This gave a beautiful rosy colour to the
face.

Because of the wickedness of tradesmen, it was probable
that many ingredients would be supplied in adulterated form.
The lady's maid would know how to make the appropriate
checks. To test a purchase of musk, she would draw a silk
thread two or three times through a clove of moist garlic, then
through the musk. If the latter was genuine, it would at once
kill the smell of garlic. Carmine made from cochineal was also
much debased, notably by the addition of red lead. The test
was to take two small silver thimbles and fill one with genuine
carmine, the other with suspect. The weight of the pure brand
would be half that of the adulterated brand. To test Balm of
Mecca, alias Balm of Grand Cairo, alias Balm of India, the
method was to pour a drop in water and put an iron knitting-
needle in. If all the drop adhered to the needle, the Balm was
pure.

It was always possible that, while engaged in her laboratory,
the maid would hear the bell ring, and have to rush from her
retorts in order to pass her mistress a book from a table a
couple of yards away. Or perhaps the mistress would wish to
remove a tight ring from her finger. The maid knew the
secret, which was to touch it with mercury, then give it a
light blow with a hammer, whereupon it would break. If the

mistress then decided she did not want the ring, so much the better.[1]

There was much else the lady's maid was required to know: not to boil the water for the goldfish (Thames water was better for goldfish than that of the New River); how to remove mourning stains; how to apply papillotes without giving her mistress a headache, earache, toothache or pimples; and how to scrub pet dogs, without envying them the use of a bath which she herself was in all probability forbidden to use.

In 1849 a shudder went through the genteel ranks of ladies' maids when one of their number was hanged, along with her husband, before 50,000 people outside Horsemonger Jail in London. This was Mrs Maria Manning, a Swiss by birth, who had been in the service of Lady Blantyre, daughter of the Duchess of Sutherland. By unhappy chance, the body of a former paramour of Mrs Manning, Patrick O'Connor, had been found buried in lime under the flags of a kitchen. A box belonging to Mrs Manning contained the Psalms of David in French, a collection of sacred poems, a work entitled *Family Devotion For Every Day Of The Year* and two letters of recommendation from distinguished individuals, one of whom described her as 'kind, affectionate and piously inclined.' On the scaffold, as became a good lady's maid, Mrs Manning was 'attired in a manner that evinced the greatest attention to her personal appearance.' In other words, she wore a cast-off dress belonging to her former noble mistress.

The Cook

Cooks were 'plain' or 'professed.' The former produced the sort of items which Mrs Beeton used to list as 'A Nice Plain Cake for Children,' 'A Nice Plum Cake,' 'A Nice, Useful Cake,' 'A Good Holiday Cake' and so on. At the worst, the plain cook's meals were so relentlessly unimaginative as to drive the master of the house to dine at his club, thus threatening the stability of yet another Christian marriage. The professed cook, with suitable assistance, would be capable of sending up a

[1] *Duties of a Lady's Maid,* and *The Servant's Guide and Family Manual* (1830).

dinner of six, eight or ten courses, but like her male counterpart (Chapter XI) she was touchy and jealous of her privileges.

The cook held her mistress's reputation in the hollow of her ladle and both of them knew it. For the mistress, as Mrs Beeton feelingly relates, the last half-hour before a dinner-party was a torturing ordeal, in which she must display no agitation before her guests 'but show her tact in suggesting light and cheerful subjects of conversation which will be much aided by the introduction of any particular new book, curiosity or article of *vertu* which may pleasantly engage the attention of the company.'[1] For families who did much entertaining, the strain of this half-hour was too heavy, and, as the Victorian age progressed, the custom grew of 'importing' the major part of the meal from a fashionable caterer.

The cook, like the housekeeper, was always 'Mrs.' She had complete domination over the kitchen and tried to keep it as impregnable as the nurse kept her nursery. Its door was a door to be knocked on, even by the butler. Most self-respecting cooks held the view that the lady of the house had no business to enter her own kitchen; others insisted that she should give advance notice of her intention to call. The cook's idea of a 'nice lady to work for' was one who 'never interferes' or 'never sets foot below stairs.' If a mistress insisted on doing so, she was made to feel that she was a busybody, a mean-minded inquisitor and, above all, no lady. Sometimes a householder might boast, 'I've always been mistress in my kitchen and that's what I intend to be,' but more often than not that boast was made by her cook.

Usually, cooks of this calibre would take umbrage if the mistress attempted to do her own shopping, or even tried to direct her which tradespeople to patronise. This they would proclaim to be a reflection on their honesty—'if that's the way of it, you'd better be getting somebody else.' The total extent of the mistress's interest in culinary matters was supposed to be her morning perusal of the slate on which the cook outlined the proposed meals for the day. Mistresses liked to think of this as 'ordering' the dinner, but cooks resented the word and preferred to talk of 'naming' the dinner.

[1] *The Book of Household Management.*

If cooks were intransigent, they had their grievances. Most kitchens were over-heated and ill-ventilated, a circumstance which encouraged the intake of liquor. Faulty flues led to lumps of soot falling into the vessels below (stir it in, said Swift, and the soup will have the high French taste). Keeping food in good condition without the help of refrigeration must have been a perpetual worry. 'When meat indicates the least degree of putridity,' said Samuel and Sarah Adams, 'it should be dressed without delay, else it becomes unwholesome. In the latter case, however, even fish as well as meat may be reclaimed by putting pieces of charcoal into the water with it when boiled or par-boiled. Tainted meat may also be restored by washing it in cold water and afterwards in strong chamomile tea and rubbing it with a clean cloth, after which it may be sprinkled with salt and suffered to remain till the next day if necessary.' In warm weather all meat was to be turned daily end for end and wiped with a clean dry cloth. Fowls could be preserved by plugging pieces of charcoal into their vents and tying a string round their necks; and the decay of fish could be arrested by means of sugar.

Anyone who has even a nodding acquaintance with Victorian cookery books will know what prodigies of enterprise were required of a professed cook to mount a formal dinner for eighteen or twenty-four persons. The hours from five to nine called for a high degree of organisation and application, and usually a rule of absolute silence was imposed. A kitchen-maid would be assigned to look after the roasts while the cook titivated the sucking pig ('well clean the nostrils and ears'), dissected larks for a pie or busied herself with *timbales* and *quenelles*, *pâtés* and *fricassées*. A full-length dinner for eighteen persons could easily produce five hundred separate items to be washed up afterwards.

The cook who could send up that sort of meal was not expected to sweep the front hall or scrub the front steps. She had cook-maids to do all the dirtier jobs and to prepare the servants' meals, for a professed cook was too accomplished a figure to waste her art on servants. It followed that the servants were fed on an endless succession of joints, often indifferently roasted by a kitchen girl, and served up cold until someone gave away the remnant at the door. There was plenty of food for everyone, and often too much; but it was so monotonous that there was a standing temptation to pilfer uneaten delicacies returned from the dining-room. These, in the normal way, were reserved for the family lunch next day, being regarded as much too good for those who prepared and carried them.

The cook's perquisites were a perennial source of grievance. By her own tradition, she was entitled to sell the household dripping to dealers, who retailed it to families unable to afford butter on their bread. Frugal mistresses thought that the household dripping ought to be used in the household cooking, instead of the butter with which cooks were dismayingly prodigal. Henry Mayhew tells how women with large baskets under suspiciously large cloaks used to call at kitchen doors in the fashionable districts of London, before householders were awake, to collect lumps of dripping, estimating the value by eye. Often the transaction would include lumps of butter, cupfuls of stock, pieces of meat and loaves; and occasionally silver spoons. To the indignation of householders, dealers distributed handbills at tradesmen's entrances offering 'The Highest Price for Kitchen Stuff and Dripping'—a standing inducement, it was said, to roast the last ounce of fat out of the meat. Some housewives closed their eyes to what they could not prevent; others tried to fight it and as a result 'kept the house in hot water.'[1]

No servant had such opportunities to underline a grievance as a disaffected cook. If forced to trade with a greengrocer who gave no commission, or did not keep a gin bottle, she would ensure that the vegetables served were stale; and if the butcher did not give a percentage she would take her revenge on the meat. To suspect such activities was easy; to expose them was almost impossible.

The vocational failings of cooks were insobriety and dishonesty. Many a mistress was willing to put up with dreary cooking if only she could be confident that the cook would not be found dead drunk an hour before dinner or was not giving away joints of meat to the itinerant woman who made a living by cleaning steps for cooks with hangovers. Although

[1] *London Labour and London Poor* (1851).

one might not realise it from the records of the times, there was a considerable army of sober and honest cooks whose mistresses went to great pains to keep them contented and who never had to advertise for places (how good a cook, one wonders, was the advertiser who called herself 'a good churchwoman and regular communicant, understands meat dishes, soups, jellies, etc'?).

Cooks were supposed to have a partiality for policemen, entertaining them to bounteous meals in the kitchen. In nineteenth century London householders grumbled more particularly about the locust swarms of Guardsmen who depleted their larders. In 1847 Henry and Augustus Mayhew wrote an extravaganza, *The Greatest Plague Of Life*, in which a housewife in Albany Street, near the Guards barracks, is made to complain of moustachioed rovers 'looking down every area like so many dealers in hare and rabbit skins, crying out "Any affection or cold meat this morning?"' She adds: 'I don't know if any of my courteous readers have been in Albany Street when the bugle is sounded for the fellows to return to their barracks, but upon my word the scene is really heart-breaking to householders, for there isn't an area down the whole street but from which you will see a Life Guardsman with his mouth full ascending the steps and hurrying off to his quarters for the night.' David Copperfield and his child-wife, it may be remembered, were vexed to find that their cook was maintaining a cousin in the Life Guards, but the trouble eventually resolved itself: 'Mary Anne's cousin deserted into our coal-hole, and was brought out, to our great amazement, by a piquet of his companions in arms, who took him away handcuffed in a procession that covered our front garden with ignominy. This nerved me to get rid of Mary Anne.'

Cook-maids, kitchen-maids and scullery-maids lived under what Tennyson called 'the sooty yoke of kitchen vassalage' and served to absorb the cook's bad temper. Their manners were not always good enough for the servants' hall and they might be required to take their meals in the kitchen, or even in less salubrious parts. Sam Weller, invited into the magistrate's house at Ipswich, asked Mr Muzzle, the footman, how many maids there were. This conversation ensued:

'Only two in our kitchen,' said Mr Muzzle, 'cook and

'ousemaid. We keep a boy to do the dirty work, and a gal besides, but they dine in the washus.'

'Oh, they dines in the washus, do they?' said Mr Weller.

'Yes,' replied Mr Muzzle. 'We tried 'em at our table when they first come, but we couldn't keep 'em. The gal's manners is dreadful vulgar, and the boy breathes so very hard while he's eating that we found it impossible to sit at table with him.'

'Young grampus,' said Mr Weller.

'Oh, dreadful,' rejoined Mr Muzzle, 'but that is the worst of country service, Mr Weller; the juniors is always so very savage.'[1]

The Nurse

Nurses came in two categories, wet and dry.

The specifications for a wet nurse were that she should be not less than twenty years old and not more than thirty, of sound morals and in perfect health, with a vigorous appetite for the right foods; her breasts were to be 'full, round and elastic' and the nipples 'erectile and firm.' She would be unaddicted to snuff or spirits. Mrs Beeton was very insistent that the wet nurse should not be a person likely to gratify her own inclinations at the expense of the child; in other words, the type who would sit down and gorge on pickles, cucumbers, fried meat 'or other crude and injurious aliments, in defiance of all orders given or confidence reposed in their word, good sense, and humanity.'

Although wet nurses were forbidden spirits they were permitted large quantities of beer. Mrs Beeton thought it reasonable to allow half a pint of stout at eleven o'clock in the morning, a pint of porter at one, a half-pint of stout at eight in the evening and a pint of porter at ten or ten-thirty.

It was a poor estate which could not produce a wet nurse at the right time from among the tenantry. If the tenants failed, the net would be cast in the adjacent villages. The 'Personal' columns of the quality newspapers were usually sprinkled with offers of 'a good breast of milk' for hire, accompanied by assurances as to the owner's health and morals. The lowest type of

[1] Charles Dickens: *Pickwick Papers.*

Nurse and children
From 'The Servants' Magazine'

wet nurse was very low indeed; perhaps a trollop who had
unloaded her infant on the parish, or who had insured it in
the hope of wringing a profit out of its death. In Preston a
mistress wishing the services of a wet nurse heard of a young
woman whose infant was ill, and offered to send her own doctor
to attend it. 'Oh, never mind, ma'am,' was the answer, 'it's in
two burial clubs.'[1] An official of a burial club in that town said
that hired nurses sometimes took out insurances in respect of
infants committed to their care, by way of a speculation.

Dry nurses varied from the young girl who had 'practised'
on her small brothers and sisters and whose parents thought
she might as well be paid for cuffing somebody else's children,
to honest, forthright 'bodies' like David Copperfield's Peggotty
and the stern, dignified 'Nanny' who is part of our folklore,

[1] Joseph Kay: *Social Conditions and Education of the People.*

the nurse described by Sir Alan Herbert as 'Britannia's virgin dam'—

> That, old as mountains and as stout,
> From child to child is passed about
> Till childless yet, she passes out,
>   The lonely British Nanny.[1]

An experienced, forceful head nurse was a formidable person to have in the house. Samuel and Sarah Adams laid it down as her responsibility to see that near-by ponds and rivers were fenced in and that all windows from which children could fall were barred; if the master would not co-operate in these matters, a conscientious head nurse could hardly remain in his service. She would reject feather beds and bed curtains for her charges, on the ground that these caused debility, and would also condemn low beds, being aware, even if her mistress was not, that 'the most pernicious stratum of air is that nearest the floor.' She would also insist on proper fire precautions. A desirable accessory in a children's bedroom was a large strong sack on the end of a stout rope, for lowering children from the window, care being taken that they were not lowered on to spiked railings. The nurse, if an athletic type, might even expect a knotted rope to be provided for her own safety, though it is not easy to imagine the traditional Nanny performing such a descent.

The head nurse ran an establishment within an establishment and did her best to keep it inviolate. Usually, the lowest ranking footman was at her beck, but neither footmen nor housemaids enjoyed nursery attendance. There were constant demarcation disputes and sooner or later the nurse antagonised the cook by her demands or rejections. As a rule, she took her own meals in the nursery, but she qualified to eat in the house-keeper's room on special occasions. Parents were not encouraged to enter the nursery, fathers being regarded as particularly tiresome because of their addiction to romps. The children were sent to the drawing-room for parental scrutiny between five and six in the evening, a period which was long enough for many mothers. During the rest of the day the children were

[1] 'Nanny,' in *Humorous Verse* (ed. E. V. Knox).

dressed, undressed, and redressed like dolls, in between out-
ings. In aristocratic families the head nurse wheeled the heir,
leaving second or third sons to the nursemaids; and the heir was
always referred to as 'the Marquess' or whatever his rank was.

The nurse's authority over the children was almost absolute.
She could rule by suasion, by example, by deprival or by
'dosing'; so long as the children were not manifestly terrified,
nobody interfered. Any notion they acquired of justice, of
right and wrong, stemmed from her. It was at her knee that
they said their prayers and it was she who described to them
the internal arrangements of Heaven and Hell. In a sense, her
position was that of a drill sergeant who laboured hard to polish
up a batch of raw recruits and to put them on parade clean and
well behaved at the appointed hour; and the respect which she
sought to engender in them towards their parents was akin to
that which non-commissioned officers try to breed in recruits
towards their officers. Parents, like officers, had funny ways
and their standards were not always as strict as those expected
of the lower ranks, but they were nevertheless set over us in
ultimate authority and merited all possible respect. Governesses
were not real officers, only education officers. There was another
point of comparison between nurses and drill sergeants: their
sayings were treasured by their charges and passed from one
generation to another.

Sage though they were in essential things, nurses had their
superstitions and their medical and scientific knowledge was
often of the most primitive. Some of them believed that the
baby's bath water could be warmed by pouring brandy into it.
At least one guidebook[1] censures the practice, not on the
grounds that it is a waste of a noble spirit but because the
admixture of brandy has the opposite effect from that intended.
In cold weather coachmen used to pour brandy into their boots
in the belief that it would warm their feet.[2]

A nurse of any stature required nursemaids to do the washing,
ironing, sewing and mending for her, but in smaller homes the
nursemaid was, in effect, the nurse; and if she merely refrained

---

[1] *The Servant's Guide and Family Manual.*
[2] In *The Compleat Servant Maid* (1677) chambermaids are advised to
wash their faces in brandy and brimstone.

from dropping her charges on their heads she earned her money. The anxious mistress would interrogate her closely on her methods. Did she know that tight head bandages could affect, not only the shape of the head, but the sanity of the wearer? Did she know that threatening children with bogeymen, sweeps, gypsies and so on could have the same result? Had she heard the story told by Sir W. Ellis, who was in charge of the County Lunatic Asylum at Hanwell, about a nurse who dressed up a figure, put it at the foot of a little girl's bed, and warned her that if she moved or cried it would get her? The child's mother was out, but some instinct prompted her to return and she found a servants' ball in progress. She ran upstairs and found the figure at the foot of the bed . . . and her child with its eyes intently fixed upon it but to her inexpressible horror quite dead.'[1]

A greater menace to the nursery population was the unscrupulous administration of lethal 'sleeping stuffs.' Sometimes a nursemaid drugged her charge to save herself rebukes for not keeping it quiet; sometimes in order to ensure an unbroken night's sleep for herself; sometimes in order to attend a place of amusement. A druggist giving evidence at an inquest at Carnarvon said that, every Saturday night, he usually dispensed laudanum to some sixty servant girls for the purpose of stupefying their charges, thus leaving them free to enjoy themselves unharassed.

The Lancet, attacking the 'venial' use of poisons in its issue of June 21, 1856, said: 'Children are daily drugged with Godfrey's Cordial, syrup of poppies, paregoric elixir, laudanum or some other medicinal preparation containing opium. This is professedly for the purpose of keeping them quiet or sending them to sleep—a sleep, alas! from which hundreds never wake and others revive to have the dose repeated again and again until it produces hydrocephalus or some other affection that renders the unhappy child in all its after life an effete being and an incumbrance upon its relations or on the poor rates.'

It was recommended that nursemaids should, within reason, toss their charges about. This was why a girl should wear loose-fitting clothing, to leave her limbs free. The author of

[1] *A Treatise on Insanity* (1838).

one manual said: 'When I see a large child remarkably quiet, with fat white-looking cheeks, I conclude that it seldom gets tossed about.' To the knowledgeable, this was always the sign of a lazy servant. Instructions on how to exercise older children out of doors read oddly in these traffic-ridden days: 'As soon as they are upon the road, let them run about as much as possible, taking care that they do not go so far away as to be out of your sight or beyond your assistance and that they avoid the middle of the road wherever there is much traffic. Families residing in a town and having no garden or piece of ground to play in must get their exercise on the road, for the fields in the neighbourhood are usually all cultivated. . . . A quiet, prim walk out and home will not give children sufficient exercise; but while running races, trundling hoops, playing horses or the like they may be joyous without rude noise or violence.'[1]

In exercising her charges the nursemaid was to walk only where her mistress directed her to walk, and not to take the children to visit any of her acquaintances. If she met other nursemaids she was to avoid discussing unsuitable topics within earshot of her charges. Always she was exposed to perils peculiar to her station:

'There are persons in the situation of gentlemen who on pretence of knowing or admiring the children under her care enter into conversation with a girl and treat her with a familiarity which in her ignorance she may think is condescension but which in fact is insult, since it presumes her to be a girl whose virtue is already lost or from whom it may be bought at the small expense of flattery, false promises or money.

'Where there is one maidservant who marries a gentleman there are ten thousand betrayed and ruined. . . . A nursery maid is perhaps more exposed to danger than any other class of servant. She walks out a good deal with no other companions but children who are not old enough to understand what is said and whose presence affords a pretence and an excuse for addressing her. It is always dangerous to give ear to a man who is either too proud or too poor to marry you.'[2]

Nursemaids took all their meals, except dinner, in the

[1] *The Nursery Maid* (Houlston's Industrial Library).
[2] *Ibid.*

nursery. If, in the evening, they heard sounds of jollity from below stairs they were to resist any temptation to run down and see what was happening, for in those few moments a child might wake, get out of bed and fall downstairs. After the children were put to bed, it was time for the nursemaid to commune with her own heart and stiffen up her resolution, rather than to gossip profitlessly with her fellow-servants. She was advised not to say her prayers until she was in a quiet frame of mind.

In the daytime, attacks of melancholy could be dispersed by holding romps with the children, or by discovering new ways to entertain them. One idea was to make them a pair of scales. Lead was 'easily procured,' and it could be melted down into ounces, half-ounces and drachms; in this way children would get a good idea of different weights. Killing beetles or other creatures was not to be regarded as an entertainment; any vermin were to be slaughtered quietly, without comment. If the nursery contained boys as well as girls, they were not to be allowed to express their natural wants or to expose their persons in each other's presence. 'Even where there are only girls this care is desirable. But on the other hand you must be exceedingly careful that the delicacy which is so desirable should not be forced upon children so as to make them attach any interest to such circumstances and thus perhaps lay the foundation of a real indelicacy.'[1]

Mistresses who handed over control of their children to nursemaids for twenty-three hours out of the twenty-four often complained that their offspring were speaking in uncouth accents, dropping their h's and using vulgar street chaff. 'Well, Mary says it,' would be the defiant answer. The onus of correcting bad habits of speech eventually fell on the governess. From nursemaids, children also learned deceitful ways. The dexterity with which Mary slipped a French novel under a cushion as her mistress entered the nursery might pass unnoticed by her mistress but not by her charges. Often, nursemaids bribed or cautioned children against telling their parents about untoward occurrences in the nursery or romantic encounters in the park. Sometimes parents instructed their children to inform them

[1] *The Nursery Maid* (Houlston).

about all such lapses. For an unscrupulous child, willing to play off one side against the other, the system had wonderful possibilities.

The Housemaid

If it was the privilege of the lady's maid to be the last into bed, it was the privilege of the housemaid to be first out of it.

Her duties varied with the size of the staff. Where there were footmen, or parlourmaids (the equivalent of footmen), or chambermaids, her lot was much lightened. If the household consisted of a cook and a housemaid, the cook would undertake to clean strictly defined parts of the hall and the front steps. When the housemaid was the sole maid of all work in a big family under a tyrannous mistress her duties could be nearly as arduous as those of the women who worked at the coal face. Among her vocational hazards was 'housemaid's knee,' defined in medical terms as 'chronic inflammation of the patellar bursa in front of the knee, due to too much kneeling'; and judging from the illustration in Miller's *Surgery* it was as unsightly as it was painful. The condition could be reduced by rest, counter-irritation or surgery. Whether a housemaid looked after her knees was her own business, but her mistress expected her to take good care of her hands; not in order to encourage vanity, but because she had to be able to tackle dirty work *and* clean work. A housemaid had the consolation that 'though her work may be hard she has no anxiety of mind'; that is, she did not need to worry where her money was to come from. 'A maid of all work who receives kind treatment from her employers has not, therefore, so hard a place as the good, industrious, careful wife of a working man.'[1]

The housemaid rose between five and six, lit the kitchen fire and opened the shutters. Then she cleaned out the grates in the sitting-room and dining-room, laying down druggets to do so, swept and dusted these rooms and polished everything capable of being polished, including the 'brass furniture.' She cleaned the candlesticks and lamp glasses, whisked a broom over the front hall and the stair carpets, brushed the outside

[1] *Instructions in Household Matters for Young Girls*, by 'A Lady' (1844).

steps and polished the knocker. It was then time to light dressing-room fires for those who were entitled to them and to carry up hot water for the family baths. After this she put on a clean apron and sat down to her breakfast, to fortify her for the more arduous labours of the day. It was important not to fall behind in her early duties, for the gentlemen of the household greatly disliked seeing housemaids at work. They preferred that young women should carry heavy coal buckets at a time when no question of offering chivalrous assistance could arise. They also liked to be able to walk about landings and corridors without falling over brooms or buckets.

The maid might or might not be expected to cook the family breakfast and wait at table. After breakfast came airing and bed-making. It was the housemaid's duty 'to keep the dwelling as well aired throughout as if the family lived in the open fields,'[1] and one would like to think she carried out these instructions to the letter. Mattresses were to be turned daily, pillows were to be smoothed so that no quill could prick the sleeper, bedding was to be switched with an old riding whip and not a wisp of 'sluts' wool' was to be left on the floor under the beds. The use of long-handled mops and brushes was scorned by the dedicated housemaid, who got down on her knees and took the risk of prepatellar bursitis. If a manservant was kept, his help was on no account to be solicited in the making of beds; 'a buxom wench has been known to ask a favourite footman to assist her and the request has been attended with bad consequences for herself.'[2] There was another delicate matter attendant on bed-making: 'the housemaid should not complain of the trouble of taking down the whole bed each time it is found that there is a bug in it.' To dismantle involved less trouble in the long run. It might seem difficult to justify the existence of bugs in an orderly Creation, but very probably this creature was introduced by Providence 'with a view to provoking acts and habits of cleanliness which otherwise would not be insisted upon, and thus tend to check accumulations of dirt which might lead to outbreaks of disease.'[3]

[1] *The Housemaid* (Houlston's Industrial Library).
[2] *Domestic Management or the Art of Conducting a Family* (Anon.), c. 1800.   [3] *The Housemaid.*

Beds, whenever possible, were to stand in the middle of the room, and not against a wall. 'We know from experience,' says Dr Kitchiner, 'that a flash of lightning, should it unfortunately strike a building, or enter through any of the windows, uniformly takes its direction along the walls without injuring the furniture in the centre of a room.' The maid's own bed would probably have to stand against the wall because of the exiguous size of her bedroom, but this was, perhaps, a necessary reminder of her station.

The housemaid also emptied the wash-basins and the chamber-pots. Some of the earlier manuals cautioned against emptying utensils out of the window; the more genteel ones enjoined her to smuggle the chamber-pots down the stairs when no one was about, as the family had sensitive feelings in these matters.

When the bedrooms were tidied, the housemaid got on with her work in the downstairs rooms, polishing the last curlicue on the door plates, wiping the last cupid on the mantel, cleaning out the bird cage and lighting any other fires that were necessary. A clever housemaid was expected to be able to light the drawing-room fire with seven pieces of wood, and even a not-so-clever housemaid was supposed to light four fires from one bundle of wood. There was no excuse for any of the fires smoking and even less excuse for the lazy, dangerous habit of carrying hot coals from room to room, or of leaving the poker in a fire to fall out and burn the carpet.

An especial vexation to the conscientious housemaid was the master's study, especially if the master was a literary man. The rule was that no papers were to be moved, and if books were dusted they were to be put down again in the identical place. Ordinarily, 'dusting round' an object was to be censured, but an exception could sometimes be made in respect of an author's books. 'A housemaid should never exercise her own taste in arranging books in a gentleman's study.'[1] Legend has it that the stupidity of a housemaid was responsible for the burning of the first manuscript of Carlyle's *The French Revolution*, which had been lent to John Stuart Mill; but investigation shows that the housemaid's share in the

[1] *Common Sense for Housemaids*, by 'A Lady' (1850).

manuscript's destruction was much less culpable than has been supposed.

During her morning's work the housemaid would be expected to answer front and back doors, and every front door ring meant putting on a clean apron. The rules said that she should not peep from behind the front door at the caller, but a maid was usually anxious to show no more *déshabille* than she could help; it was bad enough to have to present a soot-smeared face crowned by tumbled hair. Callers could be very difficult. The *Servants' Magazine*, published in the 1860s, told its readers about the Rev. Dr Nettleton whose custom it was to knock at doors and ask, 'Does Jesus Christ dwell in this house?' If the maid merely said, 'Come in,' he would reply, 'Oh no, if Christ is not here I cannot come in.'

After lunch and its resultant washing up the maid would change her plain working dress for a black gown and a tidy, modest-looking bobbinet cap tied with a quiet ribbon. She would then sit down with her needle to mend linen, patch carpets and darn the family's stockings. She would, of course, sit where she could readily hear her mistress's bell and the door bells. 'Anxiety to get on with her work must not lead her to forget the time for laying the tablecloth for dinner'—or for ringing the bell half an hour before dinner to inform the family that it was time to dress. At dinner she would wait on the family, set the decanter before the master, fill the finger-bowls with tepid water (if it was that kind of house) and, after seeing that the drawing-room was tidy and the fire well stoked, go for her own meal. After that there was little more to do except help with the washing up, empty the bedroom slops again and refill the ewers, fold down the beds and light the bedroom fires as required. If a warming-pan was demanded, she would be careful to select only the reddest coals and to sprinkle a little salt on them, in order to kill the sulphurous vapour which otherwise would linger in the bed. In the absence of a lady's maid the housemaid would lay out her mistress's night clothes, arrange her brush and comb, stretch her curl papers or cut fresh ones. She would resist any urge to run her mistress's comb through her own hair or to trim her corns with the master's razor.

Later in the evening the family would call for tea. Here is a description of the process: 'The tea urn keeps the water boiling by means of a heater in the inside. The heater, a long round piece of iron with a ring at the top, fits the inside tube or chimney of the urn; it ought to be red-hot and takes about half an hour to heat in a good fire. The water having been boiled in a kettle is poured while boiling into the outer hollow, or basin, of the urn; the heater is then taken from the fire by means of a small poker hooked at the end and put into the chimney of the urn.'[1] This infernal machine was then carried upstairs and stood on the tea table or on a rug.

On top of this ordinary programme, each day had its special duties which fell to be carried out periodically. All carpets were to be swept with wet tea leaves once a week. If there was a scarcity of tea leaves the used ones had to be put through hot water and used again. Nasty-minded mistresses tested their housemaids' industry and honesty simultaneously by planting coins under the carpet; it was for the maid to hand over the coin quietly, place it where her mistress would see it, nail it to the floor or give notice, according to her inclination. Periodically the wallpaper had to be cleaned with bread three days old and the imitation wainscot washed down with sour porter. The instructions for cleaning marble began: 'Take a bullock's gall, a gill of soap lees, half-gill of turpentine and make into a paste with pipe clay . . . or beat pumice juice to an impalpable powder and mix it with verjuice. . . .'[2] Old and unglazed paintings which appeared grubby were to be washed gently with cold water but on no account touched with soap. The master was apt to be touchy about the cleaning of his paintings and on the whole it was better simply to flick a feather duster over them. All the silver plate, of course, had to be polished regularly. Periodically, the springs of the beds were to be 'anointed' with a solution of corrosive sublimate in spirits of wine, and boiling water poured into the joints of the bedsteads, to discourage bugs. (Many houses swarmed with vermin, it was explained, because of contaminated pine wood imported from America and Canada.)

Another periodical task for the housemaid was to clean the

[1] *Instructions in Household Matters.*
[2] *The Servant's Guide and Family Manual.*

insides of the windows and sometimes even the outsides. Not a few maids attempting this latter feat fell to their deaths, being impaled on area railings. This caused a certain amount of fussing by busybodies, but in the days of crinolines there was an even stronger reason for not sending housemaids out on to window sills. In *The Girl With The Swansdown Seat*, Cyril Pearl tells how in 1853, Mrs Lowe, of Victoria Grove, Kensington, was prosecuted for permitting her female servant 'to stand on the sill of an upstairs window in order to clean it, whereby the life of the servant was endangered and the public decency shocked.' Such incidents were reported to the authorities by public informers concerned for the morals of the Metropolis.

It was necessary to work especially hard on Saturdays in order that there should be no obstacle in the way of church-going on Sunday. The secret, as everyone said, was for the housemaid to organise herself properly and take proper fore-thought, and not fritter her time away by taking cups of tea and gossiping at the back door.

A very vexed question was that of breakages. 'In some houses it is a rule that a servant is forgiven if she instantly gives information of having broken any article. With a truly careful, conscientious servant this may answer very well, but it has been found to render others only more careless as they get over the shame and distress of such incidents and it may well be that they should be made aware that in proportion as these accidents (as they are always called) happen a part of the price of each article will be required. . . . Remember that the fault of concealment is infinitely the worse fault of the two; it is not only mean and dishonourable to an earthly master, but it is a sin against God.'[1]

What were the rewards of a housemaid's life? One of them was the sight of a drawing-room in exquisite order, a delight undimmed by the knowledge that she was unworthy to sit in it. But her main reward, it was widely agreed, was simple satisfaction at a good day's work conscientiously done. In the country, on a summer evening, a housemaid could wish for no happier relaxation than to look at Nature. 'These are the hours for a walk round the garden, listening to the nightingale, or

[1] *Common Sense for Housemaids.*

seeing the convolvulus fold itself up for the night or watching
the bees coming to the hive or searching for the glow-worm on
the bank or for the brightest stars in the sky as the darkness
comes on.' Alternatively the housemaid could talk with a
fellow-servant about some book of mutual interest. 'There is
no service in England which can yield greater comfort and
more rational pleasures.' On a Sunday afternoon a housemaid
could learn a hymn or write down what she remembered of the
sermon, or better still go and nurse a sick neighbour.[1]

At night the housemaid would resist the temptation to read
in bed, a dangerous practice which had burned down many a
God-fearing house. She would, of course, be grateful to have
her own bed. 'Some ladies require the housemaid to sleep
frequently in the spare beds, which is a practice that I think
very objectionable for many reasons . . . I think it hard to
make a warming pan of her . . . and in the next place it gives
opportunities for great impropriety of conduct and I think it
more conducive to the respectability of the establishment for
all to keep to their own apartments, so that the housekeeper
can at any time ascertain their being there if she thinks proper.'[2]

In the night the housemaid was unlikely to be disturbed, but
she was supposed to keep her tinder-box ready for instant
action in case her mistress's bell rang. Before dropping off to
sleep she would pray to God to make her a more efficient
servant and plan in her mind how to get through the next day's
work to the maximum advantage of her mistress.

[1] *The Housemaid* (Houlston).   [2] *Ibid.*

XI

THE MALE BRANCH

T HE duties of menservants were never as multifarious as those of women servants. Some of them were dealt with in an earlier chapter, but the emphasis is now on the duties and deferences demanded by the nineteenth century.

The House Steward

This functionary, who was the head of the establishment in large households, remains a shadowy figure. He was there in the hall, extending his palm, in the heyday of vails-giving, but no one has much to say about him in his other appearances. Lord Ferrers murdered his steward; no steward appears to have murdered his master.

The house steward should not be confused with the land steward or bailiff. Besides hiring and disciplining all staff, he did the marketing, checked the supplies, kept the accounts and undertook confidential journeys on his master's behalf. He could write formal letters to all ranks of the nobility and to all grades of tradesmen. It was his duty to prepare the equivalent of a movement order for any servant who was being dispatched a long distance, and if valuables were to be sent between one house and another he was responsible for their packing and safe conduct. If theatrical companies visited the house he made such preparations as they needed and paid their bill; if a lady's maid married, he would organise a suitable reception in his room. At servants' balls he would lead off the first dance with the mistress of the house.

The steward was expected to have a suavity and poise of

manner suited to the dignity of the house and to be neither lavish nor penurious with his master's moneys. When Lord Pembroke's steward in London fell ill of a 'phrenzy' in 1785 his master had an idea that a good replacement might be found in Jersey or Guernsey. 'I do not mean a gentleman,' he explained, 'but I have often been assured that there were in those islands where they speak English and French men of a substantial farmering class, well brought up, both as to accounts and morals.'[1] That gives a fair idea of the type of man a nobleman sought for this office, both then and later. Though not necessarily a gentleman, the steward was often capable of mingling with his master's guests on equal terms; which does not mean that he was invited to do so. Joseph Farington says of Lord Lonsdale in 1808 (when the Earl had four large establishments—Lowther, Whitehaven, Cottesmere and London): 'He directs to his steward but never invites him to the table.'[2]

When his master entertained distinguished personages, the steward's room was conducted with much punctilio and it might well happen that more persons would sit down at his table than at that of his master. To the steward fell the honour of escorting in to dinner the visiting female servant of highest rank, usually a lady's maid, while the housekeeper went in with the highest-ranking manservant, usually a valet. On such occasions evening dress was worn by all. Writing of life at Longleat in the later years of the century, Daphne Fielding says: 'Should a visiting servant fail to bring evening dress he or she would not be allowed to dine in the steward's room but would have to eat in the servants' hall.'[3] Sometimes a valet, to avoid this disgrace, would borrow a suit of his master's.

No doubt there was much in the steward's task to drive an earnest man into a 'phrenzy.'

The Man Cook

'A French cook's notion of his own consequence is prodigious,' wrote James Boswell. By way of example, he told of a

---

[1] Lord Herbert: *Pembroke Papers, 1780–94.*
[2] *The Farington Diary.*   [3] *Before the Sunset Fades.*

Frenchman who was being considered for the post of cook to Sir Benjamin Keen, British Ambassador to Spain. Asked if he had ever dressed any magnificent dishes, the applicant said: '*Monsieur, j'ai accommodé un dîner qui faisait trembler toute la France.*'[1]

The Revolution scattered the great cooks of France. Some found employment in clubs, hotels or catering establishments; others, with many misgivings, took office in the kitchens of English milords. They brought with them, not only their sense of importance but their professional code of honour; the code which had driven Vatel, the *maître d'hôtel* of Condé, to commit suicide in the Roman fashion when it looked as though the fish would arrive too late for a banquet graced by the King. 'So noble a death!' sighed the *Almanach des Gourmands*. It proved that 'the fanaticism of honour can exist in the kitchen as well as in the camp, and that the spit and the saucepan have also their Catos and their Deciuses. . . . In *this* philosophic age all have preferred living at the expense of their masters to the honour of dying for them.'[2]

The French cooks also brought to Britain their tradition of outrageous extravagance; the extravagance which had once caused the Prince de Soubise to query the item 'fifty hams' in a dinner estimate by his cook Bertrand. Only one ham, explained Bertrand, would appear on the table; the others were needed for his *espagnoles*, his *blonds*, his *garnitures* and so forth. When his master still protested, Bertrand exclaimed: 'Oh, My Lord, you do not understand our resources; give the word and these fifty hams which confound you, I will put them all in a glass bottle no bigger than my thumb.' The estimate was passed.[3]

The English aristocrats, while regarding it as essential for their prestige to employ French cooks, declined to underwrite these mincing fellows in their larger follies, refused to let them hire all the assistants they wanted and even challenged the French custom of having a separate pastrycook on the establishment. One or two noblemen who did employ pastrycooks (usually Italians) found them no less exigent in their

---

[1] *London Magazine*, 1779; quoted in *Boswell's Column.*.
[2] Quoted in *The Art of Dining* (Anon.), 1852.   [3] *Ibid.*

demands than the cooks. Lord Albemarle's pastrycook, having
prepared a middle dish of gods and goddesses eighteen feet
high, asked his master to raise the ceiling of his parlour to
facilitate its entrance (doors and ceilings were sometimes raised
in order to accommodate ladies' extravagant coiffures).
'*Imaginez-vous*,' exclaimed Lord Albemarle's man, after a
painful interview, '*imaginez-vous que milord n'a pas voulu faire
ôter le plafond*.'[1] The Duke of Beaufort at a later day employed
a Neapolitan confectioner who took his art no less seriously.
One night the Duke was asleep when there came a
repeated knocking at his door. 'It is only me, Signor Duc,'
exclaimed the pastrycook. 'I was at the opera and I have
been dreaming of the music. It was Donizetti's and I have got
an idea. I have this instant invented a *sorbet*; I have named
it after that divine composer and I hastened to inform Your
Grace.'[2]

In the house of an Englishman whose notion of the higher
gastronomy was to eat a covey of partridges for breakfast and
then dine for the rest of the day off roasts, the lot of a French
cook was peculiarly frustrating. Squire Bramble, dining out,
had complained that the French cook provided not one substantial article for the satisfaction of an English appetite. 'The
pottage was little better than bread soaked in dish-washings,
lukewarm. The *ragoûts* looked as if they had been once eaten
and half-digested; the *fricassées* were involved in a nasty yellow
poultice . . .' and so on.[3] Captain Gronow says that in Regency
days French dishes in the main were 'very mild but very abor-
tive attempts at Continental cooking,' and were met with the
neglect and contempt that they merited.[4] 'The universally
adored and ever-popular boiled potato, produced at the very
earliest period of the dinner, was eaten with everything up to

[1] Quoted in *The Art of Dining* (Anon.), 1852.   [2] *Ibid.*
[3] *Humphrey Clinker.*
[4] In 1885 Lord Hartington, later the Duke of Devonshire, showed dis-
satisfaction with the French dishes which opened the meal at a London
dinner party. When roast beef arrived he exclaimed, in a very audible voice,
'Hurrah! Something to eat at last.' Twenty years later a man who had been
a guest at this party sought to reintroduce himself to the Duke and mentioned the occasion. 'Of course I remember,' exclaimed the Duke. 'We had
nothing to eat.'—Bernard Holland: *The Life of Spencer Compton, Eighth
Duke of Devonshire.*

the moment when sweets appeared.' Any other vegetables that were offered arrived cold.[1]

Perhaps it was the English passion for boiled potatoes that defeated Carême. He left his £1000-a-year appointment with the Prince Regent at Carlton House ostensibly because 'his soul could not live anywhere but in France,' but in fact because the Prince's taste was too *bourgeois*. The services of Felix were offered to the Duke of Wellington by Lord Seaford, and accepted; but very soon afterwards Felix called on Lord Seaford asking to be taken back at reduced wages or even none at all, rather than stay any longer at Apsley House. Asked whether the Duke had been finding fault, he replied: 'Oh no, my Lord, I would stay if he had. He is the kindest and most liberal of masters, but I serve him a dinner that would make Ude or Francatelli burst with envy and he says nothing. I serve him a dinner dressed, and badly dressed, by the cook-maid, and he says nothing. I could not live with such a master if he was a thousand times a hero.'[2]

Ude, former cook to Louis XVI and later to the Earl of Sefton, who paid him three hundred guineas a year, complained: 'In England the few assistants that a head cook is allowed in a family and the number of dishes he has to prepare often deprive him of an opportunity of displaying his abilities; nay, after ten years of the utmost exertion to bring his art to perfection, he ranks no higher than a humble domestic.' Voltaire had said: 'A cook is a divine mortal.' Some day, thought Ude, 'man will raise cookery to the class of the sciences and its professors will be *Artists*, not servants.'[3]

Even when their masters showed an intelligent interest in the mysteries set before them, French cooks were never content. They exacted unheard-of privileges and were usually at loggerheads with their English assistants, to whom was relegated the simple task of roasting. For the sake of a quiet life, many a master preferred to hire an English man cook, if he could find one; but even these, having studied under French masters, had learned to indulge in flights of temperament.

Dr William Kitchiner, himself an amateur cook of no small

[1] *Reminiscences.*   [2] *The Art of Dining.*
[3] Louis Eustache Ude: *The French Cook.*

distinction, offers some poignant glimpses of the hardships
faced by a man cook in his *Apicius Redivivus, or The Cook's
Oracle, Being Six Hundred Receipts the Result of Actual Experiments
Instituted in the Kitchen of a Physician for the Purpose of
Composing a Culinary Code for the Rational Epicure and Augmenting
the Alimentary Enjoyments of Private Families Combining
Economy and Elegance; and Saving Expense to
Housekeepers and Trouble to Servants* (1817). It is not his
aim, he says, to teach professed cooks their duties; their
function is not to allay appetite but to excite it, 'to gratify
those who live upon sauces instead of food and who see the
sun rise with no other hope than that they shall fill their bellies
before it sets.' Nor is he concerned to teach his readers how
to prepare 'fantastic dainties as the brains of peacocks or
parrots, the tongues of thrushes . . . or the teats of a lactiferous
sow.'

Dr Kitchiner quotes from 'my scientific friend, Apicius
Coelius Jr' these necessary qualifications in a cook:

'His auditory nerve ought to discriminate (when several
saucepans are in operation at the same time) the simmering of
one, the ebullition of another and the full-toned wabbling of
a third. It is imperiously requisite that his organ of smell
be highly susceptible to the various effluvia, that his nose may
distinguish the perfection of aromatic ingredients and that
in animal substances it shall evince a suspicious accuracy
between tenderness and putrefaction; above all, his olfactories
should be tremblingly alive to mustiness and empyreuma.

'It is from the exquisite sensibility of his palate that we
admire and judge of the cook; and from the alliance between
the olfactory and sapid organs it will be seen that their perfection
is indispensable.'

Faced as he was with continual heat and glare, basted with
his own perspiration, poisoned by the vapours of charcoal,
polluted inwardly by bad beer drunk to moisten his parched
throat, a cook had some difficulty in keeping his olfactories
tremblingly alive. By degrees his palate would become blunted,
and then 'indurated.' A master would know that his cook had
reached this state when the *ragoûts* came up too highly spiced
and the dishes in general had too much of the *haut goût*. This

was the signal to send for the apothecary, who would set about the work of renovating the overwrought cook. The cure would start with two days of aqueous diet and a purging potion of manna, senna and salts, followed by a day's rest, then a second purge, then two more days' rest, after which the cook would be as good as new. 'This is no joke,' warns Dr Kitchiner, insisting that such is the actual practice in those kitchens where the master is proud of the reputation of his table. 'All great cooks submit to the operation without a murmur; to prevent which it should be made the first condition in hiring them.' Any cook who refuses shows that he is not born to become a master of his art. Dr Kitchiner adds that it will do the master no harm to submit to the same cure from time to time.

The author does not indicate whether women cooks are expected to observe a similar regimen. He does say: 'An English girl properly instructed can equal the best *foreign gentlemen* in everything except impudence and extravagance and send up a delicious dinner with half the usual expense and trouble.'

The Butler

Of old, the butler was responsible only for the supply of ale and wine, which he served to his lord with suitable ceremonial. In post-feudal times, while still the custodian of the cellar, he evolved into the chief manservant of those houses which did not aspire to chamberlains and stewards. As often as not, he was kept for ostentation and sometimes for intimidation. He was expected to be deferential to his superiors and haughty towards his inferiors, which included his master's inferiors. In a populous mansion he was very necessary for the maintenance of discipline among the servants and his presence also served as a brake on the exuberance of the junior members of the family. For these reasons youthful butlers were not favoured.

The butler wore no livery but was attired in formal clothes distinguished by some deliberate solecism—the wrong tie for the coat, or the wrong trousers—to prevent his being mistaken for a gentleman. He was addressed, always, by his surname, even by those members of the family young enough to be his grandchildren; but this was one shade more dignified than being hailed by his Christian name, which had been his lot as a footman. The lower servants, over whom he had the power of dismissal, were careful to call him 'Mister.' Usually he was authorised to pay the accounts for wines, coals, flowers and all supplies which did not fall within the housekeeper's province.

Not the least qualification of the butler was that he should be a bachelor. A butler who married was guilty of selfishness as well as vulgarity. His duty was to be dignified, and the sight of a butler with a nagging wife and insolent children was as offensive and subversive to discipline as the sight of a Guards officer carrying a parcel. Moreover, a married butler spent too much of his master's time on his own affairs, and the burden of domesticity distracted his attention, sapped his efficiency and detracted from his smartness. Again, it was a great temptation for a married butler to take home food to his hungry children, or to smuggle out a half-bottle of wine to 'strengthen' an ailing wife. Not a few butlers, faced with domestic debt, would pawn an article of the master's plate, in the hope of being able to redeem it before its loss was detected. Thus, the very least that a zealous and right-thinking butler owed his master was a vow of celibacy. The law laid down that a butler who, on applying for a post, pretended to be single when he had 'encumbrances' could be dismissed instantly, like a pregnant housemaid.

It was some consolation to a butler that his social status was by no means despicable: 'He is not infrequently received at the tables of highly respectable tradesmen and thereby gains a station in society which is often advantageously employed in establishing himself as a member of the same class. Indeed, few stations afford such opportunities for a man's advancement as those which a butler may command by industry, integrity and economy in early life.'[1] The writer of the foregoing envisaged the butler setting himself up in trade, in which event he would be at liberty to marry.

The butler's duties varied with the pretensions of his master and mistress. Where many servants were kept his nominal responsibilities were increased but his practical duties were

[1] *The Servant's Guide and Family Manual.*

slight; they could mostly be unloaded on to footmen. If the household employed a butler and one footman, the latter often became the butler's drudge. If no valet was kept the butler's duties began with laying out his master's clothes in the morning; but, unlike the valet, he was not expected to comb his master's hair. As compensation for valeting, he would be entitled to his master's cast-off clothes and soiled playing cards. At breakfast the butler would bring in the food assisted by footman or housemaid and wait on the family. His morning labours, mostly discharged in the privacy of his pantry, included warming and ironing the newspapers, for any dampness in the public prints was regarded as distasteful, if not unhealthy;[1] and polishing the plate, a feat he was expected to perform without the aid of neat quicksilver, which made the articles brittle.

The butler supervised the luncheon table but was not necessarily expected to wait on the family. When his mistress left in the carriage in the afternoon he was free to go for a walk or to visit his 'club,' timing his outing so as to be back a few moments before the carriage returned, in order to hand his mistress out. If she chose to assume that he had never left the house, so much the better.

When his mistress was 'at home' the butler answered the door and announced visitors. Callers were divisible into two classes: gentlefolk and persons. Gentlefolk were led straight to the drawing-room and persons were asked to wait in the hall, or elsewhere; obviously, any error in distinguishing between them could lead to grave embarrassment. In our own times, Lady Troubridge has cited as an example of a person 'the tax collector or an agent for somebody's tea.'[2] The formula for announcing such callers was: 'There is a person who wishes to see you, Ma'am,' with as much emphasis on the 'person' as the butler cared to apply. There were also those inferior persons whom a butler did not even invite into the hall, for

[1] At least one newspaper addict preferred his newspapers moist. In the Peninsular War a Colonel Sebright of the Guards had his English papers damped by a servant when they arrived. 'Why, my papers smell as if they were printed last night!' he would say.—Captain R. H. Gronow: *Reminiscences.*

[2] *The Book of Etiquette.*

THE
SERVANTS' MAGAZINE.
No. 13. New Series.]   1 January, 1868.   [Price One Penny.

The butler in his pantry

fear they might abscond with an ornament when his back was turned. If ordered to tell callers that his mistress was 'not at home,' the butler would repeat that formula and refuse to give any further information. The reason for this, as one authority has explained, is that it would offend a caller to say that the lady of the house was too busy, and if she was merely tired a statement that she was indisposed would probably result in a stream of callers next day to ask after her health. Nevertheless, there was frequent controversy over the propriety of ordering a servant to state a literal untruth. The *Servants' Magazine* said: 'If your employer is at home and does not wish to be seen, say at once that he is engaged and you will thank the visitor to call again. On no account say "He is not at home" when he is.' Even the excuse of 'engaged' was a dubious one, however, if tendered by a butler who knew that his master was merely dozing in an armchair or that his mistress was reading a novel on a sofa. On this issue, employers fell into three classes: those who, while not tolerating falsehoods in their servants, thought it reasonable to require a servant to tell a polite untruth to suit his master's convenience; those who thought that if a servant told an untruth at his master's order, the servant was innocent; and those, a small minority, who refused to allow their servants to utter untruths or even conventional fictions on their behalf. Probably very few butlers worried about the ethics of the matter. It was useful to have a formula which avoided the necessity of framing elaborate explanations. The traditionalists among them took a gloomy and incivil pride in uttering not a syllable more than they could help; this was called discretion. A good butler, they held, could not be too careful what he said at the door. The mere fact that his master had just died did not justify him in revealing the news to an unauthorised caller, or to the representative of an inquisitive press.

The dinner table was mostly laid by the footmen but the butler was responsible for its showpieces. He rearranged such items as he did not like and finally gave his nod of approval. It was on the dinner table that he would be chiefly judged. If too much calcined magnesia had been used to bring up the bloom of the grapes, if too much laundry blue had been applied to the plums, if the filberts had not been sulphur-fumed to a uniform colour and glossiness, the master would have cold words to say later.

When the meal was ready, the butler entered the drawing-room (there was no question of knocking beforehand) and announced: 'Dinner is served, ma'am.' He brought up the first dish, followed by the other servants. Then he stood behind his master's chair while grace was said, ready to remove the covers. Thereafter he waited at the side table and served the wine, and set and arranged succeeding courses. At the dessert stage he left to take tea in the housekeeper's room.

When the family were ready for tea, later in the evening, it was the butler's duty to hand round the cups and saucers and the footman's to carry the urn. The tea itself was made by, or under the direction of, the housekeeper. The butler's last task of the day was to see that all doors and windows on the ground floors were locked, all fires safe and all lamps extinguished.

From time to time the butler withdrew to the cellars in order to perform rites of rectification and purification which, at this day, make somewhat disturbing reading. He was expected to rise at four or five in the morning for cellar work. If the cellar was badly ventilated he would advance a candle into it on the end of a long rod. Possibly the flame would go out and he would then resort to artificial ventilation by means of a pair of bellows fitted with a long tin or rubber tube. If the entrance to the cellars faced south he would use his utmost influence to have it moved to the north. The ideal cellar, as he would inform his master, was a vaulted room which was several fathoms down, far from the rumble of horses and carts, from workshops, currents of water, sewers and water closets.

As likely as not, the butler would find the wines 'sick,' 'on the fret' or 'suffering from too much intumescence.' Foul claret could be reclaimed by popping a dozen pippins into the cask, and malt spirits improved by adding powdered charcoal, thus making it 'the equivalent of fine brandy.' When the Malmsey needed fining, the butler added about twenty eggs; other wines could be fined with the aid of isinglass, gum arabic and gelatine. If the white wine had an unpleasant taste, the butler's duty was clear: 'rack half off and to the remaining half add a gallon of new milk, a handful of bay salt and as much rice; after which beat them well together with a staff for half an hour; then fill up the cask and when you have rolled it about well, stillage it, and in a few days it will be much improved.' In order to preserve new wine against thunder, the butler would lay a plate of iron on the vessels containing it. No matter how many calculated audacities he undertook with his master's wine, he would be on the alert for adulterations committed by tradesmen. A simple experiment conducted with the aid of oyster shells, sulphur and cream of tartar would serve to precipitate the least quantity of lead and copper; a piece of chalk the size of a pea could be used to disclose the presence of *aqua fortis* and oil of vitriol; and an admixture of lime water to port would reveal any alum in it.[1]

In the country the butler would be expected to brew beer. On a suitable day when the family was absent he would dust off his thermometer, saccharometer and other apparatus and get down to mashing and sparging. Supplies of water (not from rivers or marshy ground) would be brought up by relays of footmen. The resulting product might or might not fill the butler with honest pride. According to one authority the brew was usually hard and sour and rarely made its appearance at the master's board; 'those who are obliged to drink it, if they have any opinion as to its demerits, are not in a position to express it.' Nor were they entitled to test it for the presence of marble dust or oyster shells which the butler might have added to counteract its acidity. But another authority thought it much to be regretted that so few families brewed their own beer, instead of 'the half-fermented, adulterated wash found in public-houses or the no less adulterated and impure drink called porter.'

As the nineteenth century progressed, butlers were called on less often to show their expertise in the cellar. Perhaps their skill was deteriorating; perhaps the middle-class palate was becoming more fastidious; perhaps the tradesmen were becoming more honest. Many gentlemen declined to give their butlers unrestricted access to the cellar, not so much because they were afraid of unskilled doctoring of their wines but because they thought the stocks would last longer if the butler was deprived of the key. In such households the master would dole out the bottles of wine personally and call on the butler to keep a strict account of them. Proud butlers did not accept such a system, arguing that it was a reflection on their honesty; those who surrendered to it made a point of tricking the master in every way possible to punish him for being so distrustful. The kind of master who kept the cellar keys was the kind of master who would pay all the household bills himself, in order (as he hoped) to prevent his butler exacting commissions; but even when a master paid direct, the alert butler would call on

[1] Samuel and Sarah Adams: *The Complete Servant* and *The Servant's Guide and Family Manual.*

the tradesman next day for his percentage. A really unscrupulous butler regarded his salary as the least of his sources of
income; many a one could have afforded to pay his master for
the appointment.

Ultimately the butler hoped to wed a lady's maid or housekeeper and set up a boarding-house. It was a butler and his
housekeeper wife, Mr and Mrs Claridge, trained in a prosperous household, who developed a notably well-run home-
from-home for wealthy families in Brook Street, Mayfair, their
name being perpetuated in the present hotel.

The butler's 'club' to which he repaired when off duty, and
sometimes when on duty, was in fact a public-house where he
met others of his rank (footmen had their separate 'clubs' in
different public-houses, and so did coachmen). Reputedly,
gossip about masters was the staple of conversation. None of
these clubs, perhaps, was as highly organised as the Junior
Ganymede, haunt of Mr P. G. Wodehouse's Jeeves, which has
a rule requiring all members to enter in the club book intimate
details of their employers.

It was a characteristic of butlers that their feelings were
easily bruised. The *Observer* in 1848 had a report which told
how a person of stylish appearance with a handsome walking-
stick mounted the applicants' rostrum at Marlborough Street
Police Court and begged to relate a story of ill-usage. He was a
butler who had recently engaged himself to a gentleman in
Kent (butlers were not hired, they engaged themselves). On
Christmas Eve, he said, his master ordered him to go into the
kitchen to squeeze some lemons; and when he pointed out,
with 'great civility,' that this was a duty for an inferior servant,
his master gave him an angry push, causing his tray and all its
glassware to fall to the floor. Ordered to clear up the debris, the
butler again refused, on the ground that clearing up messes
was drudgery which called for the services of an under-servant.
At this point the young master intervened, accusing him of
being either mad or drunk, pinioned his arms and packed him
off to bed. Next morning he was given his wages and ordered
from the house, without the offer of a servant to carry his
luggage. 'I do assure your worship,' he said, 'I was obliged to
carry my portmanteau and my carpet bag myself for upwards

of half a mile.' The magistrate asked why the applicant had come to court, and the answer was that he wished advice on how to obtain redress. No sympathy, however, was to be had from the magistrate, who said he thought an order to squeeze lemons was not an unreasonable one. When the butler protested, 'But it was to make punch,' the magistrate said he did not see how that affected the issue. The applicant then left the court 'with the air of a deeply injured man.'[1]

Akin in status to the butler was the groom of the chambers, an unliveried servant found only in houses with a profusion of public rooms. His principal duty was that of receiving and announcing visitors and showing guests to their accommodation. Several times a day he toured his suite of rooms, unobtrusively patting cushions and straightening chairs, adjusting blinds against the sun or placing footstools. Much ceremonial door-opening came his way, as when the guests descended from drawing-room, library and elsewhere to dinner. At meals he was expected to assist in the service. It was not the most arduous of callings, but during big house parties the groom of the chambers often persuaded himself that he was earning his money, if only by replenishing the supplies of crested writing-paper which guests removed as fast as he could set it out.

The Valet

Although writers tumbled over each other to give advice to the lady's maid, hardly anyone presumed to instruct her male equivalent, the valet. As likely as not, he was a foreigner, and foreigners went their own mysterious ways. If Frenchmen wanted to comb Englishmen's hair it was their own business. But if Frenchmen tried to butcher their English masters with sabres, as the Duke of Cumberland's valet did in 1810, it was another matter, and on such occasions even the most blameless French valets could expect the populace to manhandle them.

Valets, who did not wear livery, were more often employed by bachelors than by married men. In the days of macaronis

[1] William Kent: *London in the News.*

and dandies, their duties were no sinecure; but a really proficient man could name his salary. Easily the best polished boots in Regency London belonged to a Lieutenant-Colonel Kelly of the First Foot Guards, whose valet had a secret blacking. When the Colonel died his servant was approached by numerous men about town, among them Beau Brummell, who asked what the Colonel had paid him. The man replied that he had received £150 but it was not enough and he would require £200. 'Well,' said the Beau, 'if you will make it guineas I shall be happy to attend on *you*.' Lord Plymouth later secured this paragon for £200.[1]

Brummell's valet, who had the reassuringly English name of Robinson, used to carry away from his master's toilet armfuls of cravats which had been tried and found wanting—'Our failures,' he would explain. The failure was not necessarily in the cravat but might be the fault of the wearer, who could not always be relied upon to crush down his chin at the required angle. Preparation of cravats might or might not be the valet's task; there were highly skilled and well-paid washerwomen who specialised in turning out cravats of the appropriate stiffness.

Prince Pückler-Muskau, that fascinating rake who toured Britain during George IV's reign, thought that the visitor to these shores could be excused for mistaking a valet for a lord, especially if he cherished the delusion that courtesy and good manners were the distinguishing mark of a man of quality. Very often, in the Prince's view, the higher classes in England were deficient in these attributes, though they sometimes had other admirable and solid qualities. It may be that Englishmen went out of their way to cultivate a certain roughness, rather than attempt to compete in polite manners with their body-servants. Certainly these polite manners were much welcomed by the women of the house.

One distinguished Englishman at least professed to abhor the attendance of a valet. 'Perhaps you are not aware,' the Duke of Wellington told Lord Strangford, 'that I shave myself and brush my own clothes; I regret that I cannot clean my own boots; for menservants bore me and the presence of a crowd

[1] Captain R. H. Gronow: *Reminiscences.*

of idle fellows annoys me more than I can tell you.'[1] Nevertheless, he employed a valet who served him faithfully, even to the extent of consulting secretly with the Mendicity Office in an effort to eliminate the numerous dishonest contenders for the Duke's charity.[2]

As an upper servant the valet had the *entrée* to the steward's or housekeeper's room. Among the lower servants admiration for his polished ways did not wholly efface the distrust they felt for any servant who was too close to the head of the house.

The valet's duties were by no means confined to looking after his master's toilet and clothes. At meals he stood behind his employer's chair, both in his own house and in other men's. He accompanied his master in all his sports and diversions, standing beside him on soggy moors and loading his shotguns. It was his function to smooth out the difficulties of travel, both at home and abroad. In Europe he displayed a knowledge of those useful foreign phrases which a gentleman could hardly be expected to learn for himself. He did not jeopardise his master's health, as Brummell's valet did, by putting him in a room with a damp stranger. If necessary, he slept in his master's room to guard him against robbery and insult. He knew the quickest way to rid beds of fleas and to make noxious water potable. When the railways multiplied he had to be able to read Bradshaw. He was an expert at finding cabs where none existed, at marshalling luggage, at buying the right flowers for the right ladies, at fending off without offending. If his master, despite all precautions, got caught in the rain, the valet would rub him down with *eau-de-Cologne* before putting dry clothes on him. Like the lady's maid, the valet was supposed to know how to make his own toilet aids (shaving soap called for fresh ley, lamb suet and olive oil, exposed to the heat of the sun for fifty days; clearly not the easiest thing to make in an English climate). Much of his work was essentially trivial, but he had the art of making it seem gravely important. Jeeves-like, he could lay two trifling objects in a chest with such an air that 'it was like seeing the plenipotentiary of a great nation lay a wreath on the tomb of a

---

[1] Captain R. H. Gronow: *Reminiscences.*
[2] Richard Aldington: *Wellington.*

deceased monarch.'[1] He knew how to accept his master's cast-off garments—his main perquisite—with well-simulated gratitude and respect.

Vain young gentlemen had a way of summoning their valets to answer questions to which they well knew the answer. Brummell, when asked by a bore which of the Lakes he liked best, rang for Robinson. 'Which of the lakes do I admire most, Robinson?' he asked; and was informed, 'Windermere, sir.' 'Ah, yes, Windermere, so it is. Thank you, Robinson.'[2]

Since he lived closest to his master, the valet was the first to feel his master's wrath; and in the service of a bad-tempered employer his life could be dog-like to a humiliating degree. Occasionally the servant rebelled. In 1840 François Courvoisier, a Swiss valet in the service of the elderly Lord William Russell, in Norfolk Street, London, found that his master was incessantly finding fault with him. One night, about twelve o'clock, Lord William rang the bedroom bell, so Courvoisier went up with a warming-pan. His master denounced him for bringing it and said he should have come up first to ask what was required. Some twenty minutes later Lord William rang again, demanded the warming-pan and told the valet to pay more attention to his duties in future. Later Lord William went downstairs, found Courvoisier in the dining-room, expressed the view that he was there for no good purpose and said he would be dismissed. In the small hours the valet took a knife from the sideboard, half-decapitated his sleeping master and then went back to bed. Twenty thousand persons watched Courvoisier go to the scaffold and, says the *Annual Register*, 'the number of menservants present was remarkable as evincing the fearful interest taken in the culprit's fate by the class to which he had belonged.'

The Footman

'When a lady of fashion chooses her footman without any other consideration than his height, shape and *tournure* of his calf,' wrote Mrs Beeton, 'it is not surprising that she should

[1] P. G. Wodehouse: *Ring for Jeeves.*
[2] W. Jesse: *The Life of George Brummell.*

find a domestic who has no attachment for the family, who considers the figure he cuts behind her carriage and the late hours he is compelled to keep a full compensation for the wages he exacts, for the food he wastes and for the perquisites he can lay his hand on.'[1]

In the selection of footmen, it was frequently true that a candidate's calves were considered before his character. In 1850 *Punch* quoted an advertisement in *The Times* by a footman describing himself as 'tall, handsome, with broad shoulders and extensive calves,' who preferred Belgravia or the north side of the Park. Another stipulated 'six months a year in town and if in an inconvenient neighbourhood, five guineas extra salary.' The more footmen kept, the more difficult it was to match them physically. As late as the end of the nineteenth century, wages were related to height. Charles Booth gives the rates as follows: second footmen, height 5 ft. 6 in., from £20 to £22; 5 ft. 10 in. or 6 ft., £28 to £30; first footmen, height 5 ft. 6 in., up to £30; 5 ft. 10 in. or 6 ft., £32 to £40.[2]

The footman's livery was the fashion discarded by gentlemen of the previous century: knee breeches, silk stockings with buckles, embroidered coat with shoulder knot, powdered wig, top hat. Most masters provided a footman with his livery, which ensured a smart turn-out and gave them the chance to threaten to 'strip' an offender if he misbehaved.

The footman was addressed by his Christian name, or rather by *a* Christian name, not necessarily his own. The most usual names were Charles, James, John and John Thomas, the last of which, thanks to the wide diffusion of the works of D. H. Lawrence, has for long been in irredeemable disgrace. A footman with an unsuitable name like Claude would be told to answer to a more conventional one. There were establishments in which the first footman was always called, say, Charles, the second James and the third John. This made for simplicity above stairs, though it could cause confusion down below if James's real name was John and John's real name was James. Footmen in the main seem to have accepted this custom, though the more sensitive may have questioned a

[1] *The Book of Household Management.*
[2] *Life and Labour of the People of London.*

Dinner on the way

system in which a man could not even call his name his own.

In great households, the footman's functions were those which have been described in Chapter Two. From time to time new kinds of lamps were invented, but the same coals had to be carried, the same messages borne on Shanks's pony. The master and mistress might go to new types of entertainment, but for the servant ordered to wait outside life was no different.

Manuals which he almost certainly never read told the footman how to turn napkins into mitres and water lilies, or to fold them in such a way that they had four pockets, each for the reception of a tiny tart. The same manuals informed him that, in winter, it was for him to clear away snow and ice from the pavement; and, in the country, that it was his duty to help gather ice from the pond, stack it in the ice-house and then trample it down, like a peasant treading grapes.

Towards mid-century, the fashion was to dispense with two footmen on a carriage and make do with one. Though footpads had vanished, there were, as always, plenty of would-be boarders in the shape of street urchins. Dr William Kitchiner said: 'Spikes [on a carriage] are indispensable when you have not a footman; otherwise you will be perpetually loaded with idle people; i.e. unless you think that two or three outside

passengers are ornamental or convenient, or you would like to
have your carriage continually surrounded by crowds of children
insistently screaming, "Cut! Cut behind!" '[1]

Often, footman and coachman acting in concert would be
guilty of a form of nuisance which could be termed 'furious
arriving.' On the last lap the horses would be whipped up and
then reined back in spectacular fashion, and the footman
would leap to the ground and hammer at the door with enough
noise to bring faces to the windows all along the street. Samuel
and Sarah Adams did not wholly discourage a dashing arrival,
but they counselled a measure of restraint. 'Though he [the
footman] may indicate the importance of his family by his
style of knocking at a door, he ought to have some regard to
the nerves of the family and the peace of the neighbourhood.'

When on carriage duty, the footman lowered the steps and
helped his mistress in and out of the vehicle, producing an
umbrella as required. In cold weather he saw that the occupants
had stone hot water bottles. These attentions were graded
according to rank and not lavished, for instance, on governesses, whom it was humiliating enough to have to accompany
at all. During the journey the footman forebore from recog-
nising his own acquaintances, except by an imperceptible nod;
unless, of course, he had a passenger of no consequence, when
a greater degree of affability could be exercised.

If his mistress went out on foot, the footman would normally
walk two or three yards behind, but when she was within about
twenty yards of her destination he would advance and knock
at the required door, in order that it might be open by the
time she reached the doorstep. On shopping expeditions, he
would open the shop doors for his mistress and wait for her to
emerge, accepting any parcels she might have acquired. On
Sundays he walked behind her to church, carrying her Bible
and prayer-book.

The difference between a footman and a page was not
always easy to determine, for both performed much the same
sort of function, while despising each other's pretensions. In
great houses, pages stood in succession to the well-born
youths who had once performed intimate tasks close to the

[1] *The Traveller's Oracle.*

'Humility,' by John Leech

person. At Holland House dinner parties, the imperious Lady Holland used to send a servant whom she called a page to tell Macaulay to stop talking in order that she might listen to somebody else, or to wheel off her husband to bed in the middle of a story. Greville tells of an occasion when Lady Holland's favourite page was ill with a thigh tumour. This 'little creature,' as she called him, was a hulking fellow of about twenty calling himself Edgar. His real name, says Greville, was Tom or Jack, but he changed it 'on being elevated to his present dignity, as the Popes do when they are elected to the tiara.' In fact, his real name was William Doggett. The diarist complains that 'more rout is made about him than other people are permitted to make about their children and the inmates of Holland House are invited and compelled to go and sit with, and amuse, him.'[1] One day Lady Hardy enquired after the health of Lady Holland, who had a sprained back. 'Is it very painful?' she asked. 'Where is it?' Edgar was sent for

[1] Charles Greville: *Memoirs*.

and made to stand with his back to his mistress, who then put her finger on his 'posterior regions' and said, 'Here, Lady Hardy.'[1] Edgar later became a 'groom of the library,' a special post created for him.

At a lower level, apple-cheeked, diminutive pages, shining with buttons, were thought to offer some sort of protection to the dragon-like elderly ladies in whose steps they trod. Sometimes they were employed, instead of footmen, for reasons of economy, but in small private families, without the discipline of upper servants, a page of this type could be more nuisance than he was worth. In theory he was a symbol of gentility; in fact, he was often a cheeky, idle and mischievous incubus.

Quite a few pages were waifs or orphans who, having made themselves useful in gentlemen's stables, were trained for indoor duties; but a waif's upbringing did not always bring out those qualities most esteemed in genteel employment.

The Coachman

It was usual for a master to engage his coachman personally. What he hoped for was a man like Sir Roger de Coverley's coachman, grave as a Privy Councillor under his wig, sober, honest and of equable temperament, with the right figure for plush breeches. What he often got was a leathery old soak with a passion for peculation.

To the question, 'How close could you drive to the side of the road without danger?' an applicant might reply, 'To within an inch' or 'To within half an inch.' The wise master would reject anyone who laid claim to expertise of this order. There was so much drunken driving on the roads that even the skilful, sober coachman who maintained his distance from weaving vehicles had difficulty, on occasion, in keeping the panels of his coach unscored. In the country one of the hazards was the empty one-horse cart driven furiously to make up time spent in tippling. In the town the biggest danger was outside balls and assemblies, where bad-tempered, fuddled drivers jostled each other villainously in their efforts to pick up their

[1] The Earl of Ilchester: *Chronicles of Holland House, 1820–1900.*

bad-tempered, fuddled masters. Prince Pückler-Muskau has described the behaviour of the foul-mouthed 'madmen' who called themselves coachmen in George IV's time. 'As soon as these heroic chariot drivers espy the least opening they whip their horses in, as if horses and carriage were an iron wedge; the preservation of either seems totally disregarded.' The police, he says, regarded the chaos as no responsibility of theirs. In a grand *bagarre* outside Almack's the Prince saw one of Lady Sligo's horses with its hind legs entangled in the forewheel of a carriage, in such a way that it was impossible to release them, and a turn of the wheel would have maimed the creature. Elsewhere in the battle a cabriolet was crushed to pieces, not before it had thrust its shafts through the windows of a carriage full of screaming women. Several ladies, says the Prince, had to wait for hours before the chaos was reduced.[1]

The good coachman drove at a uniform pace and never threw his passengers to the floor in sudden halts. Drivers who were for ever 'fanning' their horses (with the whip) not only injured them but caused them to proceed in a hop, skip and jump style which was very trying for the passengers. It was up to the master to specify, at the start of a journey, the speed at which he wished to travel—four, six or eight miles an hour. Mrs Beeton considered that a mere jog-trot destroyed the *élan* of the animals; any speed less than seven or eight miles an hour was 'injurious to the horses, getting them into sluggish and lazy habits, for it is wonderful how soon these are acquired by some horses.'[2] Thanks to a law passed in the reign of George I, the drivers of hackney carriages were supposed to give way to the coaches of gentlemen, and could be fined ten shillings for failing to do so.

A coachman was expected to be able to take the road at twenty minutes' notice. In the ordinary way he started work at six in the morning, spending an hour and a half or two hours in setting the stable to rights and dressing two horses. Washing and cleaning carriage and harness would take between two and three hours and the vehicle would be at the door by

[1] E. M. Butler (ed.): *A Regency Visitor.*
[2] *The Book of Household Management.*

eleven o'clock, its windows open and the interior purged of all fustiness. The master would specify beforehand in which direction he wished the horses to face; it was a sign of an ill-managed household when the carriage had to be turned in the street. If the coachman was required to wait at the dinner table—a bone of much contention—he was to be allowed an hour and a half after returning home in order to wash down the carriage and tend the horses. Sometimes he lacked sufficient time to wash himself down and the odour of the stables was wafted to the dinner table. This distressing aura was sometimes described as 'the trail of the serpent.'

Coachmen were fond of dabbling in auxiliary occupations, like keeping pigs or goats, which ate the master's corn and annoyed his neighbours; Dr Kitchiner insisted that they should be made to concentrate on their own job. Like all servants, they had traditional perquisites, permitted and unpermitted. In the former category was the disposal of the old wheels of the coach, provided that the coachman had been in his master's service as long as the wheels. Their trade-in value against new wheels was about two guineas a set. An unscrupulous coachman might hasten the decay of his master's wheels by boring holes in the spokes.

On long journeys, the coachman who valued his reputation stood over his horse at the inn while it ate its corn, the reason being that 'some mangers have a hole in one corner and as soon as a horse rubs his nose along it the great part of the corn runs out into a nice little sack which is placed underneath to catch it.'[1] He did not sit with a pot of ale by the kitchen fire while stable boys splashed cold water on his horses and galloped them dry. He did not conspire with ostlers to pretend that certain roads ahead were bad, in order to divert his master to inns where he could pick up a commission. When weary of the road, he did not find imaginary faults in harness and equipment, or create real ones. He refrained from constantly physicking his horses, and did not assume that they must always be as thirsty as himself. He never insisted on overheating the stables to give the horses 'a nice appearance,' whereas all he gave them was a chill when they came out.

[1] Dr William Kitchiner: *The Traveller's Oracle.*

According to Dr Kitchiner, the all-in upkeep of a coach came to between £345 and £400 a year, a formidable slice of income for any man earning less than £1500. By hiring a hackney coach from a livery stable a gentleman might have to defer to the carriages of more successful citizens, but on the other hand he could secure more prompt attendance; he did not have to worry about his coachman contracting rheumatism while waiting in the rain and he was not vexed by thoughts of coachman and groom trafficking in his oats or hiring his horses out to stud. Thackeray spins an agreeable tale about a master who, unable to use his own brougham, hires one from a livery stable and is drawn all unknowingly by one of his own horses which has been lent to the stable for a consideration by his groom.[1] Augustus Hare tells a more startling story about 'Lord Tankerville's father' who was puzzled to find his horses each morning foam-covered and exhausted. One day, crossing Putney Heath with Lord Derby, he was held up by a highwayman who turned out to be his own groom. Shots were exchanged, and the man fled—with his master's horse.[2]

Although a splendid equipage was calculated to turn the heads of passers-by, vulgar curiosity was to be kept strictly in check. Says Dr Kitchiner:

'If curious children ask, "Whose carriage is that?" tell your coachman to stare fully in their face and say nothing; if they have the impudence to repeat the question he may reply: "It belongs to Mr Pry." If equivocation is ever allowable, it is to such impertinence. Those who may admire the carriage and want to know who built it will find the coach-maker's name on the axle-tree caps.'

In big establishments, where no expense was spared so long as a spanking turn-out was achieved, there might be as many as sixty horses, several under-coachmen and a long string of grooms and stable boys who also performed the duties of postillions and outriders. The stable servants usually lived over the horses in a little world of their own. There would be another establishment of horses and carriages in London, and guests travelling from one house to the other would sometimes change carriages and footmen at a half-way house (the eleventh

Duke of Bedford, according to the present Duke, applied this system to his establishment of motor-cars and kept it up until 1940, the staging-post for Woburn being at Hendon).[1] In London 'Old Q' had a personal groom, Jack Radford, who kept a pony permanently saddled at 138 Piccadilly in order—so rumour said, perhaps untruly—to follow any lady who caught his master's eye, find out who she was and where she lived. Much of the day the groom could be seen standing behind his shrivelled old master on the balcony of the house. For these, and presumably other, services the Duke left Radford £200 a year and all his horses in London and at Richmond.

The disreputable Lord Barrymore, one time crony of the Prince Regent, also kept a young groom, whom he called a 'tiger,' to ride in his elegant Stanhope and, from time to time, to run after pretty women and announce that his master would like to pay his addresses to them. It has been suggested that 'jackal' would have been a more appropriate name than 'tiger.' As the century progressed, the word 'tiger' was reserved for the smartly liveried little boy who sat to attention on the box of the carriage or stood on a platform at the rear of the vehicle, holding on to two white cords, and kicking away errand boys with his highly polished jack boots.[2]

The 'tiger' was of especial value in ringing doorbells for ladies travelling alone. Etiquette forbade the lady to descend and ring the bell for herself and the coachman made the excuse that he ought not to descend from the box in case the horses bolted. The procedure, in the absence of a 'tiger,' was for the coachman to call on a passing urchin to ring the bell and hope that he would not return too incivil an answer.

[1] John, Duke of Bedford: *A Silver-plated Spoon.*

[2] Lord Salisbury, in late Victorian days, took his exercise at Hatfield on a tricycle. A 'tiger' would help him to ascend slopes, and on the way down would jump up behind and ride with his hands on the statesman's shoulders. —A. L. Kennedy: *Salisbury 1830–1903.*

XII

NO SERVANTS, ONLY HELPS

IF a British family had good and faithful servants, the quickest way to ruin them was to take them to America. As soon as they scented the heady wind of democracy, as soon as they discovered that 'servant' was a dishonoured word, and that here was a land without 'masters' and 'mistresses,' their manner changed and they became, instead of assets, liabilities.

From America, in 1818, William Cobbett wrote feelingly on the subject. 'What a difference would it make in this country if it could be supplied with nice, clean, dutiful, English maidservants! As to the men, it does not much signify; but for the want of maids nothing but the absence of grinding taxation can compensate. As to bringing some with you it is as wild a project as it would be to try to carry the sunbeams to England. They will begin to change before the ship gets on soundings; and before they have been here a month you must turn them out of doors or they will you.'

There was a type of Englishman, Cobbett admitted, who was never happy unless he had the power of domineering over somebody or other. America was no place for such a man; 'his best way will be to continue to live under the Boroughmongers; or, which I would rather recommend, hang himself at once.'[1]

Madame d'Arusmont (Frances Wright) also stressed the folly of taking Old World servants to the New World. 'Those just released from the aristocracies of Europe, finding themselves in a country where all men are placed by the laws on an exact level, conceive, naturally enough, that they are transformed from the servants of the employer into his companions;

[1] *A Year's Residence in the United States of America.*

and at one and the same time lay aside obsequiousness and array themselves in insolence. . . . A few weeks—nay, not infrequently, in a few days—and they either become a useless charge to their employers or by making inordinate demands and assuming airs of ridiculous importance force their employers to dismiss them.'[1] Often, Madame d'Arusmont conceded, masters and mistress were to blame for trying to preserve European 'tone' in a society which resented it; and their servants, embarrassed by stares and snubs, seized the opportunity to pay off old scores.

To the European visitor, the most upsetting discovery was that Americans of wealth and position made strenuous and often open attempts to lure away his servants, whose passage money he had paid, as soon as they landed. This form of piracy was deplored by Thomas Grattan, some time His Majesty's Consul in Massachusetts, on the ground that it gave the 'servile' class 'an odious example of indelicacy and bad faith.'[2]

The domestic servants in the non-slave-owning states during the early nineteenth century comprised a few native Americans, who were proud and anything but obsequious; the last wave of 'redemptioners' from Central Europe; immigrants from Ireland, who were ignorant and feckless, but warm-hearted; and large numbers of freed Negro slaves. The latter were of very variable quality. Some were unable to shake off a habit of doing no more than they could help; others, as memories of the plantations subsided, became loyal and dignified members of the families employing them, with a pride in their work and in 'their' people (it has been said that the best servants in the world were the Negro servants of old Philadelphia).

Of all these servants, the most efficient yet the touchiest (and the scarcest) were the native Americans, the heirs of the Revolution. 'No American will receive an insulting word,' said Madame d'Arusmont. 'A common mode of resenting an imperious order is to quit the house without waiting or even asking for a reckoning.' A young English officer who found no warm shaving water in his New York boarding-house shouted

---

[1] *Views of Society and Manners in America, 1818–20.*
[2] *Civilised America* (1859).

to a 'servant': 'You d——d rascal! How do you think I am to
shave myself?' The man turned his back without a word. Later
he explained that he was not accustomed to answer to the
name of 'd——d rascal.' This sort of attitude made life
difficult for English subalterns.

Those who conceded that a man might resent being addressed
as 'd——d rascal' were baffled at the odium with which the
word servant was regarded. Cobbett thought such sensitivity
was due to 'a mixture of false pride and insolence, neither of
which belongs to the American character, even in the lowest
walks of life.' The reason, as he recognised, was traceable to
the slave system in the South. 'Englishmen, who had fled from
tyranny at home, were naturally shy of calling other men their
slaves; and therefore, "for more grace" as Master Matthew
says in the play, they called their slaves servants.' Thus the
idea got abroad that slaves and servants were synonymous. The
Pope might call himself 'the servant of the servants of the
Lord,' and Government officials might pretend to be 'public
servants,' but men and women who undertook domestic
labours in America preferred to call themselves 'helps.'

Of native-born Americans, hardly a man was willing to let
himself be dressed up in variegated livery; but as only the
merest handful of American employers, at this period, wished
to see their servants in such disguises, little difficulty arose.
The wearing of liveries, often freakish to a degree, was largely
reserved for Negro servants in fashionable quarters of the big
cities and for the retinues of the ambassadors at Washington.

In a country where all men of spirit were impatient to be
their own masters, where land was plentiful and cheap, where
booming ports offered fortunes to mercantile adventurers, it
followed that the performance of household chores made little
appeal to men, except to the unambitious, the lack-lustre, the
idle and the devious. Yet men of spirit did not necessarily
despise domestic work as such. If it had to be undertaken, as a
temporary measure to acquire some capital, the rewards and
conditions of its performance were a matter for bargaining, as
in any other type of employment. The important thing was
that there should be no nonsense about 'master' and 'man.' At
the first sign that he was regarded as an inferior, out the 'help'

would go. This led sometimes to a chip-on-the-shoulder attitude which did not make for felicity of service. If it was the family custom to keep the plate locked up, the 'help' might well regard this as a reflection on himself. The degree of his obedience would depend very much on how politely he was asked to do things. His efficiency might fall short of its maximum because his employer would be reluctant to nag him into doing things properly. When he had finished his work, the 'help' saw no reason why his leisure should not be his own; nor did he see that his employer had any claim over him on Sundays.

With all these apparent shortcomings, the American man-servant yet had his vigorous defenders. He could not be compared, declared Francis J. Grund, with the 'indolent, careless, besotted' European servant. He was literate, he understood politics, he attended public meetings and lectures, he belonged to the militia, he paid poll tax and was entitled to vote. 'His mind is constantly engaged in making plans for the future . . . no sooner has he earned a few dollars than he sets up a shop; and there are many of them who finish by becoming respectable merchants. With these hopes before him it could not be expected that he would always be a ready, cringing sycophant. . . .'[1]

Thomas Grattan thought that, if well treated and properly understood, the native American servant was the best in the country. If better wages were offered for housework than for farm work, factory work or teaching, then he was not too proud to undertake it, on the distinct understanding that he was not going to work *for* Mr So-and-So but *with* him. He would bargain for great privileges, and insist on sharing any table delicacies. He liked to think that the man for whom he worked had himself been in a similar position. Any employer who was prepared to concede these indulgences—and an Old World employer was almost incapable of doing so—would have the best servant in the country. But he must not expect blind unreasoning loyalty; Grattan knew of a servant who gave notice after two years on the grounds that he 'felt he was becoming attached to the family and thought it best to clear away in good time.'[2]

[1] *The Americans in Their Moral, Social and Political Relations* (1837).
[2] *Civilised America.*

Alexis de Tocqueville noted the same attitudes. The American servant, he said, appeared to carry into service 'some of those manly habits which independence and equality engender.' Having chosen to work for another, he scorned to cheat him, yet felt under no obligation to show him the marks of respect, still less of love and affection.[1]

In the militia it sometimes happened that servants held higher appointments than their masters. A president of Harvard University was waited on at tea by a manservant who was a major of horse. On cavalry days the servant sat at the head of the regimental table with the president on his right hand. The toasts over, he went home, took off his regimentals and waited on the president's guests at tea.

Few American households—and those only the most pretentious—aspired to the European establishment of menservants. The average American gentleman, as Francis Grund explains, seldom had more than one manservant, who was a combination of porter, footman, butler and, if necessary, coachman. He cleaned the boots, washed the windows, swept the house, waited at table, went to market and was an all-round factotum. Though his wages were high, he did the work of six Europeans, and the only airs he assumed were those he thought necessary to the dignity of man. At table he did not resent being addressed by guests as 'waiter,' a usage which revolted fastidious Europeans.

As a rule, the only servants in America who were prepared to accept inconsiderateness and rudeness from their employers were persons of low character who took their revenge by pillage. Of these, there was no shortage: deserters from the British Army in Canada, ne'er-do-wells from every land, malcontents, tired adventurers, men with a horror of tilling and sowing, the riffraff who have always followed in the wake of the pioneers. The result was that those employers who were prone to servant trouble, usually through faults of their own, were faced with a problem far worse than that which existed in the Old World. Samuel Breck, a member of the government of Philadelphia, writing in 1807, thought it a crying evil that ladies were unable to fulfil their Christmas hospitality through lack of servants. 'I have in the course of ten or twelve years housekeeping had a

[1] *Democracy in America.*

strange variety, amongst which I have heard of one being hung, of one that hung himself, of one that died drunk in the road and of another that swallowed poison in a fit of intoxication.' His diary is full of tales of ingratitude by servants. In 1822 he says:

'In my family of nine or ten persons the greatest abundance is provided; commonly seventy pounds of fresh butcher meat, poultry and fish a week and when I have company nearly twice as much; the best and kindest treatment is given to the servants; they are seldom visited by Mrs Breck and then always in a spirit of courtesy; their wages are the highest going and uniformly paid to them when asked for; yet during the last twelve months we have had seven different cooks and five different waiters. One leaves me because there is not enough to do, another because there is too much; a third quarrels with a fourth, a fifth gets drunk and absents herself for a week; in short, they are the most provoking compounds of folly, turpitude, ingratitude, and idleness that can possibly be conceived by anyone who has not lived in America. With the wages which they receive they can, if prudent and constant, lay up money enough in two or three years to buy a handsome tract of new land. I pay, for instance, to my cook $1 50 cents and the chambermaid $1 25 cents a week; to my gardener $11 a month; to the waiter $10; to the farm servant $10 etc. Now if they remain steady (with meat three times a day) for three or four years they can lay by enough to purchase two hundred or three hundred acres of new land, for their clothing does not (or at least ought not) cost them above $20 per annum.'[1]

English housewives would have said that Mrs Breck, by seldom visiting her kitchen, was entirely to blame for the discontents in her household, but they would have fared no better with the offhand 'helps' of Philadelphia.

In the qualities of independence and intransigence, the women servants of America outclassed their menfolk. They, too, had no intention of making a career of service. Said Francis Grund: 'The superiority of the women over the men, which is everywhere perceptible in the United States, extends equally to the servants; and it is consequently a rare case for one of these fair "helps" to marry a fellow domestic.' This goes some way to

[1] *Recollections of Samuel Breck, 1771–1862.*

explain why no man would willingly become a career servant; for if a woman servant would not marry him, no one else would.

Mrs Frances Trollope, not an unbiased observer, said in her *Domestic Manners of the Americans* (1832) that she would require a hundred pages to tell of 'the sore, angry, ever-wakeful pride' that seemed to torment the 'poor wretches' of maid-servants, whose lives were soured by being constantly told that they were as good as anybody else and that the most abject poverty was preferable to domestic service. She laments that maids customarily came to her in near-rags, stayed until they were given a wardrobe and then left, without grace or gratitude. One of them, when informed that she would be expected to eat in the kitchen, said: 'I guess it's because you don't think me good enough to eat with you. You will find that won't do here.' In consequence the girl rarely had any dinner and spent most of her time in tears. Mrs Trollope says that she did everything in her power (short of inviting her to dinner) to make the girl happy, 'but I am sure she hated me.' Another newly engaged maid did her housework in 'a yellow dress *parsemé* with red roses,' explaining, ' ''Tis just my best and my worst for I have got no other.' Mrs Trollope and her daughters made extra clothes for her, but received no thanks. Instead the girl asked to borrow items of adornment and was annoyed when these were refused; next she begged, unsuccessfully, for a loan to buy a ball dress and with a ' ''Tis not worth my while to stay any longer,' left. Later Mrs Trollope engaged a young woman who stipulated time off to visit the Mission House twice a week, and who turned out to be the most abandoned woman in town.

Harriet Martineau, writing of America five years after Mrs Trollope, blamed Englishwomen for carrying with them their habits of command.[1] When orders failed to achieve results, they grew afraid of their servants; and it took them a long time to discover that domestic service was a simple matter of con-tract. Miss Martineau knew that there were Englishwomen (perhaps she was thinking of Mrs Trollope) who would never be able to keep their servants unless they took the trouble to learn the first principles of democracy. She noted the existence

[1] *Society in America.*

of a system, in rural areas, by which women took in girls of eleven in a state of apprenticeship which lasted until they were eighteen. The girls had to be clothed and schooled and at the end of the period they were usually given a sum of $50 or a cow. Sometimes the girls became restless at the age of fifteen or so, when they learned of the good wages they could get elsewhere. In this way, the servant could usually be integrated more smoothly into the life of the family; for it was not easy to tell an older servant that she could eat with the family only if she dressed her hair and observed the same table manners. Maids who were unwilling to go to these lengths sometimes found it consistent with the principles of democracy to eat in the kitchen.

In the main, women servants were not prepared to shoulder all the housework while the lady of the house and her daughters did nothing, or indulged in footling pastimes. As 'helps' their function, as they saw it, was to lighten the labours of someone who already had her hands full, not to take all the work out of her hands. Sometimes, on being hired, they stipulated that the lady of the house should perform a proportion of the duties. Visiting Europeans, brought up in the new tradition of female idleness, were shocked at a system which appeared to turn American mistresses into upper servants and deprived them of leisure to cultivate the mind.

As the Revolution receded farther into the distance, servants went to greater pains to assert its doctrines of equality. Thomas Grattan told of American servants who would not answer the bell in the kitchen unless they had the privilege of ringing another bell in the parlour when they wished to have private and free speech with the lady of the house. He also told of mistresses who had so far sold the pass as to allow their servants to hold 'domestic *soirées*' in the best rooms of the house, vacated for the occasion by the family. He noted that maids refused to say 'Ma'am' and called the younger members of the family by their Christian names unprefixed by 'Master' or 'Miss.' Off duty they indulged the national vice of going about overdressed.

In Grattan's views cooks were especially intractable and irresponsible. They would walk out in the middle of a dinner if there was any interference with their self-made schedule. At

The dandy slave—in Baltimore, Maryland

the same time they were incompetent. Cooks from Ireland had learned nothing beyond boiling potatoes; they served the thick, greasy salt sauces common to their country, and far too many pickles. So rare were good cooks that Americans went to one another's doors to bribe them away, 'without ceremony or remorse.' As for chefs, 'every broken-down barber or disappointed dancing master, French, German or Italian, sets up as cook.' Grattan's sad conclusion was: 'The science of the table is in the earliest stage of infancy in the United States.'

Little though he liked Irish cooking, Grattan did not despair of the Irish as Irish. Employers, he said, felt under less restraint towards them; 'they can treat them with greater kindness, with less risk of compromising their dignity; they have a chance of meeting gratitude in return for good treatment and fidelity for trustingness. These uneducated immigrants readily admit the superiority of those whom they serve.' Employers, he thought, would concentrate on Irish servants in future, even if it meant that the gentlemen of America would be served after the fashion which prevailed in cheap taverns in Britain.

The morals of American servant girls were probably no better, no worse than those of English girls, who in theory at all events were shepherded from temptation by their mistresses. Occasionally one finds a grim sidelight on the fate of the unfortunate. When Dr Elizabeth Blackwell, Britain's first woman doctor, was undergoing her medical training in America, she took a temporary post in 1848 in the great Blockley Almshouse in Philadelphia, and was assigned to the women's syphilitic ward. 'Most of the women are unmarried,' she wrote, 'a large proportion having lived at service and been seduced by their masters, though on the whole about as many seducers are unmarried as married.'[1]

It was symptomatic of America's servant problem that, even in the early years of the nineteenth century, the institution of the boarding-house was already well developed. Newly married couples, unable to find servants or unwilling to humour them, resorted to lodgings in order to save themselves drudgery. To English visitors, the idea of young couples living communally was peculiarly shocking; the result could only be that family secrets were shared by all, and that wives would have nothing to do but gossip or quarrel. This trend towards communal living was not to be detected in Britain until late in the century, when it took a rather different form.

This is not the place for an extended account of American slavery, but it is of some relevance to see how European travellers, harassed by their own servant problem, reacted to being waited on by bondsmen; that is by 'boys' aged from seven to seventy who were engaged, not by the month, but for life; who were sedulously preserved from the dangers of knowledge; who could be debarred from marriage, their bastards being sold off by their masters; and who could be flogged on the complaint of a spiteful child.

The first surprise was the discovery that young slaves often went about almost, or even totally, naked. Elkanah Watson,

[1] *Pioneer Work in Opening the Medical Profession to Women.*

telling in later years of his travels in Virginia at the time of the Revolution, wrote: 'At a highly respectable house I was shocked beyond the power of language to express at seeing for the first time young Negroes of both sexes, from twelve to fifteen years old, not only running about the house but absolutely tending table as *naked* as they came into the world, not having even the poor apology of a fig leaf to save modesty a blush. What made the scene more extraordinary still, to my unpractised eye, was the fact that several young women were at table who appeared totally unmoved at the scandalous violation of decency. I find custom will reconcile us to almost everything.'[1]

Young women at table by no means lacked all delicacy. Mrs Trollope tells how she saw one of them encroaching on the chair of a woman next to her in order to avoid immodest contact with the elbow of the gentleman next to her. Yet she once saw this same young woman standing with perfect composure while a Negro footman loosened her stays. A Virginian gentleman told Mrs Trollope that since his marriage he had been accustomed to have a Negro girl sleep in the same room with himself and his wife. Asked why, he exclaimed: 'Good heavens! If I wanted a glass of water during the night what would become of me?'

Mrs Trollope also visited the house of a small proprietor in Maryland where the slave boys were 'considerably more than half naked.' She found it odd to hear the mistress of the house, with great dignity, say to one of them: 'Attend to your young master, Lycurgus.'

Not nudity, but the sheer inefficiency of the system depressed Miss Martineau. Servants were ubiquitous, yet they did nothing well. 'While the slaves are perpetually at one's heels, lolling against the bed-posts before one rises in the morning, standing behind the chairs, leaning on the sofa, officiously undertaking and invariably spoiling everything that one had rather do for oneself, the smallest possible amount of real service is performed.' All visitors noticed how carefully everything in the house was locked up. The mistress was always being asked to unlock something for her slaves, which meant that she was almost as much of a slave as the child who trotted perpetually

[1] *Men and Times of the Revolution.*

behind her carrying a basket of keys, and whose instructions were never to stray from her mistress's sight. If she was not unlocking something she was superintending some simple operation, or straightening out some trivial difficulty, or settling a petty quarrel. The daughter of the house would say to a guest: 'Oh, you must not touch the poker here. The Negroes will be offended and it won't do for a lady to do so.' Nothing struck Miss Martineau more forcibly than the sheer patience of slave owners. 'Persons from New England, France or England, becoming slave-owners, are found to be the most severe masters and mistresses, however good their tempers may always have been previously. They cannot, like the native proprietor, sit waiting half an hour for the second course or see everything done in the worst possible manner; their rooms dirty, their property wasted, their plans frustrated . . . themselves deluded by artifices.'

Since slaves were there to do every task, it followed that all physical work was degrading. Sons who rebelled against a life of idleness migrated elsewhere. Only immediate fear of starvation induced 'poor whites' to earn a crust by labour. Freed slaves also felt it incumbent on them to attest their liberty by performing the irreducible minimum of work.

British visitors agreed that slave-owners conscientiously discharged many responsibilities towards their slaves, supporting children before they were able to work and maintaining the old who could no longer do so. The mistress who would summon a slave to pass her a handkerchief would herself apply medicaments to that slave if he was sick; a master would battle at gravest personal risk to bring his slaves through the horrors of cholera. By contrast, freed slaves were nobody's responsibility and their lot was often ten times as bitter as it had been before. A Negro, asked whether he was not better off as a free man, said that if he fell from a river boat as a slave the captain would stop the ship, rescue him, give him a glass of whisky and twenty lashes. If he fell from the boat as a free man the captain would say 'It's only dat dam nigger' and go ahead.

Always, of course, there was a suspicion that slave owners, in their good deeds, were concerned primarily to preserve their property. 'Unhappily,' says Mrs Trollope, 'the slaves too

know this and the consequence is that real kindly feeling very
rarely can exist between the parties.' Miss Martineau mentions
an ex-State governor who had drawn on himself unpopularity
after a slave revolt by refusing to have his participating slaves
hanged; 'this was imputed to an unwillingness to sacrifice his
property.' She also tells of a young white woman who was rash
enough to tell her slave girl, while she was being undressed,
'When I die, you shall be free.' Soon afterwards she found
poison in her food; but unable to bear the thought of having
the girl hanged she did the next best thing and sold her. At
Montgomery, Alabama, Dr J. Marion Sims was called in by a
slave owner to examine three girls whose condition rendered
them useless to him. Risking his reputation, he carried out on
them the first operation for vesico-vaginal fistula and they
returned to their duties. They were probably as grateful to their
master as to the surgeon, but over this episode, too, reared the
question: was the master a humane man or was he anxious to
preserve an investment? Probably he was both. One thing is
certain: that if Anarcha, Lucy and Betsey had been freed slaves,
or if they had been English 'slaveys,' they would simply have
been left to suffer.

In society's eyes, the worst offence a slave owner could
commit towards his slaves was to educate them. If reflection
were to be encouraged in fallow minds, if black men were to
learn about the things that made white men no happier, the
whole system would collapse. So, in the State of Alabama, the
maximum penalty for attempting to teach a slave, or freed
slave, to spell, read or write was a fine of not less than $250
and not more than $500. The maximum fine for encouraging
literacy was $200 more than the maximum fine for administer-
ing torture.

The slaves employed as domestic servants enjoyed an easier
life than those in the plantations; and often it was the threat
of the plantations that kept them docile. How the men and
women in the fields were treated we know from the advertisements for runaways; the wretches with iron collars, with their
masters' brands burned on their cheeks, foreheads or buttocks,
with ears cropped and teeth punched out for easier identifica-
tion, with gunshot in their arms or 'much marked by irons' or

'much scarred by the whip.' These were the men who might be tied to a post and curry-combed to cure them of sullenness, whose wives and children were sold, like cows and calves, in the market and were sometimes described as such.

Yet domestic slaves, for all their privileged status, were freely trafficked in by their owners. Miss Martineau tells of a pretty mulatto slave who asked her mistress to protect her from a young man who wanted to marry her. The suitor persisted, saying he could not live without her. 'I pitied the young man,' explained the mistress, 'so I sold the girl to him for $1500.'

Possibly the least delectable aspect of the whole system was that there were owners who helped to keep up the labour supply by intercourse with their female slaves and selling their own offspring. Alexis de Tocqueville met an old man in the South who had lived in illicit relations with one of his negresses. Often he had thought of bequeathing his several children their liberty, but the legal difficulties were too much for him. As he was about to die his mind was vexed by the picture of his sons dragging from market to market, and these horrid visions drove him into a frenzy.[1] But other slave breeders were of sterner stuff.

That was the vile side of the picture. Yet, even in slavery, there was often a state recognisable as happiness and something which passed for pride. Household slaves of a distinguished family would refrain from contact with slaves of a less distinguished family, which is doubtless as it was in ancient Rome. If the master wanted an overweening footman or coachman— well, even a slave knew how to overween. Attitudes and manners were readily copied from the householder and his family. The household slaves regarded themselves as part of the family. Knowing they were the *élite*, they repaid trust with loyalty, as much from affection as from fear. It was not unknown for a slave to be described, on his tombstone, as a faithful friend, even if the master had never called him that during life.

[1] *Democracy in America.*

XIII

THE DIVINE ASPECT OF DRUDGERY

The rich man in his castle,
The poor man at his gate,
God made them high or lowly,
And ordered their estate.
—CECIL FRANCES ALEXANDER, 1848

IF Victorian servants were slow to appreciate that, in serving man, they were serving God, the fault cannot be laid at the doors of their masters, who belaboured them with Bible texts showing that the Heavenly Master had put them there to carry the coals and empty the slops.

Had not Christ come from Heaven in the form of a servant? Surely this alone was enough to prove that the calling of servant was a holy one. The least that a maidservant could do on awakening was to kneel and thank God not only for setting her in a bright and beautiful world but for placing her in honourable and useful employment.

The author of *Advice To Young Women On Going To Service*, issued in 1835 by the Society for Promoting Christian Knowledge, said, succinctly: 'Had [God] seen that it would have been better for your eternal good that you should be great and rich He would have made you so; but he gives to all the places and duties best fitted for them.'

An anonymous butler of twenty-five years' service, who wrote 'with the aid of Divine Grace,' put it this way:

'The rich cannot do without servants any more than servants can do without the rich. God has wisely arranged that they should mutually help each other. . . . There is no sphere in this world, however humble, beneath His notice or unimportant in His sight, nor one in which we may not glorify God in being serviceable to others. To suppose the contrary would be a reflection on the wisdom of Divine Providence. If we look upon the world around us, the animal or vegetable world, we see nothing that occupies an unimportant position; everything appears to be of some use and answers the end for which it was there placed. And servants are situated in the very sphere intended by their Creator and should not fail to answer that end. Let us always strive to honour and glorify God by faithfully performing the part and discharging well the duties allotted to us.'[1]

The poets and the hymn-writers also commended the Creator's wise direction of labour and stressed the spiritual benefits to be derived from a whole-hearted compliance with it. Sometimes quoted was George Herbert, who wrote, none too neatly, in *The Elixir*:

> All may of Thee partake:
>   Nothing can be so mean
> Which with this tincture (*for Thy sake*)
>   Will not grow bright and clean.

> A servant with this clause
>   Makes drudgery divine:
> Who sweeps a room, as for Thy laws,
>   Makes that and th'action fine.

And there was John Keble (1792–1866):

> The trivial round, the common task,
> Will furnish all we need to ask,
> Room to deny ourselves, a road
> To bring us daily nearer God.

The sections of the hymnals entitled 'Domestic Praise' yield many verses in similar vein:

[1] *Hints to Domestic Servants* (1854).

> The task Thy wisdom hath assigned
> O let me cheerfully fulfil;
> In all my works Thy presence find
> And gladly do Thy holy will.
>
> While time with silent step steals on,
> And life glides fast away,
> Let none the sacred work postpone
> That claims our care today.

One verse which, perhaps, was sung with especial fervour by elderly servants, not without a sidelong glance at the earthly master, contained this appeal to the Almighty:

> Cast me not off when strength declines,
> When hoary hairs arise;
> And round me let Thy glory shine
> Whene'er Thy servant dies.

The Servants' Magazine, which flourished in the 1860s, printed a number of poems purporting to come from below stairs. One, *The Song of a Tired Servant*, began:

> One more day's work for Jesu,
> One less of life for me!
> But Heaven is nearer,
> And Christ is dearer
> Than yesterday to me. . . .
>
> One more day's work for Jesu,
> Sweet, sweet the work has been. . . .

In the search for useful Bible texts, masters and mistresses did not shrink from identifying themselves with 'rulers' and 'powers that be.' St Paul said, clearly enough, in *Romans* xiii: 'Let every soul be subject unto the higher powers . . . the powers that be are ordained of God. . . . For rulers are not a terror to good works but to the evil . . . do that which is good and thou shalt have praise of the same.' What was this, if not an instruction to servants to obey their masters and get on with the work?

Easily the most quoted text was *Ephesians* vi. 5–7:

'Servants, be obedient to them that are your masters according to the flesh, with fear and trembling, in singleness of your heart, as unto Christ; not with eyeservice, as men-pleasers; but as the servants of Christ, doing the will of God from the heart; with good will doing service, as to the Lord, and not to men.' Almost as popular was *Ecclesiastes* ix. 10: 'Whatsoever thy hand findeth to do, do it with thy might.'

In *Titus* ii. 9–10 St Paul reprehended the vice of 'answering back.' He said: 'Exhort servants to be obedient unto their own masters, and to please them well in all things; not answering again.' St Peter also lent his support: 'Servants, be subject to your masters with all fear; not only to the good and gentle, but also to the froward' (I *Peter* ii. 18). This, one authority explained, meant that a reprimand should be borne meekly even though it might be given with needless severity. The author of *Advice To Young Women On Going To Service* said: 'Instead of being angry that any of your open faults are reproved, think how much more blame you deserve for all those secret sins which are known to God only.' If those who were rebuked felt any injustice let them remember that persons who were never found fault with were far more to be pitied than those who were; for 'he that heareth reproof getteth understanding' (*Proverbs* xv. 32). If the censure was really unjust and the matter not a trifling one, a servant might respectfully raise the issue later, 'when you have quite cooled down and have had time to reflect on it.' The anonymous butler's ruling was: 'A servant may properly speak his mind on any matter provided he do it respectfully; but let him remember that his master's judgment is to determine, however opposed to his own.' Humility in a servant was his true dignity; it was for him 'to give honour to whom honour is due and cherish esteem for his master as his superior.'

Obviously rulers and powers that be had a responsibility to watch over their servants. The Bible laid this down too. In *Proverbs* xxxi mistresses were reminded of the qualities of the virtuous woman, whose price was far above rubies. One verse

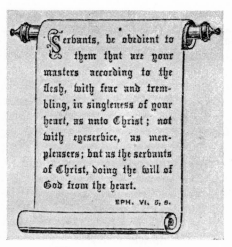

The most-quoted text

said: 'She riseth also while it is yet night, and giveth meat to her household, and a portion to her maidens.' This, explained one authority, was not intended to be taken too literally; 'that is to say, she has to provide with forethought and care, and the comforts and interests of the family are watched over by her.'[1] There was, of course, no question of the mistress getting up early to feed the maids. More happily expressed, perhaps, was verse 27: 'She looketh well to the ways of her household, and eateth not the bread of idleness.' A Glasgow pamphleteer interpreted this as follows: 'She observes the motions and inspects the matters of everyone there and neither suffers them to go abroad at their pleasure nor to labour at home without proper instruction—a concern which might alone be thought sufficient to employ her, insomuch that if she did nothing else she would yet deserve the bread she eats.' Verse 22 was welcome as indicating that it was the mistress's duty to dress herself in more expensive clothes than her maids: 'She maketh herself coverings of tapestry; her clothing is silk and purple.' In other words: 'The furniture of her house is noble. Her own apparel corresponds with it. She is not ignorant of what belongs to her rank; and she supports it with a magnificence so much the more

[1] *Instructions in Household Matters* (Anon.), 1844.

conspicuous for being principally her own handiwork.'[1] Another authority, stressing the importance of discipline in the home, wrote: 'Had Lot regulated his household with the wise government which distinguished that of his uncle Abraham it is fair to presume that the dreadful fate of Sodom might have been averted, since the Lord promised Abraham that he would not destroy it "for the sake of ten righteous," if so many could be found in that city. In Lot's household the ten would probably have been found had it been righteously governed.'[2]

If the earthly master refused his servant permission to attend church on Sunday—and some masters loudly proclaimed that they would not have their households disorganised by 'canting hypocrites'—what course should a servant take? This was a delicate matter indeed on which to give advice. 'A Lady' writing on behalf of the Sunday School Union Depot was anxious not to say anything to weaken domestic discipline. Normally, she said, permission ought to be given, but sickness might render this impossible. 'It cannot be supposed that the attendance [at church] of anyone can be either pleasing to God or profitable to themselves if they are thereby neglecting any duty which their situation calls them to perform; to go out to a place of worship without leave is not the way, I am sure, to derive any spiritual good from the service; for God will surely not accept that service which is offered Him by breaking His commandments, for He has commanded servants to honour and obey their masters and to serve them without fear.'[3]

This writer did not mention that God also commanded masters not to demand labour from their menservants and maidservants on the Sabbath. In fashionable circles, it was usual to hold Sunday dinner parties; this bore heavily on pious servants, but 'it is the custom and they must submit.' There were compensations. It would be strange, one writer thought, if in the course of waiting at Sunday dinner a servant did not hear something which was worth remembering or which awakened some good thought or feeling.[4] This advice was odd as well as

[1] *The Young Housekeeper's Book* (1856).
[2] *Instructions in Household Matters.*
[3] *Friendly Advice in a Letter to a Servant* (1820).
[4] *The Housemaid* (Houlston).

fatuous, for servants were usually told on no account to listen to the conversation at table or anywhere else. A servant's idea of something worth remembering did not necessarily accord with that of his master.

The Rev. Richard Cecil, writing on behalf of the Religious Tract Society, told the story of a maid called Elizabeth whose desire to attend church on Sunday had been frustrated by an otherwise admirable mistress. She therefore felt it her duty to seek another place. Questioned by her mistress, she spoke bluntly of 'her regard for God's command, the benefit she had found in attending His house, the value of the soul, the awful approach of Eternity and the shortness and uncertainty of the time allotted her to prepare for it. She mentioned also the exceeding great love of her Master and Saviour, Jesus Christ, in dying for her and the innumerable benefits obtained thereby.'

The mistress said: 'You seem to be very sincere and I cannot but respect your piety; but on many counts I should not choose to alter the rules of my family.'

The maid replied: 'Madam, though I am obliged to leave you I hope I shall never forget the many kindnesses I have received. I can truly say that your favour is more to me than that of anyone except God's, but He tells me that I have a soul which must be saved or lost for ever. I find I cannot live without hope; and I have no hope but in His ways. May He abundantly bless you and your family while I trust Him to provide for me.'[1]

This seemed a very reasonable solution of a difficult problem, in which both sides retained their dignity. If the mistress chose to imperil her soul, it was unfortunate; but what was the good of being a ruler if one could not, occasionally, lay down the rules?

Time and again, servants were reminded that it might be their privilege to convert a household to Christianity, that the influence of one godly servant in the home could be immeasurable. If forced to share a room with someone who did not pray, the good servant would continue to kneel morning and night, no matter how much derision this conduct drew. Prayers were not to be said in bed; 'when you have got so far they will soon

[1] *Friendly Advice from a Minister to the Servants of His Parish* (1793).

be left off entirely.' Nor was the morning prayer to be skipped
on the grounds that there was a great deal of work to do, 'thus
showing that you prefer a few minutes' sleep to the honour of
serving God.'[1] One pamphlet said that it might be impossible
to escape the presence of an irreligious fellow-servant but 'talk
to her as little as you can. Be always civil and kind but not
familiar.'

In certain circumstances, God expected servants to carry
tales. 'If you see your mistress wronged by behaviour of which
she ought to be informed, you must not then hesitate to speak
of it. This duty may be disagreeable to you and will probably
procure you the character of a mischief-maker and a tell-tale;
but this you must not regard if your own conscience tells you
that you do it from no ill nature or secret wish to bring a fellow-
servant to disgrace, but from a real sense of duty and a desire
to prevent sin.'[2] It was only fair, however, to give warning to
the wrong-doer that any repetition of an offence would be
reported.

There was, indeed, no limit to the good that a religious
servant might do. By eschewing finery (the labour on which
was a theft of the mistress's time) she could save money and
thus help others. 'Time is not yours to give,' but a penny a
week to missionary societies would serve the cause of God. It
was the more important that servants should make financial
sacrifices, since their own needs were small, even negligible.
As that anonymous butler pointed out: 'The labourer has rent
and taxes to pay on his Quarter Day; but the servant has only
to receive.' The Society for Promoting Christian Knowledge
published a pamphlet called *Good Servants Make Good Places*,
the writer of which said: 'I know a young servant who gave
her father a sovereign when he broke his leg and she was not
seventeen; but then she did not dress in smart clothes as many
girls do.' Developing the theme of finery, he said: 'You
promised at your Confirmation to renounce or give up all the
'pomps and vanities of this wicked world and all the sinful lusts
of the flesh'. . . . So, Mary Jane, be always well-dressed and
thoroughly clean and respectable, but leave ear-rings, feathers,
flounces and bright flowers alone. Remember St Paul's words

[1] *Advice To Young Women on Going To Service.*   [2] *Ibid.*

to St Timothy about women dressing themselves in 'modest apparel'. While you are in service don't copy ladies. Wait until you have the same income and a house of your own.'

That other pamphleteer of the Society put it this way: 'You would think it ridiculous to see your mistress dressed in a coloured apron and handkerchief with a coarse gown and coloured stockings such as would be proper for you to wear; and she would be wrong to dress so because we ought all to appear according to our different stations; but is it not as absurd in you to appear in laces and ribbons which may be very proper for those in a higher rank but which are very unsuitable to your station?'[1]

For servants whose flesh was weak there were compilations of short and simple prayers, including a series of 'ejaculations' like these:

'*When tempted:* Lord help me and enable me to resist and overcome this temptation.

'*When the clock strikes:* In the hour of death and in the hour of judgment, good Lord deliver me.'[2]

A prayer for Monday morning contained the appeal: 'Keep me from wasting my employer's goods, from vanity and love of dress. . . .' On Tuesday evening the servant rendered thanks for 'not allowing me to be utterly overcome by the temptations peculiar to the station in which Thou hast placed me.'

There were special prayers for individual servants. The butler and housekeeper prayed: 'O Lord God, Thou hast placed me in a position of trust. Help me, O my God, to fulfil my duties with fidelity to my employers and with scrupulous exactness and honesty. . . .' The lady's maid begged to be invested with a meek and gentle spirit—'give me patience under rebuke and set a watch, O Lord, before the door of my lips . . . preserve me from idleness and from wasting the time which is another's. . . .' The manservant prayed: 'Give me the spirit of temperance and sobriety . . . take from me all slothfulness and let my recreations be lawful and moderate.'[3]

---

[1] *Advice To Young Women on Going To Service.*
[2] *Simple Prayers For Servants* (1872).
[3] *Daily Prayers for Servants*, S.P.C.K. (1853).

Housemaid at prayer
From 'The Servants' Magazine'

A well-known Church of England hymn, included in a special compilation for servants, contained this verse:

> O may our inmost hearts be pure,
> From thoughts of folly kept secure,
> And pride of sinful flesh subdued
> Through sparing use of daily food.

Not only did God dislike to see servants cheating, drinking and guzzling, but He disapproved of the restlessness which drove them to change their places unnecessarily. The *Servants' Magazine* in 1867 reproduced a slogan suitable for hanging in a cook's quarters:

> NEVER CHANGE YOUR PLACE
> UNLESS THE LORD CLEARLY SHOWS
> YOU IT WILL BE
> FOR YOUR SOUL'S GOOD

Occasionally, servant girls were reminded that two of their number had been canonised, but they were rarely told what St Zita and St Notburga had done to merit this honour. A glance at the saints' biographies will give a clue to the reasons for such reticence. Zita, the maid of Lucca, went into service at the age of twelve. Every morning she gave up an hour's sleep to go to Mass; every day she handed most of her food to the poor; and often she relinquished her bed to beggars and slept on the floor. In spite of these self-imposed hardships, she was always amiable and efficient at her work. Her fellow-servants, exasperated by her good works, tried to blacken her character in her mistress's eyes and insulted her with lewd conduct. She scratched the face of a male servant who made an attempt on her virtue, but held her tongue when an enquiry was conducted into his injuries. Eventually, she won the respect of her fellow-servants and her mistress appointed her housekeeper. More than once, Providence showed appreciation of Zita's conduct by saving her from embarrassments brought about by her generosity. There was a difficult moment when her master decided to inspect the household's reserve stock of beans, with a view to disposing of it. Zita, who had given away much of the reserves to the poor, 'could but tremble in her shoes and send up an earnest prayer to Heaven.' To her relief and surprise, 'no diminution could be detected in the store; that it had been miraculously replenished seemed the only possible explanation.' On another occasion Zita prolonged her devotions until sunrise, forgetting that it was a baking day. Hurrying home, she found a row of loaves had been miraculously prepared, all ready to be placed in the oven.

The qualities which earned Zita her status as patroness of domestic servants were not really those which Victorian housewives looked for in their maids. Any girl who ceded her bed to a beggar would have been out in the street next morning, without a character; and no good would have come to a girl who persistently gave away the household food. Housewives may have thought that, in the matter of the beans, it would have been more honest for Zita to confess her depredations to her earthly master. Was it a good thing to encourage girls to escape punishment by praying for a miracle?

St Notburga, who also lived in the thirteenth century, was
a kitchen maid in the household of Count Henry of Rattenberg,
in the Tirol. She, too, persisted in giving away food to the
poor, not only her own meals but the family's left-over scraps
which the Countess specifically told her to put in the pig-
buckets. This caused grave domestic strife, but Notburga's
virtues were tardily recognised and she, also, was appointed
housekeeper. She is the patroness of poor peasants and hired
servants.

It does not appear that any footman was canonised.

The virtuous servant could be fairly confident that, when he
died, the preacher would repeat over his coffin the words from
St Matthew xxx. 21: 'Well done, thou good and faithful servant:
thou hast been faithful over a few things, I will make thee ruler
over many things: enter thou into the joy of thy Lord.' With
luck, the first seven words might be inscribed on his tombstone. The servant had no exclusive claim on these words, for
in death even masters were sometimes content to be described
as faithful servants. This made the inscription even more of a
privilege.

Servants who loved their masters and mistresses, and who
knew their affection was reciprocated, would beg to be buried
near them. Did not King George III erect a tablet in St
George's Chapel, Windsor, to Mary Gaskoin, aged thirty-one,
'in testimony of his grateful sense of the faithful service and
attachment of an amiable young woman to his beloved
daughter,[1] whom she survived only three months' and whose
bones were buried 'near this place'?

The qualities usually commemorated on a servant's tombstone were long service and thrift, but sometimes there was a
reference to probity ('a useful servant and an honest man')
and the ability to take it ('for 26 years ... without giving
offence or making complaint'). Often, the more striking epitaphs
of an earlier day were quoted for the edification of nineteenth-
century servants. Many agreeable examples are to be found in
a collection by Arthur J. Munby.[2] Of Elizabeth Chapman, of
Wanstead, it was said that

[1] Princess Amelia.   [2] *Faithful Servants* (1891).

By her prudent conduct
And her continuance with great credit
45 years in the same family
She acquired a decent fortune
for the benefit
Of her relations and family.

William Woolley, who died aged eighty-six at High Ongar, Essex, was a man whose thrift, prudence and caution 'supplied the comforts required by old age.' William Cummins, of Wickham, Hampshire, arrived a poor servant in the parish about 1763—

And having fulfilled his humble duty
with uprightness and fidelity
for sixty years
bequeathed at his death £800
in gifts of gratitude
and in charity to poor persons in this place
and neighbourhood.

The independent spirit of Samuel Cane, who died at Epsom in 1782, inspired his master, the Reverend William Price, to write:

Here lies a pattern for the human race,
A man who did his work and knew his place. . . .
In spite of bribes and threats, severely just,
He sought no pension and he broke no trust.

Not that reverend masters really grudged paying a pension; but if they did, it was right that they should receive some credit. Thus, of Jane Trawley, who died at Felpham, Sussex, at the age of eighty-one, it was said that:

at the earnest wish of the
deceased her mortal remains
were deposited near those
of her former master
Cyril Jackson DD
whose bounty had
secured to her
an ample provision for her old age.

On the tombstone of John Quinny, fifty-six years a servant of Sir Henry Chester, at Tilsworth, Bedfordshire, the inscription ended:

His master left him an annuity of £8.

Shabby treatment by the master was also put on record. A tombstone at Langley Marish, Buckinghamshire, read:

Sacred to the Memory of
Mrs Sarah Wall
the old and faithful but ill-requited
servant of Lord Carrington
who departed this life June 1832
aged 70 years.

Munby explains that Mrs Wall was annoyed because Lord Carrington did no more than instal her in an almshouse. Apparently her executors shared her indignation. The vicar of the parish ordered his sexton to paint out the words 'but ill-requited,' with the ironic result that the paint preserved these words when all the rest was almost obliterated.

There were servants who were in the happy position of being able to requite their masters. In 1760 died Ann Arnold, of Gloucester, for more than forty years the servant of Charles Brereton:

Amidst a great corruption of manners in that
class of people she retained an unblemished
simplicity and innocence, discharged her
duty on the genuine and disinterested principals [sic]
of affection and Christianity. She ordered
by her will that the little fruits of her labour should
at length return to the family in which she had
earned them and from whom she had deserved
much greater.

Munby also cites the epitaph of Elizabeth Gay, whereabouts unknown—

who after a service of
40 years
finding her strength diminished
with unparalleled disinterestedness
requested that her wages might
be proportionally lessened.

The epitaph did not say whether this offer was accepted.

The virtue of sobriety was not overlooked. Magnanimously, the proprietors of a brewery erected a stone at High Wycombe to Benjamin Johnson, whose honesty and sobriety were 'an example worthy imitation.' John King served the Valentine family of Beckenham for sixty-one years 'from father to son without ever quitting their service, neglecting his Duty or being disguised in Liquor.' Susanna Prince, who died in 1774 at Acton, Middlesex, aged twenty-five, was

Sober, Diligent, Honest and Virtuous
And was never caught in a Lye,
Rare character in these degenerate days!

The second line could, perhaps, have been more happily expressed. The third line appeared, with variations, on many tombstones, at many periods of history.

Black servants also qualified for epitaphs. At Teston, Kent, was buried, at the age of thirty-six, 'Nestor, a black. By robbers torn from his country and enslaved, he attached himself to his master.' His bones were laid near the tomb of his master, the Rev. James Ramsay. At Hampton, Middlesex, was buried Pompey, Lady Thomas's black, who 'behaved himself lowly and reverend to all his betters, civil and kind to all his equals.' Chaste, sober and virtuous, he 'subdued the prejudice his colour raised.' It is comforting to think that Pompey was able to find equals.

Of course, there were scores of epitaphs which were neither patronising nor sententious, but which were worded with warmth and dignity, with affection and gratitude. An example was that of Ann Pearce, a Nanny, who died at Walthamstow:

Ann Pearce died 1822
in the house of Sir Robert Wigram Bt
in whose family she lived 48 years
and faithfully discharged her duty as Nurse
to his 23 children; of whom
19 survive her
and retain a grateful and affectionate
remembrance of her tender care and love
towards them.

'Lord, now lettest Thou Thy servant depart in peace,
according to Thy word.'

The *Servants' Magazine* reproduced, with appropriate moralising, the epitaph on Mary Ashford, a farmer's daughter, who came to a sad end at Sutton Coldfield:

As a warning to female virtue
AND A HUMBLE MONUMENT TO FEMALE CHASTITY
This stone marks the grave of
MARY ASHFORD
who in the 20th year of her age
having incautiously
REPAIRED TO A SCENE OF AMUSEMENT
without proper protection
WAS SHAMEFULLY ILL-USED AND MURDERED
on the 27th day of May 1817.

It appears that Mary went to a dance alone, was accosted, raped and murdered. The clergyman who quoted this epitaph in the *Servants' Magazine* said: 'Remember, my young friends, it was in a ballroom that Mary spent the last evening of her life.'

XIV

VANITY FAIR

THACKERAY, when deflating the pretensions of Vanity Fair, spared neither masters nor servants. The sight of powdered wigs and plush breeches inflamed him as much as it gratified those gossips who boasted, over the tea cups, that they had seen dear Lady So-and-so's livery in the Park that afternoon, and dear Sir John's in the Mall the day before.

Thackeray has a memorable picture of Sir Brian Newcome's family at breakfast in their mansion in Park Lane. The period is 'the reign of George IV,' but the picture is equally valid for the early Victorian years. A bell has rung for family prayers calling all the staff, including nurses and governesses, to the breakfast-room.

'The urns are hissing, the plate is shining; the father of the house standing up, reads from a gilt book for three or four minutes in a measured cadence. The members of the family are around the table in an attitude of decent reverence, the younger children whisper responses at their mother's knees; the governess worships a little apart; the maids and the large footmen are in a cluster before their chairs, the upper servants performing their devotions on the other side of the sideboard; the nurse whisks about the unconscious last-born and tosses it up and down during the ceremony. I do not sneer at that—at the act at which all these people are assembled—it is at the rest of the day that I marvel; at the rest of the day and what it brings. At the very instant when the voice has finished speaking and the gilded book is shut, the world begins again, and for the next twenty-three hours and fifty-seven minutes, all that household is given up to it. The servile squad rises up and marches away to its basement, whence, should it appear to be a gala day, those tall gentlemen at present attired in Oxford mixture, will issue forth with flour plastered on their heads, yellow coats, pink breeches, sky-blue waistcoats, silver lace, buckles in their shoes, black silk bags on their backs, and I don't know what insane emblems of servility and absurd bedizenments of folly. Their very manner of speaking to what they call their masters will be a like monstrous masquerade.'

The public know no more, says Thackeray, about the race that inhabits the basement floor than of the people of Timbuctoo, to whom they send missionaries. The servants answer the bell for prayers as they answer the bell for coals and for exactly three minutes in the day all the household kneel together on one carpet. Then:

'Exeunt servants, save those two who warm the newspaper, administer the muffins, and serve out the tea. . . . Ethel whispers to her mother, she thinks Eliza is looking very ill. Lady Ann asks, which is Eliza? . . . If she is ill, Mrs Trotter had better send her away. Mrs Trotter is only a great deal too good-natured. She is always keeping people who are ill. . . .'[1]

Here, parenthetically, may be told the story of a real-life Eliza who had some cause to look pale at family prayers. She was Eliza Squirrell, a housemaid who died suddenly in a house at Ipswich in 1829. Just before the servants were called to evening devotions in the parlour she had been quarrelling with Thomas Churchyard, a footman. Eliza looked unwell, worsened rapidly and died that same night, from no obvious cause. A surgeon who conducted an autopsy found embedded, almost transversely, in her body a small cheese knife, the point of which had penetrated her stomach. It emerged that in the course of the quarrel Churchyard threw a box of knives at the maidservant. The jury were invited to believe that one of these had penetrated her like a dart—or that she had thrust the knife into herself. Evidently the jury believed one or other of these theories, for they acquitted Churchyard.[2]

As Thackeray said, masters and mistressess little knew what went on in the basement.

In *Frazer's*, Thackeray handed over his pen to 'Charles

[1] *The Newcomes.*   [2] *Annual Register*, 1829.

'Let them ring again,' by George Cruikshank
From 'The Greatest Plague of Life'

Yellowplush' and in *Punch* to 'Jeames,' each of whom presented
a mis-spelled, condescending, flunkey's-eye view of the world.
One of Jeames's more anguished moments was when he read
that British footmen in Paris had been mocked and manhandled
by the revolutionary mob of 1848. These series seem to have
been just as popular with those who kept footmen as with those
who did not.

The novelist was shocked, too, that men and women should
so lightly put their secrets within the keeping of their servants.
Did they know that everything they did became the subject of

a servants' inquisition? He pictured a laughing, happy woman holding indiscreet court amid her admirers. Then—

'Discovery walks respectably up to her in the shape of a huge powdered man with large calves and a tray of ices—with Calumny (which is as fatal as Truth) behind him in the shape of the hulking fellow carrying the wafer biscuits. Madam, your secret will be talked over by those men out at their clubs at the public-house tonight. Jeames will tell Chawle his notions about you over their pipes and pewter beer-pots. Some people ought to have mutes for servants in Vanity Fair—mutes who could not write.'[1]

Punch kept up a running fire against flunkeydom, and what Thackeray did not say with his pen John Leech said with his pencil. There was a series of items called 'Flunkeiana,' in which the same 'plush Adonis' would be seen ignoring the 'libery bell' on the grounds that 'It's my Sunday out and I'm at church,' or protesting to a maid that the red livery ill suits his complexion, or moaning at a complaint that he no longer matches Joseph and must get his fat down or be sacked, or threatening to resign because the master has been seen 'on the top of a homnibus and I couldn't after that remain any longer in the family.' Asked by his mistress, 'Have the goodness to take up some coals to the nursery,' one Adonis replies, 'H'm, Ma'am. If you ask it as a favour, Ma'am, I don't so much object; but I 'ope you don't take me for an 'ousemaid, Ma'am.'

Under the heading of 'Servantgalism' *Punch* had a similar series of jokes ridiculing the airs of female servants; as, for example, a maid refusing a place because there is no skating rink in the vicinity, a cook asking for *The Times* 'when the master has finished with it,' a maid objecting to going to church in the morning on the grounds that 'in my last place I was never as'ed to go an' 'ear a curate preach.'

The maids in question usually bore names like Eliza, Betty, Sarah, Susan, Mary, Martha and Mary Anne, but *Punch* was quick to note that humble families were beginning to christen their children with names like Eugenie, Victor Albert, Evelyn Ada and Edith Amelia. These in due course became servants'

[1] *Vanity Fair.*

names and the upper classes took over the once despised names of Betty, Susan and so on.

There is a theory that all these jokes at the expense of servants played a big part in goading the domestics of a later generation into taking revenge—'We'll see who laughs last.' In fact, *Punch* had a fair leavening of jokes directed against snobbish and insensitive employers. In one, a 'charming lady' showing a 'benevolent old gentleman' over her house indicates an insanitary corner where the housemaid sleeps. 'Dear me!' says the old gentleman, 'Isn't it very damp? I see the water glistening on the walls.' The reply is: 'Oh, it's not too damp for a servant.' In another, a child with a dog says, 'Mamma, don't you think Pug ought to be vaccinated?' His mother replies, 'What nonsense, dear! They only vaccinate human beings,' only to be told, 'Why, Lady Fakeaway's had all her *servants* vaccinated, Mamma.'

Like Thackeray, Dickens also looked with deep distaste on flunkeys—'those long and languid men, flabby in texture, would appear to take the function of the slave on the car of the Roman general. Their terrible equanimity and monotonous whiteness appal.' But the non-liveried menservants equally failed to impress. In *David Copperfield*, Dickens has a telling picture of Steerforth's servant, Littimer:

'It would have been next to impossible to suspect him of anything wrong, he was so thoroughly respectable. Nobody could have thought of putting him in a livery, he was so highly respectable. To have imposed any derogatory work upon him would have been to inflict a wanton insult on the feelings of a most respectable man. And of this, I noticed that women servants in the household were so intuitively conscious, that they always did such work themselves, and generally while he read the paper by the pantry fire.' Nobody knew Littimer's Christian name: 'Peter might have been hanged or Tom transported; but Littimer was perfectly respectable.'

Elsewhere, Dickens has much to say on the tyranny of elderly servants:

'They think something is due to the credit of the house and rather stand up for all impositions. They keep us in a decent bondage, the ladies in a sort of terrorism; and grave consulta-

tions have to be held, and mutual support conceded, before
John or William can be asked to go out on some message, or
worse, have the news broken to him that Mr and Mrs Brown
are coming to dinner. . . .

'The face of the ancient retainer as he opens the hall door to
admit some new modern "notion"—say, a fern case carried in
by two men—is worth study, bearing an expression compounded
of disgust, wonder, contempt and anger. He looks after the
object with a muttered, "Well, well, after *that*! Now *this* ends
it!" As for the "Rosshian" system as applied to dinners, *that*
"goes beyond the beyonds." In his eyes it is next to sitting down
with savages and pulling the meat with our fingers. . . .'

Then comes the day when the retainer falls sick—mortally
sick, as he thinks, 'when he moans and crones over himself and
more than hints in faltering accents that it is the overwork of
the cruel family who have brought him to this sore pass, but
whom he forgives, with a "No matter *now*," dating it all from
the night of the party, when all that weary, weary work was
laid on his back.' Concludes Dickens: 'It is we who are in the
service of these "treasures," not they in ours.'[1]

In fact, the flunkey, 'the great man's overfed great man,' as
Carlyle dubbed him, was now on his way out. He was becoming
as much of an anachronism as his livery. By mid-century
gentlemen no longer had to be guarded with cudgels against
footpads. In gaslit streets there was no need for attendants with
flambeaux. Gentlemen who had taken to driving about town
with only one footman began to wonder whether even one was
superfluous. The middle classes, while anxious enough to
maintain outward style, grudged the money they paid to idle,
fuddled giants in fancy dress; men who were too lazy to work in
factories, too badly educated to work in offices, and too flabby
to join the Army. The real work about the house was done
increasingly by women, who needed less money and less time
off and were more readily put upon than men. Ah, for a neat-
handed Phyllis, even if her name was Eliza, a simple virtuous
girl who lived only to glory in 'her sensible face reflected in the
mahogany!'

A fair cross-section of neat-handed Phyllises crops up in the

[1] 'Old and New Servants,' *All the Year Round*, July 20, 1867.

'Here's Missus'—the interrupted party, by George Cruikshank
From 'The Greatest Plague of Life'

voluminous letters of Thomas and Jane Carlyle. To Carlyle they were mostly geese, cows or moon-calves, or big beautiful blockheads. He seems to have raised no objection to his wife's habit of using these beautiful blockheads to warm his bed ('I have put the women to sleep in your bed to air it. It seems so long since you went away'). His manner of dismissing inefficient servants was untempered by civility. To a 'mutinous Irish savage' who tossed down the plates on the table as if they were quoits he commanded: 'To your room at once. Wages tomorrow morning. Disappear!' Jane Carlyle showed compassion to her servants, even to the drunken ones, and kept their friendship in later life. One of her maids married a physician at St Leonards, exercising 'completest silken dominion' over her husband; and when Jane paid a visit her hostess was not too proud to bring up the hot water. At Cheyne Row the maid's function was to be 'the least bit of a valet' to Carlyle (which included lighting his clay pipe for him in the morning) and the least bit of a lady's maid to his wife. When the Carlyles rose to the dignity of two servants, difficulties started. Both maids joined in an alliance against their mistress and began holding solemn consultations over 'your dinner' and 'our dinner.' Says Jane: 'A maid of all work, even in London, will tolerate your looking after her, and directing her; but a "cook" and a "housemaid" will stand no interference; you musn't set foot in your own kitchen, unless you are prepared with their giving warning. Either of these servants by herself, provided she were up to the general work of the house (which neither of them is) I could be tolerably comfortable with. But together, O dear me! Shall I ever get used to it?'

It was a predicament in which many a Victorian mistress, unused to employing servants, found herself as the family fortunes expanded.

Occasionally, Jane Carlyle obtained a close-up of how great folk treated their servants. In 1851 she attended the servants' Christmas ball at Lady Ashburton's home, The Grange, at Alresford, Hampshire. The servants' hall was decorated with banners reading 'God Save The Queen' and 'Long Live Lord And Lady Ashburton.' Some forty-eight children from the estate were among those called up by name to receive presents; and so was 'Thomas Carlyle, the scholar,' who was presented with a jigsaw map of the world. Mugs of tea and slices of currant loaf were served to all, and there was much condescension. The whole thing, Jane thought, had a very fine effect, but what worried her was the knowledge that the forty-eight presents had been bought for £2 12s. 6d. 'in the Lowther Arcade, the most rubbishy place in London.' This regard for economy might have been commendable in 'the like of us,' but not in 'a person with an income of £40,000 a year—and who gives balls at the cost of £700 each, or will spend £100 on a

china jar.' How much better, she thought, if each child had
been given a frock; 'but everyone has his own notion on
spending money.'[1]

How to give a party for the servants without debauching
them was a problem which worried middle-class mistresses.
'A Practical Mistress of a Household' offered some advice in a
pamphlet *Domestic Servants As They Are And As They Ought
To Be*, published in 1859. She explained that if servants once
began to measure their desires and their deserts by the doings
of the class above them, they would place themselves on an
assumed equality and there would be no possibility of meeting
their demands. Significantly, this writer says that, if a servants'
ball must be held, the mistress should select a day when the
gentlemen of the family are likely to be absent. The servants
should be allowed to invite a limited number of friends, the
only male guests being close relatives or *authorised* suitors. The
event should start early, about four or five o'clock, and stop at
ten. The mistress and her female relatives should take an
interest and 'provide suitable amusements which may afford
rational enjoyment,' also suitable food, such as a good substantial cake, a few oranges, apples and nuts and a little *British
wine*, thus furnishing 'a feast at once wholesome and satis-
factory.' Tea might not unreasonably be provided as well. The
function should end with an hour's dance, a musician being
engaged for the purpose.

Naturally all these temptations could not be provided without
a serious warning: 'It should be announced to the servants by
their mistress that she does not wish to interfere with their
pleasure, at the same time she expects that they will be moderate
in their merriment and that it will depend upon themselves
whether they are permitted the same indulgence again.'

In this writer's view the greatest mistake a mistress could
make was to say, 'If the servants must have a party, they shall
have it when I am at So-and-So's and then they will have the
house to themselves and can do as they like.' A well-regulated
party, with moderated merriment, was the surest way to prevent
'many of those clandestine nocturnal assemblies which are

[1] Quoted in *Jane Welsh Carlyle* by Trudy Bliss. There is an excellent
chapter on the Carlyles' servants in D. M. Stuart's *The English Abigail*.

so detrimental, if not ruinous, to the character of female servants.'

Although tea allowances were a perquisite of long standing, many mistresses worried because their servants were the slaves of a beverage unsuited to their station; a beverage which, while sustaining the energies of ladies, sapped those of servants. Girls who were not paid a tea allowance actually squandered on this unhealthy drink money which should have gone into the Savings Bank. If they *had* to drink tea, why could they not be content with the tea left over from the parlour? If that had been too heavily diluted, surely they could refresh themselves adequately with milk? For a girl earning £8 or £9 a year, an expenditure of £1 on tea was clearly uneconomic; 'there are families,' scolded one writer, 'in which the master and mistress deny themselves one dessert and common table luxuries which cost far less in proportion to the money they have to spend than their servants' tea does to their wages.' And how disgraceful it was for housemaids to spend money on tea when their younger brothers and sisters were growing up in ignorance because there was no money to send them to school!

Many a mistress thought it far better for servants to drink beer than tea, but the temperance reformers were now trying to dissuade employers from providing unlimited quantities of beer for the servants' hall. They also tried to put down the custom whereby a mistress gave the wash-day maid a tot of whisky before she got down to tubbing; this was supposed to lead to the ruin of many a good laundry-maid. 'Beer money' was often paid in lieu of beer and even teetotal servants claimed it, since it was a valuable perquisite. In temperance circles there was a belief that a cook by the sheer excellence of her dishes could eliminate any craving for drink on the part of the family.

The writers of etiquette books tried tactfully to explain to mistresses how servants should be treated. According to one writer, they were to be spoken to in a special voice:

'It is better in addressing them to use a higher key of voice and not to suffer it to fall at the end of a sentence. The best-bred man whom we ever had the pleasure of meeting always employed in addressing servants such forms as these—'I will thank you for so-and-so' or 'Such a thing, if you please'—with a gentle

A girl leaves home for service
From 'The Servants' Magazine'

tone but very elevated key. The perfection of manners in this
particular is to indicate by your language that the performance
is a favour and by your tone that it is a matter of course.'[1]

Mrs Beeton insisted that a servant was never to sit in the
presence of master or mistress; never to offer any opinion unless
asked for it; and never to say 'Good morning' or 'Good night'
except in reply to those salutations. One pundit is said to have
ruled that a gentleman on meeting his housemaid in the street
was under no obligation to take off his hat to her; but Louis XIV
stood with head uncovered in the presence of a maidservant.

Etiquette and justice sometimes clashed on the question of
whether an employer should apologise to a servant for an
unjustified rebuke. If it *had* to be done, it was important that
it should be done with the minimum loss of dignity. The Duke
of Wellington's method was to call in the servant he had
maligned, and ask him some routine question. Then, when the
answer had been given, the Duke would reply in a kindly tone,
'Thank you, I am much obliged to you.' The servant would

[1] *Etiquette* (Anon.), 1857.

understand that this meant, 'I have done wrong. Pray forgive me.'[1]

Hippolyte Taine, that sharp-eyed Frenchman who visited Britain in the 1860s, was fascinated by the Englishman's attitude to his servants. Like his predecessors, he noted the gulf between the two—'this fundamental difference is always cropping up, the difference which divides the land of hierarchy from the land of equality.' But Taine was much impressed by the way the English householder called his servants to family prayers, calmly assuming the role of chaplain and asserting his moral leadership while spreading a community feeling; a situation without parallel in France.[2] But that community feeling in the English home did not always extend to public places of worship. Periodically, down the long Victorian years, there were protests about the segregation of servants in churches. In 1846 a reader of *The Times* complained that in Rawstone Street Chapel, Brompton, servants in livery were relegated to the back seats of the gallery, 'an extraordinary arrangement which would necessarily exclude all wearers of livery coats from partaking in Holy Communion.' Perhaps, suggested this reader, it was thought that the sight of a family crest on a canary-coloured coat would distract others? If that was so, would a gaily attired cornet also be excluded from the ground-floor pews? 'Let these persons know,' said this critic, 'that at St George's Church, Hanover Square, the real aristocracy of the land are separated from their liveried domestics by a mere oak panelling.' *Punch*, commenting on this, suggested that the sign 'LIVERY SERVANTS AND DOGS NOT ADMITTED,' which used to hang over the gates of Kensington Gardens, should be set up outside the Brompton chapel.

Protests like this seem to have had no effect, for more and more churches relegated servants to the gallery, keeping them penned there after the service until the gentlefolk had left. In 1871, during a Commons debate on the Parish Churches Bill, Beresford Hope said that some years previously, having selected a possible church for his family, he had asked for a pew plan, and had chosen a pew close to the pulpit. Unluckily, something he said aroused suspicion. 'You don't mean that you will be

<hr>

[1] Richard Aldington: *Wellington*.   [2] *Notes on England, 1860–70*.

taking the pew for your livery servants?' he was asked. 'Yes, I
am.' 'Then I cannot let it to you, for if livery servants were to
go to the pew the ladies and gentlemen in the neighbouring
pews would cease to attend.' Another Member said he did not
believe the humbler classes would wish churches to be managed
in such a way as to allow a costermonger a seat opposite that of
a duchess.

The coming of the railways brought its own peculiar servant
problem. On post coaches, all servants except the more
privileged valets and ladies' maids had travelled outside,
refreshed by the healthy breeze. Logically, therefore, the place
for servants on the railways was in open trucks, but it was a
harsh master who could condemn his retinue to a prolonged
ordeal by wind, water and hot coals, not to mention boulders
dropped from bridges. On no account could they be admitted
to first class, since first was designed (in the words of the
Railway Times in 1841) for those anxious 'to avoid the risk of
mixing even temporarily with any other than persons of the
same apparent standing in society.' It was very largely for the
benefit of servants, therefore, that a middle, or second, class
was instituted. The railway companies were unhappy about the
consequences of this concession, for it became apparent that
certain gentlefolk preferred to travel in a class below that which
Providence and the companies had assigned for them, and the
directors did not see why loss of self-respect in travellers should
involve the companies in loss of revenue. Sometimes, refresh-
ment rooms bore signs which read: 'For Second-Class Passengers And Servants,' which was thought to be a cunning way
of forcing sensitive gentlefolk into first-class. One disadvantage
of the system was that gentlefolk could not communicate with
their servants during the journey; the master might be lying
bludgeoned amid his luxury but the valet would not know this
until he reported with a brandy and soda at a suitable stop; the
mistress might be fighting for her honour while the maid who
was supposed to be guarding her from molestation was reading
a French novel several compartments away. By mid-Victorian
times a special family coach was available for large, affluent
families. It had a parlour in which the head of the family sat
between padded arm-rests with his brood extending on each

side of him, along the arms of a 'U,' in descending order of seniority. Just outside the parlour was a lavatory and on the other side of the lavatory was a second-class compartment for servants.

From mid-century onwards two laments were increasingly voiced by the middle classes: 'girls are too proud to do housework' and 'education is ruining our servants.' In 1861 a woman who founded a school at Norwich to train servant girls described her disillusionment in a letter to the *Norwich Mercury*. Her object had been to give her pupils a good general education, plus a knowledge of sewing, cutting out and 'practical acquaintance with cookery and housework under my excellent housekeeper.' After four years the school had to be closed down because parents were making every excuse to preserve their daughters from doing any household work and many had withdrawn their children for that reason.

Punch, quoting this letter, shook its head sadly. It had been strongly advocating that girls should be trained for domestic duties. That same year it reproduced a statement by a clergyman in the Minutes of the Council of Government Education: 'For want of good schools for girls, three out of four of the girls in my district are sent to miserable private schools where they have no religious instruction, no discipline, no industrial training; they are humoured in every sort of conceit, are called 'Miss Smith' and 'Miss Brown,' and go into service at fourteen or fifteen skilled in crochet and worsted work but unable to darn a hole or cut out a frock, hating household work and longing to be milliners or ladies' maids. . . . No wonder that people cry out that education is ruining our servants and doing more harm than good.' These minutes also disclosed that, at a school for girls intended for service, scarcely one girl in 150 had a handkerchief but almost every one had a hoop crinoline or a very good imitation of one, worn with 'enormous masses of petticoat.'

Whether they liked it or not, these girls would find that, in the better-class homes of the 'sixties, they would be expected to wear what in effect was a uniform: the black dress, with white apron and cap, which was to survive, with modifications, into our own times. Hitherto, a maid had been distinguished

PROFESSIONAL DIGNITY.

Lady. "RESIGN YOUR SITUATION! WHY, WHAT'S WRONG NOW, THOMAS? HAVE THEY BEEN WANTING YOU TO EAT SALT BUTTER AGAIN?"

Genteel Footman. "OH, NO, THANK YOU, MA'AM—BUT THE FACT IS, MA'AM—THAT I HAVE HEARD THAT MASTER WERE SEEN LAST WEEK ON THE TOP OF A HOMNIBUS, AND I COULDN'T AFTER THAT REMAIN ANY LONGER IN THE FAMILY!"

from her mistress largely by the inferior quality of her clothes. The Victorians preferred 'livery' for their women servants as well as for their menservants.

It was all part of Vanity Fair. The middle classes, though they might discard a flunkey or two, continued to raise their standards of display. In 1858 readers of *The Times* debated whether a young gentleman could afford to marry on £300 a year (the correspondence arose from a suggestion that the Haymarket drabs existed only because the cost of marriage was prohibitive). Among the letters were several from householders revealing their personal budgets. One of the more frugal was from a man with £300 a year who spent £12 6s. on the combined wages of a woman servant and a nursery girl, £25 on rent, £3 12s. on taxes and £22 on meat (the biggest item after rent). He still had £69 14s. left over—enough to pay the wages of four or five more servants.

XV

VIRTUE STILL IN DANGER

IN his explorations of the London underworld, Henry Mayhew was depressed by the low standard of morals he found among maidservants, 'more commonly known as Dollymops.'

'In small families,' he says, 'the servants often give themselves up to the sons or to the police on the beat or to soldiers in the parks; or else to shopmen whom they meet in the streets. Female servants are far from being a virtuous class. They are badly educated and are not well looked after by their mistresses as a rule.'[1] He notes that Marylebone has recently been classed as one of the seven black parishes of London, in that half the women sent from the workhouses into situations turned out prostitutes. 'I have no means of corroborating the truth of this declaration,' he admits. He quotes some figures showing that, out of the total of disorderly prostitutes arrested in London in 1850–60, 400 were servants, 418 laundresses and 646 milliners. Over a ten-year period, the totals do not seem unusually scandalous.

The knowledge that any lapse was punishable by instant dismissal probably kept a good many servant girls virtuous, or at least careful. For many it must have seemed that celibacy or sin were the only courses. Mayhew says that a maidservant seldom has a chance to marry unless she is placed in a good family where, after saving some money, she may become an object of interest to a footman who is hoping to open a public-house. A virtuous girl with a reputation for saving her wages would not necessarily attract the advances of a virtuous, thrifty male.

[1] Quoted in *London's Underworld* (ed. Peter Quennell).

Mayhew falls in with those who blame the maid's downfall, as often as not, on her vanity. He deplores 'the suicidal decking in flowers and making preparation for immolation on the part of the victim herself. Flattered by the attention of the eldest son or some friend of his staying in the house, the pretty lady's maid will often yield to soft solicitation. Vanity is at the bottom of all this and is one of the chief characteristics of a class not otherwise naturally vicious.'

Soldiers, Mayhew says, are notorious for hunting up servant girls in the parks, where it is easy to accost them. The girls are always ready to succumb to 'scarlet fever,' preferring a redcoat to a manservant or to any other male. The soldier, for his part, prefers servant girls because he likes to be appreciated for his own sake, because no fee is payable and because there is no risk of infection.

Not long after Mayhew made his report to the nation, Dr William Acton published his study of prostitution, which was sold at a price to prevent it becoming 'an investment for the pocket money of school children or the savings of nursemaids.'[1] Dr Acton distressed the middle classes by assuring them that fallen women did not necessarily continue falling, as was popularly believed, but often married respectably and above their original station. His own observations in the Home Counties showed that the best servants were often found among those who had children to support. Much of the trouble began in the rural areas, where pre-marital intercourse was sanctioned by the North Country 'proverb': 'If thou houd'st I wed thee; if thou doesn't thou'rt none the waur.' But in the country a high degree of blame attached to farmers, farmers' sons, squires and squireens: 'many such rustics of the middle class and men of parallel grades in the country towns employ a portion of their time in the coarse, deliberate villainy of making prostitutes. Of these, the handsome are draughted off to the larger communities, where their attractions enable them to settle; the others are tied to the spot of their birth and fall.' The best that such women could expect was 2s. 6d. a week under a bastardy order; their fathers were entitled to sue the seducers for damages but very rarely did so. In 1843 a farmer

[1] *Prostitution* (1857).

near Broadway was ordered to pay £300 to the father of the fourteen-year-old nursery governess whom he raped when she asked him what he wanted for supper. The defendant did his best to prove that the girl had been guilty of 'conduct as shameless as would have disgraced a cyprian in the Metropolis.'

Dr Acton thought that maids' protection societies, of which several now existed, were but 'paltry, peddling [*sic*] scratches on the surface of the evil.' He held the view that the root cause of the corruption of Britain's morals was 'the single bedroom in the two-roomed cottage'; but he reserved a powerful blast for the infamous lodging-houses, no better than brothels, in which out-of-work servants were obliged to seek shelter. He was told of one in which a dozen boys and girls slept in one bed and three or four dozen persons of both sexes shared the same room, capering about naked at night and boasting about how many times they had been in jail, workhouse or lock hospital. In these dens vermin plopped continually from the ceiling like peas. An inmate told Lord Ashley (Lord Shaftesbury): 'They can be gathered in handfuls. I could fill a pail in a few minutes.' It was to resorts like these that friendless servants, turned adrift without characters by tyrannous or impatient mistresses, were likely to drift.

Dr Acton may have been right in believing that the best servants were those who had children to support. Often, the uncovenanted offspring became useful citizens. A recent biography has told the story of Joseph Ashby, of Tysoe, Warwickshire, whose mother was seduced by a member of the wealthy family which had employed her as maid. Joseph, born in 1859, grew up to be a champion of village rights, a farmer and justice of the peace, a rural stalwart whose life was commendable in every way.[1] Other children were doomed from the start; and sometimes the newspapers told of singularly macabre happenings. In 1849 Sarah Drake, a cook-housekeeper in Harley Street, was brought to court charged with murdering her two-year-old child, who had been farmed out. After strangling the boy, she packed the body in a box, handed it to the butler to address and then sent it by a footman to be dispatched by rail to her sister in the country, with a request

[1] M. K. Ashby: *Joseph Ashby of Tysoe.*

that the body be buried. The parcel was opened by the sister's husband. A few years before she had sent a dead child to the porter of the Knutsford Union, with a similar request.

Was a mistress to be accounted blameworthy for the ill-behaviour of her maids? Clearly she could not be expected to keep an efficient watch on her maidservant out of doors. If the girl said she wanted to visit an aunt at Camberwell on Sunday afternoon, her employer was not to know, though she might well suspect, that the aunt at Camberwell wore a red jacket and a waxed moustache and was stationed at Knightsbridge. To an old-fashioned mistress it was unthinkable that a maid should be regarded as the custodian of her own virtue, like a milliner or a factory girl. She did not dare take the responsibility of letting the girl out in the evenings, when unaccompanied women of any station were liable to insult or molestation. Often, it seemed that the best way to keep a maid virtuous was to keep her a virtual prisoner in the house; but how was one to protect her from 'followers'?

'Followers' could be a considerable headache. Most mistresses were concerned to exclude them, as much in the interests of their own larders as of the maids' morals. But if a girl was to be debarred followers at her place of employment, where was she to meet her friends? In the streets? In the parks? In the public-houses? Occasionally there was a plea for a more enlightened approach to the problem of followers, as in *The Young Housekeeper's Book*, published in Glasgow in 1856:

'We have known much good and no evil to result from permission being granted to young women to receive the visits of their "admirers," as they are now styled, openly and honourably, as an indulgence on one or two evenings in the week. If a servant be respectable and worthy (and who would retain a person if she were not so?) she merits the favour; an opportunity is thus afforded her employers of knowing the young man and his connections, and advising her to cease her intimacy if it should be inimical to her welfare, or of forwarding a courtship that may prove eligible. The stamp of respectability is thus given, mystery avoided, falsehood prevented, and any tendency to lightness of conduct, coquetry, promiscuous gossipings etc.

The washday whisky that led to ruin
From 'The Servants' Magazine'

checked; to say nothing of continual sore throats and colds from nocturnal back gate assignations. . .'

For one mistress who could carry out a policy of that kind with tact and delicacy, there were a dozen who could not. The servant girl of spirit did not see why, out of all the world's workers, she should be denied free choice of a mate, why she should be expected to limit her attentions to those young men who had been questioned and screened by the woman whose ornaments she dusted.

The writer of the passage quoted thought that the idea of encouraging followers was especially well suited to country areas. In certain parts of Wales, however, followers were allowed to take liberties that astounded visiting moralists. The Rev. William Jones, Vicar of Nevin, told an investigator that the vice of bundling was everywhere tolerated. 'I have had the greatest difficulty,' he said, 'in keeping my own servants from practising it. I am told by my parishioners that unless I allow the practice, I shall very soon have no servants at all and that it will be impossible to get any.' The Rev. J. W. Trevor, chaplain to the Bishop of Bangor, complained that the householders of Anglesey tacitly undertook, when hiring servants, to give facilities for fornication.[1]

In Glamorganshire the superintendent of police said that servants of both sexes often slept in the same room. Unmarried men ranged the countryside at night demanding admission to the female servants' quarters. 'I heard the most revolting anecdotes of the gross and almost bestial indelicacy with which sexual intercourse takes place on these occasions,' he reported.[2] It also appears that much misbehaviour occurred among Welsh girls returning from chapel meetings at night.

Another fount of misconduct was the 'mop' or hiring fair. This old-fashioned occasion was a strong tradition in Wales, in the south of Scotland and the north of England, notably in Cumberland and Westmorland. In preceding centuries domestic servants as well as farm servants were widely hired at these functions, but by Victoria's accession fewer domestics were presenting themselves. Those who sought employment were supposed to carry some emblem of their speciality—a broom for a housemaid, a ladle for a cook, and so on. Young men indicated that they were disengaged by wearing a straw in the mouth. Sometimes the proceedings bore an uncomfortable resemblance to a cattle auction. Burly farmers and their wives would look over the available 'stock' with a practised eye and were not above giving a playful prod. Before the bargain was sealed, with the transfer of a shilling, each party had an opportunity to discover the other's character and reputation. Young girls were usually under the charge of mothers or older sisters, who helped to negotiate a fair wage. For a shy girl it could be quite an ordeal, since all the town turned out to watch the fun, to stare the girls out of countenance or to make ribald proposals. Shy girls, however, were in the minority; many of the candidates were happy enough to be publicly appraised and could banter or blister with equal skill.

[1] Joseph Kay: *Social Condition and Education of the People* (1850).
[2] *Ibid.*

When the bargains were sealed, the young men invited the girls into the public-houses and there were scenes ranging from 'great heartiness and mirth' to 'gross excesses.' Often there were free-for-all fights, with the girls egging on the combatants or even lending a hand. Then the fighting would subside suddenly and the fun continue, until the next quarrel. This sort of thing could be expected, observers said, so long as servants were given so little time off that they had to pack a quarter's revelry into twelve hours. An attempt at Penrith in the 'sixties to suppress the hiring fair and substitute a registry office failed. The young men and maidens valued the convivial aspects of the fair too highly to let it go.

In some areas there was a periodical 'runaway mop,' at which servants who had made a bad bargain could try for a better place; but only bad servants and publicans were really happy about this indulgence.

XVI

THE RULING TOPIC

Housekeepers! Do you then, like those of yore,
    Keep house with power and pride, with grace and ease?
No, you keep servants only! What is more,
    You don't keep these.
    —KATHARINE BURRILL, 'The Servant Question Again,'
                        Chambers, September 8, 1906

'She was a good cook as cooks go; and as cooks go, she went.'
                    —SAKI, *Reginald* (1904)

FROM about the 1880s onwards the most obsessive topic of conversation among Englishwomen of the middle and lower middle classes was the Servant Problem. By this was meant, primarily, the growing shortage of good servants, but the phrase was a useful cover-all for the restlessness, intractability and all-round cussedness of the race below stairs. Sometimes, mistresses did not wait until the maids were out of the room before they got down to the subject, taking the view that the creatures might as well listen openly as at the keyhole. Aware that they were regarded as a Problem, servants went out of their way to be one, rather like the delinquent young of our own times.

Mistresses did not make much serious effort to diagnose the causes of the unrest in attic and basement, which they supposed to be due to the inborn ingratitude of the lower orders and the impossible pretensions of young women seeking to share the emancipation intended for their betters. They blamed with much bitterness the new folly of compulsory education in Board Schools, where teachers helped to sharpen class-con-consciousness and inculcated in the young a distaste for domestic service. One deplorable result of popular education was that servant girls were publishing pamphlets criticising their mistresses, claiming twelve free hours a week and all Sundays off, and even demanding that mistresses should produce references.

Among the factors that had produced the servant shortage were: the increased flow of young women into factories, where mass-production was beginning to make headway; into offices, where operating a typewriter was being looked upon as a moderately refined occupation; into hospitals, where Florence Nightingale had made nursing respectable; into the postal and telegraph service; and into shops and stores, which were multiplying with a fast-multiplying population. Every year, thousands of young women were emigrating to the Commonwealth, where domestic servants enjoyed a higher status and better wages. Even families in which domestic service was a deep-rooted tradition were allowing their daughters to choose their own careers. As a result Britain increasingly drew its servants from those who were too timid or feckless or undisciplined to work in shops or factories. There was never any shortage of women in search of employment, but there was a chronic and ever-growing shortage of women with the desire and the aptitude to work in other people's houses.

The chief, the inescapable, reason for the Servant Problem was the failure of the mistresses of Britain to lighten the conditions of service at a time when the nation was raising its social standards and shaking off old injustices. Factory Acts had improved the lot of factory workers, but no Home Acts relieved domestic oppression. Increased wealth continued to breed a prosperous class who thought their importance best expressed by ostentation and a tyrannous attitude towards servants. Mistresses, while deploring the fact that shop girls were employed for fourteen hours a day, kept their own servants on duty for sixteen. Sometimes an enlightened voice was raised to suggest that a twelve-hour day was enough for a servant, and that one day off per month was not an exorbitant demand.

The bitter truth was that the occupation which employed most women had nearly the lowest social rating and any incentive to shine in it was thus negatived. Factory girls were

called 'Miss' and were not constantly summoned by bells to
pass things or pick things up; on the works floor they may have
suspected that they were toiling on behalf of a richer, idler
class, but they were not hectored by them daily or bullied by
their children. They were employees working for a barely
glimpsed employer, who paid them their wages and left them
alone, whereas in the home the relations were those of master
and servant.

The slights which servants had to endure, in a world growing
more liberal and humane, were all too numerous. The parlourmaid had only to look out of the window and an urchin would
cry 'Skivvy!' At a village dance the 'wallflowers' would
invariably be servant girls; and at a church social the wives of
traders and artisans excused themselves rapidly if they found
that they were condescending to somebody else's kitchen staff.
Servants were still expected to describe their next-of-kin as
'encumbrances' and to be ashamed of them. Denied the
privilege of being called 'Miss,' they were rebuked if they
referred to the baby of the house by its Christian name,
unprefixed by 'Miss' or 'Master.'

There were mistresses who locked out maids if they arrived
back a few minutes late, leaving them to spend the night in the
coalhouse (the idea of giving a maid a latchkey was unthinkable).
There were mistresses who went round turning off the gas every
night to stop the servants reading in bed. There were mistresses who intercepted servants' letters at the front door, in an
effort to discover whether they were carrying on affairs or
trying to get a better job; who provided the servants' hall with
knives and forks inscribed 'Stolen from ———'; who locked the
rooms to keep out maids who had no business in them; who
gave soft blankets to their dogs and rough ones to their maids.
And so on.

Often, of course, the master was as inconsiderate as the
mistress. He would sympathise openly with the maids in their
complaints, grumble at his wife for not handling them properly
and for failing to maintain the discipline he helped to under-
mine, and then commit some act of thoughtlessness which gave
the maids something else to protest about; but by then he
would be at his office.

Even in 'good' places, much hardship was caused by a regard for fashionable practices or simple selfishness: the selfishness that could keep up a lady's maid into the small hours, night after night throughout the Season, just to undo a few hooks and eyes when her mistress returned. In the 'nineties, a vogue for going to balls on Sundays had grown up and the custom of Sunday dinner parties still persisted. A large section of the middle classes had resigned themselves to eating a cold dinner on Sunday evenings, but a hot Sunday dinner was a sign that the servants were not yet the masters. Soames Forsyte at this period regarded a hot dinner on Sundays as 'a little distinguishing elegance.' The servants, he pointed out, had nothing else to do but play the concertina.[1]

In the smaller homes, domestic service had a loneliness experienced in no other calling. Especially was this so in the lower reaches of suburbia, with its ever-extending avenues of one-maid homes. The girl of thirteen or fourteen from a large, rumbustious family found herself sequestered in a small house in a road where nothing happened, under a mistress who, while benevolent according to her lights, made it clear that the girl was in no sense one of the family. The thrill of having a bedroom to herself for the first time was a short-lived one; if loneliness was the penalty of privacy, then privacy was less desirable than she had supposed. It was, of course, very splendid to have a lavatory and even a bath of one's own, but the maid's enjoyment of these amenities was tempered by the knowledge that she was regarded as unfit to use the family plumbing, though eminently qualified to clean it. The servant lived on the edge of other people's wealth, she saw them enjoying privileges from which she was shut out, she heard them addressing her in that special voice. They did not understand why she could not be happy in her work. If she was a nursemaid, she could love her charges; but if she was a maid of all work, was she to love the slops and the coal buckets? So, at the first crisis, or even before any crisis, she would vanish, possibly to work in a factory where there were others of her kind; and there would be another tale of ingratitude to tell over the tea cups.

To editors of popular papers, any proposals for a servants'

[1] John Galsworthy: *The Forsyte Saga*.

union, or for strike action by servants, were usually a theme for
levity. In practice, however, the servants of Britain, unorganised
though they were, were beginning to operate an outstandingly
successful nation-wide strike. When it came to walking out of
bad conditions, they could show the tub-thumping, banner-
carrying working men a thing or two. They passed no resolutions, they raised few cries for solidarity, they just walked out.
Attempts were made, in 1872, in Dundee and Leamington to
form unions of domestic servants, but the scattered nature of
their employment and the difficulty of attending meetings
rendered these efforts fruitless. Early in the 'nineties the London
and Provincial Domestic Servants Union was founded, with the
patronage of eminent clergy, including Archdeacon Farrar, but
it never had much following; nor had any of its successors. A
major obstacle was that upper servants had no wish to join in
an agitation by lower servants. The valet regarded himself as in
another world from the tweeny, and the scullery maid was not
fool enough to suppose that the cook or housekeeper would
fight her battles for her. As it happened, the diffused nature of
domestic service was a source of strength as well as weakness,
for there was no possibility of victimisation or lock-outs on
the part of employers. Domestic servants, though essentially
individuals, were the most powerful combination of all.

If the popular press dealt facetiously with the servant
problem the serious press did not. All the weekly and monthly
reviews gave it a great deal of attention. *The Spectator*, worried
by suggestions that mistresses should provide references as to
character, explained to its readers what it believed to be the
fundamental difficulty in domestic service; namely, that no
contract could ever be drawn up, specifying the servant's duties
as a factory girl's or a shop girl's duties could be specified. 'The
essence of the matter is that within reasonable limits she is to
do as she is bid; and if she is to cherish an attitude of mind
which renders her habitually disinclined to do as she is bid
without getting a good reason for it she can never be either a
happy or an efficient servant.'

All of which, as the writer admitted, was semi-feudal, but
'one woman cannot do happily the will of another woman simply
because it is her will, without looking up to her in some degree;

and the more genuinely she looks up to her the more the latter deserves to be looked up to, and the more the servant is able to see that she deserves to be looked up to, the more happy the relation will be. A servant who accustomed herself to sit in judgment on her mistress's character and to point out its defects to applicants for a place in her household . . . will never take kindly to domestic service. If domestic service is to be tolerable there must be an attitude of habitual deference on the one side and one of sympathetic protection on the other.'

The Spectator thought that if a servant were to give a mistress a reference it would inevitably read like this:

'Jane Smith regrets to say that Mrs Harrison is always meddling in her kitchen and that no servant of spirit would remain in the place for a month. She is mean in her house-keeping, has a bad temper and it is impossible to please her; and the wages are not paid punctually.'

As a testimonial it might be true, but would this sort of thing conduce to more cordial domestic relations all round? *The Spectator* thought not.[1]

Many attempts were made by individuals and organisations to befriend, shelter, educate, and otherwise assist servant girls, but the girls looked on such endeavours warily. Were the organisers genuinely out to help or were they trying to mould servants nearer to their hearts' desire, to put them under an obligation? How did these eloquent organisers treat their own maids? In the 'eighties the Countess of Aberdeen founded the Haddo House Young Women's Improvement Association, which aimed to draw mistresses and servants together, to give girls useful interests in life, to dissuade them from everlastingly changing their jobs and to try to raise the whole tone of young women in service. Girls who joined the Association found they were given essays to write and sums to do. Periodically they would be rounded up and awarded prizes by the Countess. She would tell them: 'I should like to think that the girl who will not give up a difficult sum until it be correct will also be the one who will dust not round but under the cupboards' (laughter); or 'People are often afraid that education will prevent girls being good housemaids and good servants. Education should

[1] August 9, 1890.

make a cook a better cook, a housemaid a better housemaid, because they think about what they do.' This did not produce laughter, possibly because the audience had some obstinate notion that education ought to lift them out of domestic service altogether.[1]

One notion for alleviating the servant problem was to recruit 'lady helps,' a proposal much canvassed during the 'nineties and the following decade. As always, there was a large body of gentlewomen in reduced circumstances who were trained for no occupation, and there was also a considerable number of educated women who, having fought for the right to maintain themselves, were given little or no opportunity to do so. The more fortunate were absorbed in offices and shops; others, who at one time would have been regarded as competent to instruct in 'the arts,' could produce no certificates and were an embarrassment to their relatives. The only field of labour left wide open was that which was now being rejected by a lower class: domestic service. Perhaps this career could be invested with a new status? If gentlewomen called themselves 'ladies' helps' they would not be losing caste, but would merely be reassuming some of the traditional responsibilities of gentlewomen in an earlier age. That was the argument.

In practice, the idea did not work out. Like the governess the lady help was neither in one world nor the other. In a house with several servants, she was inevitably a source of friction. *The Spectator*, tackling this problem in 1892, referred to a report that lady servants operating under a body called the Household Auxiliary Association proposed to eat apart from the other servants and to do no scrubbing, blacking of boots or carrying of heavy objects upstairs. In 'an ordinary household where the servants number between four and nine,' such discrimination, in *The Spectator's* view, was undesirable. Servants were quick enough to humiliate the governess for her pretensions—'she has to earn her living like the rest of us'— and it would be ridiculous to spread this attitude in kitchen and pantry. Therefore, thought the journal, lady helps must do all the work of the house. They did not really object to hard work

[1] The Countess of Aberdeen: *Mistresses and Maidservants* (1884).

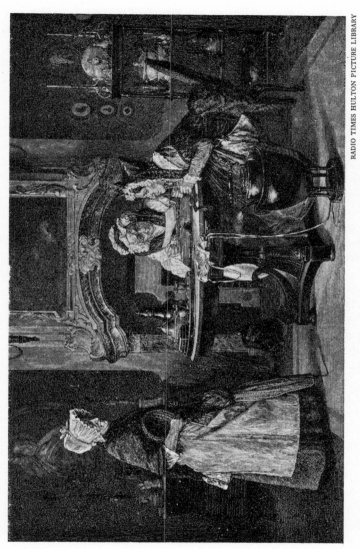

Her character. From the painting by Bakker Korff

but 'they cannot and will not face associating day by day with those who belong to a lower caste than themselves.' Rather than face bad manners in the servants' hall they would eat wretched meals in holes and corners, to preserve their self-respect. The trouble was, said *The Spectator*, that there was no camaraderie among women. Gentlemen could adapt themselves to the life of barracks or mining camps, and knew better than to assert their social superiority when thus situated. But the servants who worked under the same roof as a lady help would recognise her superiority only too well and would punish her for a refinement they did not themselves possess. All of which, *The Spectator* thought, was a great pity, because people of education and cultivation were usually amenable to orders. Ordinary servants entirely repudiated the type of discipline observed in offices ('I ain't agoing to be ordered about by anybody') but the educated person saw the folly of such an attitude and was prepared to say 'It's her house and if she wants it that way, all right.' The journal thought there might be possibilities in a non-resident body of lady charwomen, who would eat out; they would give better service than most maids.

A pamphlet entitled *Lady Servants* (*For and Against*), published in 1906, quoted varying experiences of lady helps. One of them, who had taken a training course, started in her first place with enthusiasm, which dwindled when she found that her food was doled out slice by slice and her milk drop by drop. She was spoken to as if she was a dog, had to ask permission to go out to post a letter, and was expected to work a seventeen-hour day. She had no interest in bandying chaff with the butcher and baker or in ogling passers-by from the area steps, but these were the only recreations open to her. As a result of her service her respect for the lower orders had increased, her respect for her own class had decreased. Other lady helps had been more fortunate; one of them had enjoyed three hours to herself daily, the use of a pleasant sitting-room in which she could entertain her friends and had the services of a boy to do the rough work. Another said: 'In taking up domestic work ladies do not sink to the level of the ignorant servant class; rather they, by their actions and example, should raise their work to a

¹ July 16, 1892.

high and honourable standard; and thus educated persons with small means can gain a livelihood in a way that is as yet little known.'

The least successful lady helps started with no domestic knowledge and hoped to muddle through. Others underwent training by such organisations as the Guild of Aids, at Bath and the majestically named Guild of Household Dames, at Cheltenham. It is a pity that we have not a record of the principal's parting words of advice to her tremulous Household Dames before sending them out into a world which wanted only household drudges. In the main, the most successful and contented lady helps were those who secured posts as companions with tolerant old ladies employing no other domestic help.

Another school of thought rejected the whole idea of lady helps as intolerable and against the natural order. Surely the solution to the servant problem was not to reach higher but to reach lower? Of what use were parish institutions if they could not be made to yield a supply of domestics? 'In the future we will draw our servants from the Union,' declared Mrs Eliot James, in *Our Servants: Their Duties To Us And Ours To Them* (1883). They would first have to go through the 'purifying process of boarding out.' This experiment, as we have seen, was tried in the previous century and all too few orphans survived the purifying process; but in Scotland, in the nineteenth century, a system of putting out orphans to foster-mothers in the country had worked tolerably well, and the products of such training had been found places in England and Ireland. The idea was to give the feel of home life to those who would otherwise be pariahs. England had pauper schools where children were industrially trained, a more expensive system than that of boarding out. Mrs James's idea was that ladies, instead of joing in the hue and cry against servants, should help to turn orphans into useful members of society. They should not be too proud to read to servants who were unable to do so.

The problem of training up workhouse girls was one which caused concern to the Girls' Friendly Society (founded 1875). 'They are too frequently the offspring of sin,' said the Society's journal in 1880; moreover, many of them laboured under 'the sad heritage of an inherited disposition to vice.' In the workhouse they acquired 'a hopeless sort of knowledge with no spirit in it.' They tended to grow up dull and heavy, knowing nothing of a life of freedom, but they picked up some of the arts of deceit, as in the hoodwinking of workhouse inspectors. At the age of thirteen (fourteen in some urban workhouses) they were deemed ready for service, but the only available places were those which had been rejected for good reasons by girls who could afford to pick and choose. The sight of even modest luxury and plenty demoralised the orphan girls. Accustomed to seeing their diet carefully weighed out, they were often unable to resist the temptations of a well-stocked larder; even if they did not raid the larder, they ate wolfishly whatever was given them. They picked up pretty objects they were not supposed to touch and tried on clothes they found lying about, almost as if they were South Sea Islanders and not the product of a benevolent workhouse system. They were ignorant of the names and functions of many ordinary household articles; they had scrubbed floors but had never cleaned carpets or polished mahogany; they had washed heavy crockery, not delicate glasses. For their shortcomings, the girls would be dismissed by impatient mistresses, possibly with a passport to ruin in the shape of an indifferent character. Others returned to the workhouse at the age of seventeen or eighteen, unwanted and not infrequently pregnant, or consumptive, or both. In the servants' hall they were looked on without sympathy. 'I never knew a servant from an orphanage or institution shine in my time and they were often given the cold shoulder by others,' writes William Lanceley, a former servant.[1]

The chief merit of orphan girls was that, being simple-minded, they were easily cheated of their wages. Relieving officers were supposed to see that they were well and fairly treated and the associates of the Girls' Friendly Society also undertook to visit them. If a girl lost her moral character, she lost the attentions of the Girls' Friendly Society; but by that time she probably did not care. One difficulty was to keep workhouse girls out of the hands of relatives who were on the look-out for an unpaid drudge, but who were not willing to 'give her a good home' until she was old enough to slave.

[1] *From Hall Boy to House Steward* (1925).

In London orphan girls were looked after by the Metropolitan Association for Befriending Young Servants. The minimum wage specified was £5 a year and there was a stipulation that time off should be allowed on Sundays and that girls should be regularly visited by members of the Association. Records were kept of girls' behaviour. If they failed in two situations, they might be sent to a training home for a year, a proceeding which usually had good results. The Association also maintained a lodging-house for girls out of work; it had free registry offices all over London; and it had a sick fund to which girls were invited to subscribe.

As the shortage of good servants grew more acute, private registry offices came in for more and more criticism. While they no longer trafficked in dishonour, they had an interest in maintaining a rapid turnover in servants, since each replacement meant an additional fee. To mistresses, good or bad, they offered an inexhaustible supply of trained maids who did not exist, and to maids they offered high wages which were equally unobtainable. In the main, their chief source of revenue was the bad employer. There was a saying 'When down and out, start an agency for servants.' Some of the more responsible registries tried to clean up their profession, but with little success. Between 1905 and 1910 the London County Council succeeded in enforcing a scheme of compulsory registration for agencies and imposed rules for their operation.

Amid all the welter of talk about the Servant Problem, one judgment, by a man who had taken the trouble to study the issues for himself, stands out conspicuously. It is that of Charles Booth, whose famous survey *Life and Labour in London* appeared in 1889. Domestic service, he points out, revolts those who are accustomed to free speech and bold criticism.

'It is, in fact, almost necessary to have an inherited aptness for the relationship involved—a relationship very similar in some respects to that subsisting between Sovereign and subject. From both servant and subject there is demanded an all-pervading attitude of watchful respect accompanied by a readiness to respond at once to any gracious advance that may be made without ever presuming or for a moment "forgetting ourselves." It is a fine line not to be overstepped in either case without risk of humiliation, but those, whether in courts or households, who are gifted with the tact or the experience to tread safely are not only able to keep with perfect comfort within the line, but even acquire an exceptional dignity of their own which is very far removed from servility. But this perfection of personal relationship in domestic service is a rare flower and very vile weeds grow in the same soil.'

Booth deals with the servant problem in London only. Of the female servants in rough single-handed places—that is, the homes of artisans and well-paid labourers—he says that those who remain in such employment as mature women are, as a rule, either incapable or of doubtful character. They come from homes with a low standard of behaviour and cleanliness, and often the homes to which they go are not much better. On the next grade are the servants who are daughters of artisans or policemen, who work for the wives of small clerks, women who often take great pride in their houses. These servants look for places only when times are slack in factories or they feel like a change.

Among the lower class of servants Booth discerns a very independent spirit. They will arrange to take a place, and then fail to turn up, having changed their minds or decided the neighbourhood is too far away. 'Another curious feature is the frequency with which girls will run away from their places instead of giving notice of leaving, due, it seems, to a feeling of alarm at the formality of giving notice.'

Booth notes that menservants are vanishing from all but the most wealthy households. Because of restricted accommodation, coupled with high living, footmen are much addicted to drink. 'As failures, male servants are perhaps the most hopeless of all failures and are the source from which the ranks of cab runners[1] and sandwichmen are, it is said, most largely recruited.'

A butler contributed a far from flattering picture of his fellows to the *Nineteenth Century* in 1892. 'I will begin,' he said, 'by accepting the general verdict and at once admitting that the average manservant is a very poor creature indeed. Aim

[1] These were men who ran behind cabs bound from railway stations to the suburbs in the hope of picking up tips by unloading baggage.

he has none beyond that of gaining a sordid livelihood.' In his
spare time the manservant drank, gambled; his ambition never
rose beyond owning an inn or lodging-house. He entered
service for the same reasons that his master's sons entered the
Church: he was fit for nothing better. Though his duties were
light, he was fed like a navvy on beef and beer, 'the coarse fare
of the Middle Ages.' Those who could not face endless cold
joints had the choice of going hungry or pilfering from the
family dishes. Copious beer for servants was the cause of
'disgusting animalism,' but at least it was a solace against bore-
dom. A manservant's duties were so easy that they could be as
easily performed drunk as sober.

   With the new century, however, a new and more responsible
manservant was beginning to enter the service of the rich: the
chauffeur. Although he wore livery, he preferred to think of
himself as a gifted artisan rather than as a servant.
   The first 'shuvvers,' as they were dubbed, were French, for
the sufficient reason that most of the early cars were French.
Their mechanical knowledge was sound, but their manners
were indifferent; they omitted to shave, they reported for duty
in clothes covered with grease, they smoked incessantly and
they drove with unnecessary dash, raising the bile of other road
users. Also, they were ruthless in squeezing commissions from
garage men. Though manifestly too big for their boots, they
had to be tolerated because they were the only persons capable
of keeping a car on the road. By about 1905 the proportion of
foreign drivers was diminishing, but the name 'chauffeur' was
still borne by their native successors. These were recruited,
very often, from bicycle works or car factory and were
untrained in the ways of personal service; but at least they
were more adaptable than the Frenchmen. Very few chauffeurs
came from the ranks of coachmen and grooms, who deeply
despised the new form of transport.
   The rich man's motor-car, like his carriage, had a 'box' which
the chauffeur shared with a footman, an observance which was
kept up until 1914. Usually, the vehicle required a good deal
of maintenance, and for this reason, but more especially on
grounds of prestige, the early chauffeurs were indignant that

they should be expected to dig gardens, polish boots, chop fire-wood and ring church bells, all for 30s. or £2 a week. The posts of chauffeur-valet and chauffeur-gardener ought to be 'left for the Chinese or other amiable aliens,' advised a writer in 1905.[1] But masters were unwilling to concede that looking after a single motor-car could be a full-time occupation for an able-bodied man; and the masters won. They then grumbled because their chauffeur-footmen introduced the odour of petrol to the dinner table, as their groom-footmen had once brought the odour of the stables.

The author of *The Chauffeur's Companion* (1909), calling him-self 'A Four-Inch Driver,' said that more chauffeurs lost their positions through rudeness than through neglect of their vehicles. 'Let not the chauffeur be offended if his master is not inclined to listen to his conversation and tells him so,' said the writer. He also informed his readers that it was their duty, when fetching guests from the station, to carry the luggage upstairs and free it of any heavy straps.

Passengers had to be prepared for some exciting manœuvres. The author of *The Chauffeur's Companion* said:

'If . . . on a fairly broad and slippery road you have the alternative of going on and killing someone, or stopping, and you find you cannot stop, there is one desperate remedy which may or may not come off, and that is to try and swing the car round with the bonnet pointing to where the back was. To do this (and I only advise it in cases of absolutely dire necessity) swing your steering wheel hard round and at the same time time open your throttle and jam in your clutch with a jerk. This should skid the car and when you are round you must get the wheel over on the other lock, and head her straight along the road again. The impetus of the car forcing her in the original direction and the engine pushing her the reverse way (when you have got her round) will neutralise each other and she should stop almost dead.'

The short-lived *Professional Chauffeurs' Club Journal*, launched in 1914, deplored the fact that over the years an undue number of 'wasters' and 'rotters' had been attracted into the ranks of chauffeurs. 'When Tommy, the bad boy of the

[1] A. E. S. Craig: *Motor Driving for a Living.*

family, has received the Order of the Boot from everyone in the neighbourhood who has been weak enough "to give him another chance," his fond mama, who is the only person who realises the awful way in which he is misunderstood, gets an inspiration and says, "Let us make him a shuvver," and forthwith it is done.'

A few years earlier, according to the *Journal*, feckless persons like this would have been packed off to Canada, and good riddance to them.

XVII

SPECTRE OF CHANGE

THE suggestion that a middle-class family could re-shape its
life in order to do without servants was not one which the
Edwardians liked to contemplate. Lady Bunting, writing
in the *Contemporary Review* in 1910, invited sympathy for the
mistress temporarily without servants: 'No one to cook the dinner,
answer the door, attend to the children and carry out the many
other requirements of an ordinary household. In many cases
the mistress is absolutely incapable of taking on the duties
which the servant has done and she finds herself far more of a
"dependant" than the servant, who can go forth with light
heart and soon find another place . . .'

This reads comically enough now, but there were thousands
of mistresses who had hardly done a hand's turn in their life.
Gwen Raverat, a grand-daughter of Charles Darwin, in her
most agreeable book *Period Piece*, introduces us to her Aunt
Ettie who, at the age of eighty-six, had never made a pot
of tea and never gone out in the dark alone, even in a cab; who
took a maid with her when she travelled by train and even when
she went to the dentist. 'I am sure that she had never sewn on
a button and I should guess that she had hardly ever even
posted a letter herself. There were always people to do these
things for her. In fact, in some ways she was very like a royal
person.' At the age of thirteen the doctor had told her to have
breakfast in bed for a time and she had had it there all her life.
These 'royal persons' never doubted that it was their right, and
even their duty, to live like this; and they usually had a cheerful
word for those who came up two flights of stairs to pass their
shawls.

The higher ranks of society were full of women who were dependent on their personal maids to a wholly ridiculous degree. Young or old, they were incapable of dressing their own hair; 'a great many of my generation cannot do it up even now,' says Lady Clodagh Anson, writing in 1957.[1] Nor could they dress or undress for formal occasions without assistance, for the *fin-de-siècle* corset was an intractable engine. It was intended, according to the philosophers, to show that the wearer was a woman who in no circumstances was to be expected to work, or to do things for herself. To be able to move with any grace in corset and hobble skirt required deportment lessons. At this period, as Sir Edward Hulton recalls,[2] working women were quite unable to ape their superiors with success; they could pinch their waists but they could not move in hobble skirts without raising cruel mirth—unless, of course, they were ladies' maids.

Neither the upper-class nor the middle-class mistress could conceive that it might be possible to reorganise life in such a way that servants would be unnecessary and that it would not be a betrayal of civilisation if a gentlewoman boiled an egg for herself. The idea of scrapping all the ornamental rubbish from the drawing-room, leaving a room that could be dusted in two minutes, would have seemed preposterous; still harder to envisage was a state of degradation in which the mistress of the house would wash the dishes and the master would wipe them.

Labour-saving devices were coming in only slowly. Gas lighting had replaced candles and electricity was replacing gas, though not necessarily in the servants' quarters; and gas stoves were ousting those ranges that swallowed coal by the hundredweight. Baths with piped hot water were beginning to save the housemaid one of her major chores; yet how slow were the bulk of householders to instal bathrooms! The ritual of the hip bath on its mat in the bedroom, with the steaming jug of hot water and the neat, warm towels, and—with luck—a bright fire was one the older generation were reluctant to give up. What was the use, they asked, of installing expensive drudgery-saving devices when the whole function of servants was to do the drudgery? This argument applied with special force to the vacuum cleaner, which arrived in the early years of the century. It was an expensive, extremely cumbrous apparatus and even in its more sophisticated later guise it was looked on with distrust both by mistresses and the older generation of maids (it would be a gross error to suppose that all servants welcomed the devices that were intended to save their energies). The telephone had arrived, to make the footman even more super-fluous; but, of course, there had to be somebody to answer it. Advertisers had begun to make the most of labour-saving soaps, labour-saving polishes and labour-saving foods. Maids were portrayed excitedly holding up tins of the latest cleanser, with the same light of glory in their eyes that is now to be discerned in the housewives in television commercials. 'The *servant problem* is helped by the advent of ———'s Porage Oats, which require no over-night preparation, no *soaking*, no trouble . . . the servant appreciates the saving of time in the morning,' ran a typical advertisement.

The most important labour-saving device of all was still lacking: a sensibly designed house. True, the basement fashion was going out, but the new Edwardian houses were not con-ceived to be run without servants. In America, at the start of the nineteenth century, society had turned to boarding-houses; now at the end of the nineteenth century, Britain turned to flats. And not only to flats. In the *Nineteenth Century*, in 1893, a writer put forward what he called a reasoned plan for doing without servants and establishing a central restaurant for several blocks and streets of the London West End. His estimate for building and fitting a supply kitchen with a manager's residence, stabling, steam engine, boilers, refrigerators, ovens, lifts and so on to supply 3500 persons a day was £43,000. This included the supply of fifty heated carts and one hundred horses to carry the cooked meals to the homes of subscribers, who would have gas-heated closets. This was but one of many proposals for communal living, either in 'federalised' flats, or boarding-houses.

The new blocks of flats which began to soar at the start of the present century still contained rudimentary quarters for servants; and in the view of *The Lancet* in 1905 these quarters

were often abominable enough to merit the attention of Medical
Officers of Health. Perhaps the slaveys in the hot attics of Eaton
Square or the shrubbery-guarded dank basements of Clapham
were better off after all. *The Lancet* expressed surprise that
persons who had so far succeeded in life as to pay rents of
£150 to £250 a year (very high rents in those days) 'should be
content to house their servants under conditions in which they
can never enjoy direct sunlight and where even diffused light
is but a matter of a few hours daily in midsummer.' It was lack
of sun, bad ventilation and cramped quarters that caused 'the
pale-faced, anaemic appearance sometimes seen in servants in
the employment of the better-off classes.' The national press
took up this scandal, discovering, for example, maids' rooms
containing two ship-style bunks against opposite walls with
only enough room between for one person to dress at a
time.

Perhaps the answer was for servants to live out, in hostels?
This proposal had been frequently discussed, but was usually
criticised on the grounds that no one could be sure that women
servants would go straight to their hostels; that they might be
waylaid on the way there; and that they would not reach their
place of employment in the morning in time to light fires and
make the breakfast. The real objection, perhaps, was that housewives liked to have servants under their roof all the time, ready
to answer the bell at any hour.

The servant problem, by almost any standards, had become
a Great Human Drama and one observer was convinced that it
was a drama eminently suited to the stage. Constantly, Max
Beerbohm urged playwrights to tackle a theme which had
scarcely been touched since *High Life Below Stairs*. In 1902 he
was suitably delighted by Sir James Barrie's comedy *The
Admirable Crichton*, the message of which is that, given a change
of surroundings, the servile may by their innate worth readily
establish an ascendancy over those who tyrannise over them.
British audiences do not seem to have resented this heresy—
after all, it was only a play—but Barrie was fascinated to hear
that people had walked out of the theatre in New York because

a fashionable actor, Gillette, had so far demeaned himself as to play the part of the butler.[1]

Crichton is (in his own words) 'the son of a butler and a lady's maid—perhaps the happiest of all combinations.' He is devotedly attached to Lord Loam who, 'in his opinion, has but one fault, he is not sufficiently contemptuous of his inferiors.' Lord Loam causes intense embarrassment and friction among his domestic staff by holding a monthly tea party in the drawing-room at which family and servants are under orders to fraternise.[2] 'Remember this, Crichton,' says Lord Loam, 'for the time being you are my equal. I shall soon show you whether you are not my equal. Do as you are told.' His lordship's precious daughters have been warned that 'the first who condescends, recites.' The conversational exchanges are on the level of Lord Brocklehurst's enquiry to Tweeny:[3] 'What sort of weather have you been having in the kitchen?' A lady's maid is offended because Lord Loam asks a kitchen wench to have a second cup of tea before he asks her. Crichton admits to Lady Mary that he had to dismiss a pageboy after the previous month's party, because in an outburst of equality the lad called him Crichton. His summing-up of the situation is: 'His lordship may compel us to be equal upstairs, but there will never be equality in the servants' hall.'

The Admirable Crichton helped to establish the literary convention of the drily witty, accomplished and always 'deadpan' manservant. In eighteenth-century plays, witty butlers are a rarity, but Oscar Wilde's butlers figure in exchanges like this, from *An Ideal Husband:* 'Lord Goring: Extraordinary thing about the lower classes in England—they are always losing their relations. Phipps: Yes, my lord. They are extraordinarily fortunate in that respect.' Mr P. G. Wodehouse's Jeeves, not a butler but a gentleman's gentleman, is a continuation of the tradition. No good purpose can be served by trying to find social significance in these stage and literary menservants. If they have helped to give gentlemen's gentlemen a reputation for

[1] Cynthia Asquith: *Portrait of Barrie.*

[2] Barrie may have got this idea, says Laura, Lady Troubridge, from the Countess of Aberdeen who, rumour said, used to give drawing-room parties for those below stairs.—*Memories and Reflections.*

[3] The between-maid (see page 285).

tact, resource, omniscience and a knowledge of form (including racing form) far beyond anything they normally possess, no great harm has been done.

The early years of the new century saw two notable truces in the war between maids and mistresses.

The first occurred in 1901, just after the accession of Edward VII. Queen Alexandra, aware that domestic service was still the biggest single source of employment for women, decided that it was time something was done to honour the abigails of Britain. She therefore invited ten thousand London maids of all work to attend a series of 'Queen's Teas.' Hitherto, royalty had not shown any excessive interest in the welfare of servant girls. The Prince Consort had cut the wages of palace housemaids from £45 to £18, an act of discipline much approved by the middle classes; and the old Queen Victoria had neither wished to see housemaids nor to be seen by them. That Queen Alexandra should seek to recognise the existence of female servants was hailed as an act of most praiseworthy and liberal patronage, and the mistresses of Britain developed similar symptoms of solicitude. The only difficulty was how to make sure that no undeserving girls received the benefit of royal hospitality. At first the Bishop of London, to whom the Queen gave the task of organising the Teas, seemed to be persuaded that the choosing of the girls should be left entirely to such bodies as the Metropolitan Association for Befriending Servant Girls, the Girls' Friendly Society and the Ladies' Society for Aiding Friendless Girls, but there were demands that girls who belonged to no such societies should also be included. Eventually the Teas were held in about thirty districts of London. The Queen does not appear to have attended any of them, but the guests dutifully sang the National Anthem and sent her messages of loyalty and gratitude. All the girls paraded in their best black dresses, aprons and caps, and were waited on by ladies, wearing the finery appropriate to their station. The fare ranged from tea and buns to tea and strawberries, and the entertainment from sing-songs to roundabouts or 'a scamper through the woods.' In the Zoo Gardens torrential rain soaked the guests and bedraggled the banner: 'GOD BLESS OUR GRACIOUS QUEEN, THE GIVER OF OUR FEAST.' The Bishop of London, who dutifully addressed these gatherings, read to his dripping guests a message from the Queen expressing the hope that they were all enjoying themselves, which produced loyal laughter from under the tables. He then said he proposed to send a message to the Queen saying that they were indeed enjoying themselves very much, which produced even louder loyal laughter from under the tables. These formalities over, the company adjourned to the Lion House.

The second truce, in 1911, was sudden, spectacular and, as it turned out, ill-founded. Weeping affectionately on each other's shoulders, the old enemies united in shrill resentment against a common enemy: the Chancellor of the Exchequer.

Mr Lloyd George, it appeared, was bringing in a National Insurance Bill which threatened the sanctity of the British home. He was demanding no less than threepence a week from employers and servants alike in order to insure the latter against the hardships of ill-health, which was a damnable insult to those millions of generous employers who nursed their sick servants through thick and thin. He proposed to collect this money by the foul and unhygienic method of making mistresses or servants, or both, lick stamps and stick them on cards, as the disgusting Germans did. It was the responsibility of the employer to collect the threepence from the servant; thus the ladies of Britain would be tax-gatherers in their own homes.

The clamour against the Bill was led by the Northcliffe newspapers, and in the view of Mr Lloyd George it was 'the meanest agitation which has disfigured the annals of the press.' Among the supposed perils of the Chancellor's plan were that it would lead to wholesale sacking of servants as soon as they became sick, and that inferior State-appointed doctors would be appointed to treat them. But there was another, perhaps graver, danger. According to 'A Solicitor,' who was privileged to write the *Daily Mail's* lead story one day, inspectors would have powers under the Bill to enter any drawing-room in the land and order the staff up from the basement to show their cards and be questioned. The cook might be in the middle

The pleasures of polishing

of a *soufflé*, but the Bill said the inspector must not be 'wilfully delayed.' If the inspector, looking through the window, saw a gardener busy in the flower beds he could summon him too, 'muddy boots and all.' He could also send for the French governess and, since it was unlikely that he would know any French, call upon the mistress to interpret. As it happened, Mr Lloyd George had already tabled an amendment to remove any threat to the nation's drawing-rooms, but it was a good story while it lasted.

The readers of the *Daily Mail* outdid the indignation of its leader writer. Rita, 'the famous novelist,' called for a strike of mistresses against the tax and received many promises of support. One came from a woman who said she had provided the best medical attention for her servants for more than seventy years. She would refuse to pay any tax, or any fine for refusing to do so; 'it remains to be seen whether an aged English gentlewoman will be dragged off to prison in order to force her to pay an infamous tax.'

A reader wrote: 'If the Insurance Bill is passed, I shall hold myself both legally and morally discharged from the slightest obligation to look after my domestic servant in future.' Another said: 'My intention is to give my servants notice and then to re-engage them (or substitutes) at a wage reduced by the amount of insurance I shall have to pay. I do this because the insurance is supposed to be for the servants' good, not mine.' Said yet another: 'Many of my friends assure me that if this odious tax becomes law they will not renew the leases of their houses but will live in boarding-houses or apartments.'

A number of mistresses had no doubt that, if the Bill was passed, servants would stipulate, when applying for jobs, that their insurance contributions should be paid by the employer, as already happened in Germany. Day after day the *Daily Mail* printed a large reproduction of a German servant's insurance card, as a reminder of the shame to which Britain was descending.

The Medical Officer of Health for Onsett, Essex, detected a danger that others had missed. Millions were to be called upon to lick stamps, irrespective of the state of their health. 'Will not this act as a disseminator of such dread scourges as con-

sumption, diphtheria, smallpox and scarlet fever? On whom
will the duty devolve of disinfecting cards stamped by a consumptive mistress or master?' He himself would have no
hesitation in destroying all stamped cards found in an infected
house. This danger occupied many who had never worried
about the risk of infection by sticking postage stamps on
envelopes and who assumed there was no other way of moisten-
ing a stamp than with the tongue.

Cartoonists were much stimulated by the controversy. One of
them, wide of the target, showed a row of bright, clean servant
girls ('Those who pay') and a row of down-at-heel pipe-smoking
loafers ('those who will receive'). Haselden in the *Daily Mirror*
portrayed a maid protesting that 'at my other places they kept
a boy to lick the stamps'; a doctor examining the tongue of a
page—'just a little gum poisoning'; and a man saying to his
wife, 'I wish you'd tell cook to be more careful, my dear. This
is the third time I have found a stamp in my soup.'

Obviously the agitation, to be really successful, needed the
support of servants themselves. One householder reported that
his cook was already most indignant at the idea of paying
other people's sick bills. Letters began to appear from servants,
or bearing the joint signatures of mistresses and maids. All over
the country, reported A. A. Milne in *Punch*, mistresses and
servants were asking each other how to spell 'scandalous.'

The servants who joined in the agitation, or who appeared to
join in it, were of various categories: those who had been
looked after generously in wealthy homes and considered it
unlikely that Lloyd George would provide them with the soups,
jellies and port wine to which they had been accustomed in
illness; those who thought it tactful to be indignant if the mistress was indignant; those who resented the fundamental
notion of taxation; and those who believed that domestic
servants were a caste apart, not to be bullied by politicians or
anyone else.

Not all servants, of course, were taken in by the agitation.
Many thought that a proposal which roused their mistresses to
such a pitch of fury must be fundamentally a sound idea. The
notion of being paid 7s. 6d. a week sick benefit for twenty-six
weeks, with free medical attention, seemed on the whole better

than being cast adrift with a high temperature and one month's wages. Before the furore started, the *Daily Mail* had published letters from medical men telling how some householders discharged their responsibilities towards their servants. A Surrey doctor said that when, after being called to attend a servant, he sent in his bill to the householder, he would receive a curt note from her saying she 'never pays the servants' bills,' or 'the maid in question has left and was a very unsatisfactory person,' or 'as far as I am aware I never sent for you and thus cannot be responsible.' A London doctor said that a mistress would send for him and then, after a few visits, the maid would express the hope that the bill would be a modest one, as she would have to pay it herself. In such circumstances, he thought, it would be more honest for a mistress to call in a doctor whose fees were more within the range of the patient's purse; presumably, a 'sixpenny doctor.'

In the Liberal press Lloyd George's Bill aroused as much fervour as it inspired distaste in the *Daily Mail*. Here were to be found letters like that from a former poor law guardian who had seen dozens of sick servants turned out into workhouse infirmaries, not from heartlessness, but from inability on the householder's part to pay for treatment. A medical reader of the *Daily News* defended the Bill on the grounds that 'the growth of wealth and large establishments, the impersonal relations between employer and employed have converted domestic service and servants into mere drudgery machines out of whom is to be got the maximum of work with the minimum of pay, personal consideration and leisure.' Others pointed out that under the existing system servants were much addicted to self-medication, that they visited the doctor as seldom as they could and usually when their symptoms had been badly neglected. Only the very good cook was sure of getting her job back after a spell in hospital.

Mere press agitation was not enough for the ladies who opposed Lloyd George's Bill. Petitions were got up and fighting funds were raised. The ordinary mistress who had no strong views on the issue would usually sign a petition if the lady presenting it was a person of good social standing, and she would summon her servants to sign too if the caller suggested it. In these circumstances not many servants refused, but some did. The climax of the campaign was a mass protest meeting when, in the Chancellor's words, 'the domestic servants drove up in their limousines to the Albert Hall to protest against their mistresses paying threepence a week.' Organised by the Dowager Lady Desart and Lady Brassey, it was, according to *The Times*, the most amazing meeting staged in the history of the Albert Hall. Twenty thousand women turned up on a raw November night, and ten thousand could not get in. The speeches were punctuated by shouts of 'We won't pay,' and every mention of Lloyd George was booed or greeted with 'Taffy was a thief.' An organist playing patriotic airs was also booed when, in an absent-minded moment, he struck up 'Men of Harlech.' The speakers ranged from a manservant, representing one thousand West End servants, who said that when he had been ill his mistresses had called in Sir Victor Horsley and Sir Frederick Treves, to Mr Hilaire Belloc, who discerned in the Bill a capitalist plot, to be financed by the servants, for destroying the unions. Cheers greeted a reference by Lady Desart to 'that beautiful intimacy which had hitherto so often existed between mistresses and servants,' an indication of the unusual climate of the day. By what right, demanded Lady Desart, echoing the *Daily Mail*, did the Chancellor decide to make every mistress a tax-gatherer? Would it not lead, in households, to endless wrangling, ill-feeling, hatred and malice? 'Come the three corners of the world in arms,' she quoted, 'and we will shock them.'

Two days earlier Lloyd George, at his own invitation, had received a party of mistresses and maids at the Treasury, and had gone to great pains to enlighten them on the true nature of his proposal. The leaders of the agitation had not seen fit to attend; their attitude seems to have been 'Don't confuse us with the facts.' Besides, they needed all their energies for the Albert Hall. In Parliament, after the Treasury meeting, Lloyd George said: 'I observed a great deal of enlightenment appearing on the faces of the domestic servants who were present, not unmixed with surprise, when I told them accurately what the benefits were. They were not so loud in their protests at the end of the meeting as they were at the beginning.'

The agitation continued, with slowly diminishing fervour, for weeks. After the Bill became law, there were old servants who said it had killed the personal touch between the Quality and the poor. The last word may be left to Sir Winston Churchill. In *My Early Life* he describes how he travelled up from Sandhurst to attend the last illness of his childhood nurse, Mrs Everest, and to enlist a specialist to attend her. He says: 'When I think of the fate of poor old women, so many of whom have no one to look after them and nothing to live on at the end of their lives, I am glad to have had a hand in all that structure of pensions and insurance which no other country can rival and which is especially a help to them.'

XVIII

'THE FINEST SPECTACLE'

RIGHT down to 1914, the houses of the aristocracy
continued to attract the aristocracy of domestic service,
including the type of lady's maid who insisted on serving a titled mistress because she could not bear to go into the
steward's room last.

For the distinguished visitor, it was all highly pleasurable.
Disraeli, after staying at a stately seat, is reputed to have said:
'Good-bye, my dear lord, you have shown me the finest
spectacle these islands can afford—a great nobleman living at
home among his own people.' The old order changed but slowly.
Each Christmas the same 'God bless' banners were put up in
the servants' hall, the same loyal tenants gratefully accepted
their gifts or dress lengths and their children were called to
order if they seemed insufficiently respectful. In many of these
houses footmen still put powder on their heads; though
grumbles were heard, in the 'nineties, from a few who found
it tiresome to have to wash their hair whenever they wished
to walk out.

In the Great Queen's reign there were still dukes rich enough
to indulge the most awesome eccentricities, among them the
fifth Duke of Portland, William John Cavendish Bentinck-Scott,
of Welbeck Abbey, who died in 1879. Though 'handsome, kind
and clever' in youth, the Duke developed the exaggerated love
of privacy which had marked his mother. With it he combined
a passion for grandiose building. The result was to be seen in
the famous subterranean suites at Welbeck and, not least, in
the carriage tunnel, more than a mile in length, dug under the
park to allow him to reach his seat unseen. When he drove out,

according to Augustus Hare, he did so in a black coach like a
hearse with blinds drawn, pulled by black horses. At night, if
he chose to walk abroad, he would be preceded by a woman
servant at a distance of exactly forty yards, carrying a lantern.
She was forbidden to speak to him. When he visited his London
home, the Duke travelled in a carriage, with blinds drawn,
which was loaded on a railway truck. Before it was due to arrive
at Harcourt House, in Cavendish Square, all the servants were
ordered out of the way (the garden had high screens round it).
Whenever the Duke required medical attention, the doctor
came to the door of the room and asked diagnostic questions
by way of the valet, who felt his master's pulse when requested
to do so. (This was somewhat in the fashion of an earlier
Countess of Carlisle, who was too proud to allow the local
doctor to speak to her, except through her personal maid.
Once, after a frustrating interview, she instructed her maid:
'Inform the doctor he may bleed the Countess of Carlisle.')

It is hard to know what Ude or Felix would have thought
about the Duke of Portland's kitchens, which were in a
converted riding stable. Dinner was sent, not up, but down—
down into a heated truck which then ran on rails for 150 yards
to the dining-room. It was the Duke's whim to have a chicken
roasting on a spit perpetually, so that at any time he could send
for one. He replaced the riding school by an enormous new one,
containing 4000 gas jets (8000 by Augustus Hare's count), and
at his death left ninety-four horses, attended by nearly fifty
grooms and stablemen. In the grounds he installed a skating
rink, on which his servants were expected to disport. According
to a family memoir,[1] if he came across a maid sweeping a
corridor he ordered her out to skate, whether she had any
desire to do so or not. In lesser homes, mistresses were often
indignant at the mere idea that their maids should wish to go to
ice-rinks.

Of Welbeck, Augustus Hare wrote: 'All is vast, splendid and
utterly comfortless. One could imagine no more awful and
ghastly fate than waking up one day and finding oneself Duke of
Portland and master of Welbeck.'[2] The sixth Duke, to whom

[1] *Men, Women and Things: Memoirs of the Sixth Duke of Portland.*
[2] *The Story of My Life.*

this ghastly fate fell, had a heavy struggle making the place habitable; his predecessor had lived in four or five rooms in the west wing.

It had always been the custom in great houses that servants, more especially women servants, should keep out of sight as far as possible, but in some houses the custom had hardened into a rule, which was liable to be severely enforced. Mrs Edward Ward, the artist, who was a guest of the third Lord Crewe, an aged and eccentric bachelor, reports that no house-maids were ever to be seen at Crewe Hall except in chapel, 'when a great number would muster, only to disappear mysteriously directly the service was ended.' One morning, needing the services of a housemaid, Mrs Ward looked out of her bedroom door and saw a black dress 'flash down the corridor' and vanish. She gave chase but in vain. The incident seemed so odd that she mentioned it to the housekeeper, an elderly cousin of Lord Crewe. 'What, don't you know Lord Crewe's orders?' said the housekeeper. 'None of the servants are allowed to be seen by visitors; if they break the rules they are dismissed. Lord Crewe hates women and thinks all his guests must detest them too.'[1] From the servants' point of view this ban was probably more tolerable than the rule, inflexibly enforced, that no fires were to be lit in Crewe Hall except between December 1 and May 1, irrespective of the state of the weather.

The tenth Duke of Bedford (d. 1893) also hated the sight of women servants. 'To cross his path,' says Lady Troubridge, 'unless he wished to see you, was little short of a crime, and any of the women servants who met him after twelve o'clock in the day, when their duties might be supposed to be done, were liable to instant dismissal; yet he exacted almost royal observances from them . . .' The Duke was 'decidedly peculiar,' in Lady Troubridge's view. She thought he was actuated by 'some great hidden pride in his own rank and station in life, some consciousness that he was set apart from the rest of the world by it.'[2] The next Duke of Bedford carried his dislike of being seen by underlings to a perhaps greater

[1] Mrs E. M. Ward: *Memories of Ninety Years.*
[2] Laura, Lady Troubridge: *Memories and Reflections.*

pitch: the electricians wiring Woburn Abbey used to
bundle into a cupboard when their lookout reported his
approach.[1]

The diaries of the peripatetic Augustus Hare give admirable
glimpses of the degree of state maintained in the great houses
during the latter part of the nineteenth century. He tells of
Lady Llanover, ordering her footmen and maids, the latter in
traditional Welsh dress, to perform reels and candle dances for
a royal visitor, and sending two footmen to lay red carpet on
the local railway station wherever it seemed that her visitor
might step. He tells of Worth, the excessively luxurious home
of the Montefiores, where the servants had their own billiard
tables, ballroom, theatre and pianos and were 'arrogant and
presumptuous in proportion'; and of Baddesley Clinton, proud
of its priest-holes, with 'a congregation of maids veiled like
nuns' at evening prayers, and a veiled housekeeper reading
prayers and litany in 'a priest-like monotone.'[2]

Hare had a sharp eye for the way prayers were conducted—
or neglected. One of his best stories is about Lord Cardwell's
valet who, tendering his resignation, explained: 'Your lordship
will repeat every morning—"We have done those things we
ought not to have done, and have left undone those things
which we ought to have done." The valet admitted that he
had done things in the former category, but utterly denied that
he had failed to do anything he should have done—'and I will
not stay here to hear it said.'[3]

Belvoir Castle, where an earlier duke had trained his servants
on the guns, kept up medieval observances even in the 'nineties.
Hare heard the soft-footed watchmen calling the 'all's well' at
hourly intervals through the night; and so did the young
Diana Cooper, who as a child was a guest of her grandfather
at Belvoir. Throughout the day, she recalls, bearded giants
'with a general Bill Sikes appearance' bore cans of water, on
yokes, to the upper rooms of the castle and in their wake trod
coalmen. A wizened old 'gong man,' white-bearded to the
waist, shrunken in his livery, toured every corridor and turret
sounding the time for lunch, for dressing, and for dinner.

[1] John, Duke of Bedford: *A Silver-Plated Spoon.*
[2] *The Story of My Life.*   [3] *Ibid.*

(Hare says this function was performed by trumpeters, as it may have been on occasions.) When the family went for the afternoon drive the head groom stood with a bunch of carrots at the ready for the Lord of Belvoir to hand personally to his horses.[1]

Life at Longleat, in Wiltshire, has been well described by Daphne Fielding in *Before The Sunset Fades*. When she arrived there, as wife of the son of the house, she was partnered at the servants' ball by the butler, the second in the hierarchy of menservants. From her account it appears that her husband's grandmother had the coins of her spare change washed daily and the valets ironed the gentlemen's boot ribbons. Mr Randolph Churchill gives piquant glimpses of life at Knowsley, seat of the Earl of Derby, where the household expenditure before the First World War was £50,000 a year.[2] When the King and Queen arrived for the Grand National, forty guests ate in the dining-room, sixty servants in the steward's room and sixty more in the servants' hall. Not for nothing was the Earl of Derby known as the 'King of Lancashire.' At the 'Palace of the Peak,' otherwise Chatsworth, the Duke and Duchess of Devonshire welcomed their Sovereign with medieval-cum-Oriental honours: blazing fireworks and an avenue of three hundred torchmen recruited from wherever dukes recruit torchmen. The plain man's favourite 'lord' was the Earl of Lonsdale, whose equipage, drawn by matched chestnuts, and with postillions in yellow livery, stole the show at race meetings within not-so-distant memory. This was one nobleman who did not mind how many people stared at him—the more the better. To greet the Kaiser at Lowther in 1895 he sent the Quorn servants in hunting kit, followed by a squadron of Yeomanry, two blue-coated outriders, a dark phaeton in which he himself rode, and nine other vehicles, each drawn by two chestnuts driven postillion with footmen up behind;[3] all as befitted a nobleman whose North Gate was eight miles from his South Gate. Until 1914 the Earl had a private band of

[1] *The Rainbow Comes and Goes.*
[2] *Lord Derby, King of Lancashire.*
[3] Capt. Lionel Dawson, R.N.: *The Authorised Life of Hugh Lowther, Fifth Earl of Lonsdale.*

The footman at the start of the nineteenth century

twenty-four musicians on his permanent establishment, who accompanied him on his visits abroad.

The children of the rich were still brought up almost entirely by servants. That jest about the society woman who was able to greet her infant in the park only because she recognised the nurse was not so wide of the mark. Parents were persons to be greeted formally once a day, not to be climbed over and tugged about. Until children were reasonably tamed, it was for servants to bear the brunt of the attack; and when they were reasonably tamed it was time to send them off to boarding-school. The children did not resent this arrangement. In her account of her childhood at St James's Palace, Loelia, Duchess of Westminster, testifies that often 'there was plenty of fun and warmth "upstairs" or in "the back regions" ' and that 'nurses were loved as much as any mother, butlers respected more than most fathers, cook and housemaids considerably preferred to some aunts.'[1] Sir Osbert Sitwell

[1] *Grace and Favour.*

The footman's dress uniform, 1902
and at the start of the 20th century

says: 'The female child sought shelter with nurse and housekeeper and cook, the male in the pantry.' He claims to have
learned more from the instinctive wisdom of butler and footman at Renishaw than from more academic sources. Certainly
Henry Moat, Sir George Sitwell's butler who became an
innocent member of the Camorra, emerges as a very likeable
figure.[1] All too few writers recalling those times pay tribute to
menservants; the usual awards are a bouquet for Nanny and a
cabbage for the governess.

In the great homes, vails were still offered and accepted,
but there were exceptions. All over Woburn Abbey,
seat of the Dukes of Bedford, were printed notices asking
guests not to tip servants. At Mount Stewart, Lord

[1] *Left Hand, Right Hand.*

Londonderry also discouraged the practice.[1] Among the more determined gratuity-hunters were the gamekeepers who arranged the mass slaughter of pheasants and partridges. For a day's partridge shooting, the head keeper expected a tip of one sovereign; for a good day's pheasant shooting, two sovereigns. 'A gentleman who does not tip or fee up to this mark is not likely to find himself too well placed in a *battue*,' remarks an expert on the etiquette of the day.[2] It was wise, also, to show a certain open-handedness towards the servants who, in between sessions at the butts, laid out in the open air tremendous champagne luncheons, complete with plate and flowers.

Unscrupulous servants in great houses had another unofficial source of income, to judge from revelations published by *The Times* in 1911. A householder wrote to say that her butler, wishing to change his situation, advertised in the *Morning Post* and received a letter from a woman journalist representing a number of American newspapers. This letter suggested that if he had half an hour's leisure once or twice a week he might care to turn it into cash by writing her a 'long, gossipy letter' about the well-known Society people with whom he came into contact. The American press 'insisted' on having current gossip and amusing stories. 'Anything about Lady Gerard and the De Forests is "good copy" on account of the slander case between them now coming on; also about the Dillon jockey on account of the Marie Lloyd divorce suit, in which he is co-respondent; also about Lord Howard de Walden's suit for libel against Mr Lewis.' Perhaps, suggested the gossip broker, the butler might like to put her into touch with any friends of his on the staffs of Lord Howard de Walden, Lady Gerard, Baron de Forest, Sir Thomas Lipton, Sir Ernest Cassel and Mrs George Keppel, or in the employ of the Turf Club, White's, the Marlborough, Claridge's, the Savoy, the Gaiety or the Waldorf. The writer of the letter said that she regularly bought 'large quantities' of chatty letters from servants, paying liberally and settling monthly. If the butler would care to double or triple his income he should write a specimen letter and then terms could be discussed.

[1] John, Duke of Bedford: *A Silver-Plated Spoon.*
[2] 'A Member of the Aristocracy': *The Management of Servants.*

This 'abominable letter' was discussed the same day by *The Times* in an extremely angry and self-righteous leading article. Here was 'a complete revelation of a system often suspected but never so completely exposed'; here was 'a disgusting invasion of the sanctities of private life'; here was 'a lurid light upon the tastes, the ideals and the standards of life which we regret to say are fostered by a democratic press.' Only after much anxious deliberation, said *The Times*, was it decided to print the names of the Society people who were regarded as 'good copy'; they would now know that, socially speaking, there was a price on their heads. The name of the woman journalist was not published, for fear she should derive a free advertisement; she was referred to as 'Harriet ———.'

Other British newspapers expressed suitable indignation, though it is likely that several of them would secretly have welcomed the odd 'juicy bit' contributed from the pantry of a reliable butler. The *Evening Standard* thought the disclosure would do good if it discouraged guests from indulging in the sort of tittle-tattle which could be recorded by paid sneaks standing behind their chairs. The *New York Times* thought the fulminations from Printing House Square were a little forced, since everyone knew that kitchen journalism had long flourished in Britain. A reader of *The Times* contributed an apt quotation from Juvenal:

'O Corydon, Corydon, do you think the actions of the rich can be unknown? If the servants shut their mouths, the very beasts, the dogs, the posts, the marble pillars will speak out. Shut up the windows, draw the curtains close, bar the doors, put out all the lights, let all be hush, let no soul lie near; what the rich man does in the morning at three will be the talk of the next tavern before day; there you will hear the lies raised by the steward, the master cook, the butler of the family.'[1]

How much gossip was, in fact, supplied by servants to agents like 'Harriet' we can only guess. It is more probable that most of the piquant items in the press were leaked, accidentally or designedly, by guests themselves.

[1] See also Claud Cockburn on the 'Harriet' affair, *Punch*, March 15, 1961.

XIX

AMERICA CALLS FOR BUTLERS

IN 1861 there were three millionaires in America. By the century's end, there were four thousand: a buoyant, and often flamboyant, dollar aristocracy of rail operators, steel-masters, mine-owners, factory bosses, pork butchers and canners.

Whereas an English nobleman owed his lands to an ancestor who had pushed a rival off a horse, the wealthy American owed his brave new palace to a father who had broken a rival in the market. In the New World there was no hereditary aristocracy to teach form, to mould taste, to snub those whose pretensions exceeded their manners; but as it turned out there was a public opinion strong enough to discourage such antics as holding chicken and *pâté-de-foie* banquets for dogs (with a waiter to each animal) and serving up live chorus girls in pies. In their Midas dwellings the first-generation millionaires were ill at ease; it seemed to them, and still more to their better-educated sons and daughters, that the effete Europeans had the secret of what, in a later day, was to be stigmatised as gracious living. So the meat barons and the railroad kings began to import, along with other luxuries from Europe, English butlers and footmen, sometimes in matched sets, to lend much-needed dignity and efficiency to their households. Thanks to the insidious processes of democracy, it was almost impossible to find trained upper servants within America's own confines.

Even before the Civil War, leaders of New York society— the society which had snubbed Commodore Vanderbilt—had been sighing for liveried servants. George William Curtis, in his

Potiphar Papers (1856), portrays the snobbish Mrs Potiphar trying to put a manservant into feudal attire. The applicant reports for the interview in pantaloons and she is at a loss to know how to ask him to show his calves. By the 'seventies, the Revolution had been betrayed: livery was a familiar sight in New York. The sons of the rich were driven along Fifth Avenue to school in handsome carriages, accompanied by grooms; though, notoriously, the heir of John D. Rockefeller was made to walk. In their Italianate palace on Long Island the new generation of Vanderbilts could field upwards of a dozen footmen in white wigs and maroon livery; Mrs William Astor could produce an equal number in blue. Wherever the very rich congregated—New York, Newport, Saratoga—lackeys were for ever hopping down from carriages, hammering at doors, delivering cards to other lackeys and hopping up on their carriages again. By the 'eighties that ineffable dandy, Ward McAllister, who turned the American picnic into a *fête champêtre*, had created the legend of the Four Hundred (the ballroom of Mrs William Astor, his patroness, held four hundred people). It was a major dereliction not to have English servants; they were 'the expensive, smooth-running, imported mechanism without which the social race could not be run.'[1] By the end of the century American magazines were publishing picture jokes about liveried flunkeys reminiscent of those which had appeared in *Punch* fifty years earlier. It was not only in print that flunkeys were mocked. For protection against jeers and snowballs, they tended to hide their persons when opening doors. There was a type of mistress who approved of powdered hair and white stockings on the grounds that this attire kept the wearer from running about the streets.

The more austere of the imported menservants shuddered at the ways of a society which turned its tea-cups upside down, with the spoon on top, to indicate that it did not want any more tea, addressed footmen as 'waiter' and butlers as 'Jack.' In modern times, films like *Ruggles of Red Gap* have wrung most of the available laughs out of the theme of the English butler in America. But those early Ruggleses, little by little, taught their new masters some of the felicities of social intercourse,

[1] Dixon Wecter: *The Saga of American Society.*

conspiring when necessary with the female side of the house. Employers learned not to slap the backs of their servants or to invite them to sit down and have a drink, but to observe that formality and distance without which the imported servants were plainly unhappy.

It was not possible, the English butlers found, to re-create in America the system under which upper servants exacted humble deference from lower servants; but at least the little sidelines of the butler's calling could be operated with great success in this lavish society. If an employer protested at extortion, he was given to understand that he did not understand the customs of great houses and was undeserving of a butler. Yet the American *grandes dames* were not intimidated by their English menservants. Cornelius Vanderbilt, Jr, says that his mother's butler urged that in fashionable households all the bed linen should be changed daily; but his mistress ruled firmly that twice a week was often enough, even in the House of Vanderbilt.[1]

Why, the American man-in-the-street wanted to know, were such ostentatious establishments of servants necessary? Thorstein Veblen, the political economist, explained in his *Theory of the Leisure Class* (1899) that it was all part of the game of conspicuous consumption. While the possession and maintenance of 'slaves' employed in the production of goods testified to a man's wealth and prowess, the maintenance of servants who produced nothing at all testified to still higher wealth and position. Servants were necessary 'as a method of imputing pecuniary reputability to the master of the household on the ground that a given amount of time and effort is conspicuously wasted in that behalf.' Their ability to perform mechanical tasks was in itself not enough; such tasks had to be discharged with 'due form.' Indeed, thought Veblen, domestic service was a spiritual rather than a mechanical function.

'It is a serious grievance if a gentleman's butler or footman performs his duties about his master's table or carriage in such unformed style as to suggest that his habitual occupation may be ploughing or sheep herding. Such bungling work would

[1] Cornelius Vanderbilt, Jr.: *The Vanderbilt Feud.*

imply inability on the master's part to procure the service of
the specially trained servants; that is to say, it would imply
inability to pay for the consumption of time, effort and
instruction required to fit a trained servant for special service
under an exacting code of forms.'

In more modest American homes, the servant problem was
now the Irish Problem. A nation which steadfastly refused to
do its own menial tasks or cook its own food was reduced to
grabbing the first simple foreigner it could find, and the
easiest to grab—but not necessarily the easiest to hold—was
Bridget.

Those Irish famines earlier in the century had flooded the
eastern seaboard with cheap and fairly docile labour. The first
Irish girls to arrive had sent back every penny they could save
to bring their relatives across, and the process had snowballed
until the 'wild Milesian features' which so distressed Carlyle
were seen everywhere in eastern America, and apprehensive
economists complained that the Irish were sending home such
a fortune in dollars as would bankrupt America. As the numbers
of the Irish grew so did their self-confidence and they became
less inclined to admit any superiority in those who employed
them. Unfortunately, their qualifications as servants were slight.

'As a cook, Bridget is an admitted failure,' wrote Edwin
Lawrence Godkin, in 1895.[1] 'No amount of teaching will make
a person a good cook who is not himself fond of good food and
has not a delicate palate.' Bridget's palate had been nourished
on boiled potatoes and the fare she found in American pantries
seemed to her the height of sophistication. Her notions of
cooking were as unformed as her manners, but housewives
nevertheless expected from her well-cooked dishes served in a
well-bred style. As they themselves were incapable of teaching
her the fine points of her art, there was a deadlock.

'In North America,' wrote Godkin, getting a male grievance
off his chest, 'as the habit of ministering to men's tastes has
become weaker, the interest in cookery has fallen off. There
are no such cooks among native American women as there
were fifty years ago; and passages in foreign cookery books

[1] *Reflections and Comments.*

which assume the existence among women of strong interest in
their husbands' and brothers' likings, and strong desire to
gratify them, furnish food for merriment in American households. Bridget, therefore, can plead first of all the general
incapacity of women as cooks.'

Bridget was in the American kitchen, not of her own volition,
but because no one else would look at the job. She was in the
position of a volunteer at a fire. 'To anyone who looks at the
matter as a moralist,' continued Godkin, 'it is hard to see why
Bridget, doing the work badly in the kitchen, is any more a
contemptible object than the American sewing girl killing herself in a garret at three dollars a week out of devotion to the
"principle of equality." '

The Bridget of the 'nineties was well familiar with the
principle of equality, which accounted for her increasingly
offhand ways, though to Godkin she seemed 'the personification
of repose, if not of comfort' to anyone who had been rash
enough to hire an American help. Was it to be expected that
she should stay servile in a land where American males set her
an example by discharging personal tasks with 'the air of doing
forced labour for a tyrannical jailer?'

From the housewife's point of view, Bridget's handicaps were
manifold. Firstly, she seemed to regard her religious life as of
more importance than her domestic observances. She was for
ever going off to Mass when she should have been lighting the
fire and she observed an inordinate number of saints' days.
Also she was incurably addicted to attending 'wakes' with 'her
own folk,' walking in monstrous processions, wallowing in shrill
emotion and returning exhausted and near-mutinous. She liked
to swig at any bottle that was not locked up and to laugh and
chat with people, including her mistress. On top of it all she
had the tolerance of dirt natural in those who had been brought
up on earthen floors; and she handled objects roughly, having
been used to the crudest of pots and pans. When she erred, her
'royal blood' would not let her accept a rebuke without flaring
up. And when teased for being Irish she would walk out in a
huff, stay with her own folk until she had worked the resentment out of her system, and then apply for another job.

The faults were not, of course, all on Bridget's side. As a rule,

she was warm-hearted and did her best by her standards, if
not 'picked on,' or if not harried and 'sauced' by children
whose unchecked impertinences were responsible for no small
part of America's servant troubles. There were housewives who
thought that, because Bridget came from the poorest country
in Europe, she could be treated as an inferior being, and that
she ought to feel gratitude to those who 'sheltered' her. One
writer speaks of her sleeping in a little black hole off the area
kitchen, with hardly a place to hang her Palm Sunday branch
or her picture of the Blessed Virgin. Was it necessary, asked
this critic, that those who did the hardest work should sleep on
the hardest beds? Why not hang up a stocking for her at
Christmas, or give her a rocking-chair?[1] These were modest
enough proposals, in all conscience, and it is hard to believe
that there were homes in which Bridget received no Christmas
present. Inevitably, a cook who was given the irreducible
minimum of comfort was likely to insist on doing the irreducible
minimum of work. Hence such exchanges as: 'Bridget, we have
some friends coming for a visit tomorrow.'—'Dade, thin, I'll be
afther laving.'

To Bridget-weary housewives in eastern America came
reports that, on the Californian coast, women had found a
new and altogether more tractable race of servants, trained
in servility and economical ways, with a natural talent for
laundering: namely, Chinese menservants. Harriet Spofford,
discussing the possibilities, doubted whether the demands of the
joss-house would cause more interference with domestic work
than the saints' days of the Irish; but how many housewives
could really accustom themselves to the sight of servants in
pigtails and trousers? Moreover, even the Chinese were wary of
being victimised. It was said that if Ay Sin was displeased with
his employer he would write in some spot where Ay Foo could
see them a few remarks describing the sort of woman she was;
Ay Foo, on reading them, would go elsewhere.[2]

How did conditions in America impress trained servants
from England? In 1913 one of them, Alfred Child, published
a booklet for the guidance of those who might wish to follow

[1] Harriet Prescott Spofford: *The Servant Girl Question* (1881).
[2] *Ibid.*

him to the New World.[1] First, he warned that they should be careful not to give themselves airs, representing themselves as necessarily better than Irish, Germans or Swedes. The great attraction in America, he emphasised, was the growing use of labour-saving devices. Houses were steam-heated, even in the servants' quarters—'one never sees an open coal fire, that bane of the housemaid' (clearly, Child was accustomed to working in better-off households). Vacuum cleaners were 'quite the rule'; some houses had electric buffers for cleaning the silver; nearly all houses had elevators for both passengers and goods; inter-communication telephones obviated much running up and down stairs;[2] and the ritual of tin baths and pails of hot water had been superseded. All servants were equal before their employer. The second footman was not expected to open the door of the servants' hall for the butler, who was not called 'sir,' and there was no silence rule at the servants' table. The custom was to address servants, even cooks, by an unprefixed surname. Wages to be expected were: maids, £5 to £6 monthly; cooks, £8 to £16 or £20; ladies' maids, £6 to £8; nurses, £5 to £8; butlers, £12 to £16; footmen, £7 to £11 (the men had no morning clothes supplied, no laundry money and no beer money).

Girls wishing to emigrate from Britain were warned that they would find it almost impossible to enter America if they travelled third class (Cunard third fares by *Lusitania*, *Mauretania* and *Aquitania* were £8 5s). They were urged to travel second class (£13) under the auspices of the Girls' Friendly Society or Travellers' Aid Society, whose representatives would meet them in New York. These societies apparently were not allowed to meet girls travelling third class.

Liberty lifted her lamp beside the golden door, but she had a prejudice against excessively thrifty housemaids.

[1] *Domestic Service in America.*

[2] A Western Electric advertisement in 1910 showed a housewife standing proudly before an inter-phone push-button system which linked her with Hall, Stable, Laundry, Maid, Den, Kitchen, Bedroom, Library, Dining-room, Garage, Nursery, Butler.

XX

'*STOP THEIR DOLE!*'

THE war of 1914–18 gave women servants a welcome new excuse for walking out on their mistresses. It was more patriotic, as well as more profitable, to fill shells than to wash dishes, to milk cows than to pass shawls. It was also more companionable. As for footmen, only the oldest stayed in service. Sir Edward Hulton tells of a *nouveau riche* hostess who replaced her set of footmen with a row of handsome, strapping 'foot girls,' who wore blue livery jackets, striped waistcoats, stiff shirts, short blue skirts, black silk stockings and patent leather shoes with three-inch heels.[1]

During these catastrophic years great households were dispersed and many were never re-formed again. Castles and mansions, once self-supporting, were thrown on the property market. In middle-class homes mistresses perforce learned to cook and discovered how ill-designed their kitchens were, how cold their stone-flagged floors, how wet the walls. Those who were able to retain servants were forced by rationing to take control of the household food supplies, and in some instances were glad of the excuse to do so. Women with more manageable homes found that there were compensations—indeed, that there was a great deal of sheer pleasure—in being without servants; as, for instance, in being able to knit, sew or play cards on Sunday without incurring the black looks of elderly housemaids.

After the peace treaties were signed it became obvious that young women were not going to return to domestic service if they could help it. Many of them had gone straight from school into arms factories, and knew nothing of household work.

[1] *When I Was a Child.*

It also became obvious that young women would have no compunction about taking 'men's jobs' if they could get them, and that they were full of a tiresome new spirit of independence, a mood of 'I'm as good as you are.' The war alone was not to blame for this; it was part of the continuing struggle for women's emancipation. In 1918 the franchise was thrown open to women over thirty, but the mass of women servants remained without a vote until 1928, when the age limit was lowered to twenty-one.

It also became apparent that young women were willing to accept the supposed indignity of the 'dole' rather than strengthen their characters by doing domestic chores for fourteen or sixteen hours a day in someone else's home. Mistresses who regarded the 'dole' as a subsidy to slackers were to grow intensely angry with the government for not drafting unemployed girls into their kitchens.

At first, there was a campaign to persuade demobilised, out-of-work soldiers to go into domestic service. After all, they were steadier than girls and they had just undergone intensive training in the arts of scouring, scrubbing, polishing, cleaning lavatories, peeling potatoes, standing still when spoken to, accepting abuse, obeying without question and treating their superiors with an unfailing outward respect. (They had also learned the valuable arts of looking busy when they were not and making a small job last a long time.) In fact, a good many soldiers *did* drift into domestic service. Drift was not necessarily the appropriate word, for as the chaos of demobilisation deepened as many as forty ex-soldiers would answer a single advertisement for domestic help. There had been much talk about 'homes fit for heroes'; here were the homes—other people's homes. A number of batmen accompanied their demobilised masters into private life, but the loyalty which had flourished in a shared danger sometimes failed to survive the transfer into a world of unshared privilege.

The traditional edifice of domestic service did not collapse overnight. Clearly not all independently minded young women could become 'flappers' with easy jobs in offices—offices where husbands could be picked up. With some reluctance, the 'servant class' resigned themselves to service until they could

find something better. War profiteers had no intention of doing
without domestic staffs. They still had urgent need of an
obsequious, subject race behind green baize doors. If they
paid the wages, they could always buy attendance of a
reasonable standard. Servants of the old school avoided such
establishments, attaching themselves to homes where gentility
had not been blown away in the economic wind; they did not
look for a job, they looked for a family. Many of the younger
women preferred to take 'domestic' jobs in institutions or in
hotels and boarding-houses, where the hardness of the work
was offset by companionship, a prospect of tips and even the
chance of finding a mate. During the 'twenties and 'thirties
more and more young women were absorbed in this way and the
wage rates of industry began to set the standard for the ordinary
household.

From the reluctant, untrained residue householders of modest
means had to accept what girls they could find, and to humour
them in their new-found affectations, even to the point of
allowing them to smoke. Some things, of course, could not be
tolerated and failure to wear a cap was one of them; the cap no
longer had to carry those long trailing ribbons at the back, but
a cap of some sort, however useless and vestigial, there had to
be. The new generation of maids did not see why, in a freer,
easier world, they should limit their responses to 'Yes, ma'am'
and 'No, ma'am,' or why the civility of wishing the mistress
good morning should be censured as familiarity (it puzzled
them that these same mistresses who were so keen on form
became positively angry with girls who knocked on the drawing-
room door in the belief that it was ill-bred to enter rooms
without warning—'We only knock on the *bedroom* door,
Elsie!).' To keep 'familiarity' at bay was an all but hopeless
struggle. A drawing in *Punch* in 1923 showed two women discussing the maid who had just brought them tea. The caption
ran: 'She's a perfect treasure, but I do wish she wouldn't call
me "Old Thing." '

By 1923 mistresses were complaining so loudly about the
quality of 'servant material' that the Government set up a
public enquiry, under the Minister of Labour, into the
problems of domestic service. A great deal of ingenuous, and

disingenuous, nonsense was offered in evidence, and the popular press reported the proceedings with such levity that *The Times* began to wonder whether it had not been a mistake to hold the enquiry. The whole purpose of domestic service had become obscured, complained *The Times*. It existed 'simply to set those to whom it is rendered free to do work for which they are better fitted than making beds or sweeping floors.' Just as a general in the army was entitled to employ inferiors to do the chores, so were archbishops, bankers and even labour leaders. *The Times* chose not to dwell on those thousands who, by employing servants, were rendered free to do other work, and did none.

Much was heard at the enquiry about the slights to which servants were still subject. If, said one witness, there were two sisters, one working in the City and the other in service, young men would call the one 'Miss Brown' and the other 'Mary,' taking off their hats to Miss Brown but not to her sister. Lady Cunliffe, president of the Girls' Friendly Society, thought that the status of maids could be raised by more formal use of their surnames. As it was, even tradesmen and errand boys addressed them by their Christian names. The chairman said he was filled with astonishment to hear from Lady Cunliffe that persons still kept up the old-fashioned custom of omitting the prefix 'Miss' when addressing a letter to a servant.

Miss Jessie Stephen, general secretary of the Domestic and Hotel Workers Union, insisted that one half-day per week and every other Sunday off were not enough; maids should have two hours free every day. She herself had been lucky to get one hour in a sixteen-hour day. There was too much enquiry into where maids went on their afternoons off. Evening dinners, in her view, were a fetish and should be abolished unless more than one servant was kept. She made a far-sighted proposal when she suggested that each municipality should have a corps of 'mothers' helps,' to be paid according to the means of the families involved. Miss Stephen also urged the abolition of the living-in system. She talked a good deal more sense than many of the witnesses, among whom were a woman who wished universities to 'recognise' domestic service and a Member of

Parliament who hoped to raise the status of service by awarding a Gold Cross Order.

The voice of old-fashioned prejudice was heard in a woman witness who said: 'I am a Britisher, but as a middle-class woman I am bled from all sources. I have no sympathy with the girls who are out of work. They have too much help given to them.' If they were close to starvation, she was 'not particularly sorry.'

The trade union view was that it was wrong to coerce girls into service so long as there was a chance of revival in their own trade and certainly wrong to coerce them into working a sixteen-hour day. Miss Margaret Bondfield, on behalf of the National Union of General Workers, pointed out what irate mistresses always overlooked, that by no means all girls drawing the 'dole' were suitable for resettlement as domestic workers. 'Munitions work,' she said, 'develops a grip which is fatal to china.' This, however, was a trivial handicap compared with some of those under which the female unemployed laboured. If the Ministry of Labour had bowed to the housewives' storm, withdrawn the 'dole' from all who refused to become housemaids, and drafted into middle-class kitchens all the coarse-tongued, unruly slatterns on their books those same housewives would have rocked the welkin with their protests.

A Ministry of Labour official pointed out that as private domestic servants were not covered by national unemployment insurance, they were not entitled to the 'dole,' but servants in hotels and boarding-houses were. If a girl had a background of domestic service, and had been drawing benefit, the labour exchanges had some authority over her and could stop her money if she refused to take work in a hotel or boarding-house.

There were, at this stage, domestic training centres in London and Leeds run by the Central Committee for Women's Employment, with Ministry of Labour support. The superintendent of these told the enquiry that girls came for training as servants only as a last desperate resort. He thought that 95 per cent were unemployable in domestic work without training and that 60 per cent turned out successfully.

After hearing many other witnesses, including a servant who said she knew of a maid who was made to take her bath in her mistress's bath water, the Committee reported as follows: they urged the inclusion of domestic servants in a contributory scheme of unemployment insurance, or the grant of dowries on marriage, or pensions at fifty-five; a system of domestic training in both elementary, central and secondary schools; and whole-time vocational courses in suitable centres for suitable candidates. The Committee appealed to the public to do all they could to raise the social status of servants and to treat them with less ridicule. They thought that if a girl wished to be addressed as 'Miss' on first entering a household there was no reason why this should not be done. They were quite sure that, in general, employers were too prone to subordinate the legitimate desires and interests of servants to their own convenience. 'Present conditions,' they said, 'which enable inefficiency, neglect of duty and bad service to obtain the same rewards as efficiency and good service are demoralising for the workers and intolerable for the employers.'

Meanwhile, society continued to adapt itself to living without servants. It was not lack of nursemaids that drove the population to birth control, but the lack of nursemaids would have been a more distressing problem had it not been for birth control. Women had already decided to live a fuller life unhampered by domestic ties; men had decided that they wanted their women reasonably uncluttered. So the trend to labour saving and outside servicing went on. Increasingly, laundry was sent out, clothes were bought ready-made, bread was bought ready-baked, more and more foods came out of tins. Thousands of small restaurants sprang up where middle-class women could lunch out, or where friends could be entertained to dinner. In *The Work, Wealth and Happiness of Mankind* (1932) H. G. Wells was eloquent in praise of service flats, which had a system of domestic service conforming better, in his view, with modern conceptions of human dignity. A bachelor was assisted in his domestic affairs by persons whom 'he may neither rail against nor threaten nor burden with unexpected and uncovenanted tasks.' They would keep his rooms spick and span for him, a maid would wake him and bring him tea and a valet would carry away his disordered clothes. A hundred years earlier he 'would have been their patriarchal

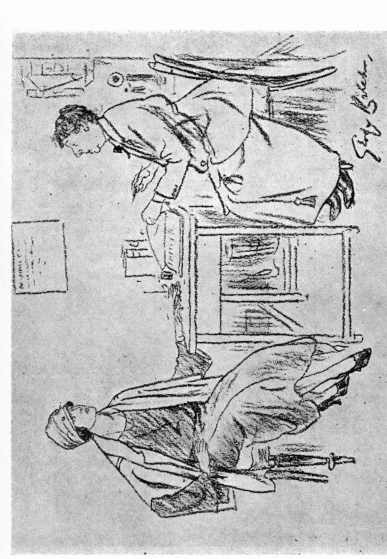

Lady. "THEN AM I TO UNDERSTAND THAT NO NURSE WILL TURN OUT HER OWN NURSERY?"

Registry Office Clerk. "CERTAINLY NOT, MADAM." *Lady.* "AND THAT NO HOUSEMAID WILL TURN OUT A NURSERY?"

Clerk. "CERTAINLY NOT, MADAM. AN UNDER-HOUSEMAID MIGHT, BUT NO SINGLE HOUSEMAID."

Lady. "THEN I SUPPOSE I MUST TURN IT OUT MYSELF?" *Clerk (much shocked).* "I AM AFRAID, MADAM, THAT WE COULD NOT RECOMMEND ANY SERVANT TO A HOUSE WHERE THE MISTRESS SO DEMEANED HERSELF."

tyrant and they (and he) would have suffered all the limitations
and inconveniences of their being fixed upon his back.'

In private service, maids began to expect the use of a gramo-
phone or 'the wireless.' The habit of working to background
music had already arrived. More and more, servants' rooms
were fixed up with bright cretonnes, proper wardrobes, soft-
seated chairs. To save drudgery, family silver was locked away
in cupboards and polished only for special occasions. Deal
tables which cooks had been expected to scrub daily were
moved out to the toolshed. The lure 'no basement' appeared
in the advertisements for help.

In outer suburbia, where hundreds of thousands of bungalows and small houses were going up, builders incorporated
'service hatches' between kitchen and dining-room—just in case
the householder was fortunate enough to find a maid. They
continued to do so long after it was obvious that no maid could
be found. A distinguished architect has described the survival
of the service hatch as a notable example of snobbishness. 'It is
an arrangement that overlooks the fact that everyone knows
there are no maids in the kitchen, and that men have at last
been allowed into the kitchen to do the washing-up.'[1] Even
today estate agents advertise tiny bedrooms in bungalows as
'maids' bedrooms.'

In homes where evening dinner was still kept up, a new
system began to be worked: maids would work from eight till
two, then return from five till eight. This left the mistress with
the fatigue of opening her door to afternoon callers, but the
alternative was to have no maid at all. For the servant, it was
still a long day, but at least there was a three-hour break when
the shops and cinemas were open. More and more maids lived
out; they were 'dailies' now. Victorian mistresses said it could
never work, but it did. It had to.

The classifications of servant were being continually modi-
fied and extended. There were more and more 'working housekeepers,' that is, middle-aged women who were employed not
only by professional men but by professional women, and who,
with the aid of labour-saving appliances, tackled nearly all the
tasks that the old-time housekeeper would have delegated to

[1] Eric Lyons, reported in *Daily Telegraph*, September 12, 1961.

others. There was a growing legion of 'cook-generals'; there
were 'mothers' helps,' who were neither housemaids nor nursemaids but a combination of the two; there were 'chauffeuses'
and 'chauffeuse-companions'; and there was a large army of
working-class wives who did not regard themselves as servants
or charwomen but who came in to 'oblige.' There were also
au pair girls from Europe, the heirs of a system under which
families of equal social status used to exchange daughters,
primarily for cultural reasons; unfortunately, the system was
already being abused (Chapter 21). The 'domestic' advertisement columns of *The Times* were a happy field for students of
delicate social and occupational distinctions. Usually the sub-
divisions were as follows: Governesses, Companions, Matrons
and Lady Nurses; *Au Pair;* Helps and Nurses; Ladies' Maids
and Maids; Lady Housekeepers, Housekeepers and Cooks;
Parlourmaids and House Parlourmaids; House, Kitchen and
Scullery Maids; Between Maids, Generals and Laundry Maids;
Married Couples; and Menservants. The section headed
'Chauffeurs' followed the domestic columns but was ruled off
by a double line.

The distinction between parlourmaids and house parlourmaids puzzled foreigners, and not only foreigners. In practice,
parlourmaids confined their labours to the drawing-room and
similar rooms, and gave occasional help in the bedrooms; house
parlourmaids were willing to do all that and serve at meals too,
and even to help in the kitchen, which the parlourmaid would
in no circumstances agree to do. The between maid, or 'tweeny,'
was a general dogsbody whose function was defined by the
Admirable Crichton thus: 'It is she, my lady, who conveys the
dishes from one end of the kitchen table, where they are placed
by the cook, to the other end, where they enter into the charge of
Thomas and John.' To the tweeny also fell many of the nursery
chores despised by the other servants. She was at everyone's
beck and her status was almost negligible. In Jessica Mitford's
Hons and Rebels is a sad tale of how the authoress's pen-friend
from a dingy part of London is found a post as tweeny in Lord
Redesdale's house—a great privilege, as she appreciates—but
leaves in tears after the briefest of stays.

One result of Lloyd George's National Insurance Bill was

that mistresses became more willing to employ elderly servants, knowing that the State would contribute towards their maintenance in old age and sickness; but still there was a tendency to pay servants less money as they grew older. At the other extreme, mistresses no longer were offered the services of those little thirteen-year-old girls tricked out in caps and aprons. It might be necessary to make do with the services of 'simple' girls, or girls with physical handicaps; these seem, as often as not, to have succeeded in obtaining the normal wages. By 1930 the wages in the leading domestic posts were roughly as follows: cook, £54 to £63; cook-general, £45 to £52; general, £40 to £52; working housekeeper, £45 to £52; housemaid, £40 to £50; nurse, £50 to £68; parlourmaid, £45 to £52; others, £40 to £50.[1]

In the depression of the early 'thirties the number of State-aided training centres for domestic servants was increased. By 1934 there were twenty-four of them, mostly in distressed areas, each attended by up to forty day pupils, aged about fifteen, on courses lasting thirteen weeks; there were also six residential centres where girls underwent a more intensive course of eight weeks. In 1937 a centre was opened to train Welsh lads as houseboys and kitchen assistants, work for which they were said to have a natural aptitude and which was rewarded by a wage of 10s. to 15s. a week. There was also a State-aided Roman Catholic training centre which helped to staff the servants' hall at Arundel Castle, the Archbishop's Palace at Westminster and Beaumont College. In their first fifteen years the various centres trained and placed about 67,000 girls; and, for twenty girls placed, two hundred mistresses were disappointed. To keep the figures in proportion, it must be remembered that the number of unemployed women varied between 300,000 and 400,000. The training centres drew in only a trickle of these and the least hint of a trade revival caused a run-down in the number of applicants.

London continued to draw nearly all its servants from the country, but the growth of light industries on the city's outskirts served to drain away thousands of potential housemaids,

[1] Sir Herbert Llewellyn Smith: *The New Survey of London Life and Labour* (1930).

and the mistresses in London had a taste of what the mistresses in Lancashire and the Potteries had endured for so long. Many of these new factories were able to offer comforts and amenities which offset such domestic baits as private sitting-rooms and radio sets. By the mid-thirties, in an area covering three-quarters of the County of London, there were only two servants to one hundred people.[1] Yet anyone willing to set up an establishment in the Welsh valleys would have had no difficulty in recruiting an old-fashioned plenitude of staff.

In general, the bigger the establishment, the easier it was to recruit reliable servants. Not for nothing did the advertisements boast 'eight footmen kept' or 'large staff of maids.' Staff tended to seek staff; even a life of bickering was better than a single-handed situation in suburbia. Besides, in the rich man's house there were valued perquisites and comforts. Despite the ravages of war and taxation, not every nobleman had been reduced to leading a life of threadbare austerity. The country's biggest landlord, the Duke of Westminster, had his town mansion, his monstrous mock-Gothic pile of Eaton Hall in Cheshire and other *pieds-à-terre*, besides a floating seat of considerable tonnage. His third Duchess says that Eaton Hall could take in sixty guests, but that Lord Fitzwilliam could put up two more than this at Wentworth Woodhouse.[2] Lord Curzon struggled to maintain four homes—Kedleston, Hackwood, Montacute and his mansion in Carlton House Terrace—and kept a housekeeper and staff of housemaids in each, moving his footmen and downstairs staff when he changed house. He also had the castles of Bodiam and Tattershall in reserve. At Hackwood and in London, says the Marchioness Curzon of Kedleston, the Marquis's footmen wore trousers if there were no more than twelve at dinner, knee breeches if fourteen or more. 'I suppose he felt that a dinner party of twelve was a domestic sort of occasion and anything larger amounted to serious entertaining,' she writes.[3] Notoriously, Lord Curzon insisted on recruiting almost all staff personally. On one occasion at Carlton House

[1] Sir Herbert Llewellyn Smith: *The New Survey of London Life and Labour*.
[2] Loelia, Duchess of Westminster: *Grace and Favour*.
[3] Marchioness Curzon of Kedleston: *Reminiscences*.

Terrace he and the Marchioness held a parade of applicants
for the post of footman; the men were made to walk up and
down in order that their gait might be assessed and their hands
were examined to see whether they were the sort of hands
suited to passing plates at the Curzon table. According to one
of his biographers, Lord Curzon inspected his footmen and
housemaids every morning, carefully checking their uniforms
and finger nails.[1] Cynthia Asquith says she once surprised him
putting soap and towels in her room and that he showed her
menus made out by himself for the Room and the Hall for the
next fortnight.[2] News of Lord Curzon's fussiness gradually got
about and there was no rush of servants to work for him; to the
end, he was vexed by domestic worries. Sir Harold Nicolson
in *Some People* has told the piquant tale of Curzon's hard-
drinking valet 'Arketall' who accompanied his master, with a
footstool, to the Lausanne Conference, disgraced himself
spectacularly at a ball at Ouchy and vanished leaving his
master trouserless. This was not the English valet at his best;
but Lord Curzon apparently had a weak spot for Arketall.

In a world of decaying morals, the servants of the old
school set their faces against irregular behaviour on the part of
their masters. Arnold Bennett, unable to obtain a divorce from
his wife, set up house with Dorothy Cheston Bennett. The birth
of their daughter, in 1926, was a matter of some scandal among
Nannies in the park. A nurse engaged to look after the child
said she could not understand at first why all the other nurses
were looking at her in such a queer way; she thought her petticoat must be coming down. Remarks were passed 'That's the
baby.' An uncle of the nurse came to see Bennett to discuss
whether the house was one in which a respectable nurse could
really be expected to serve. He agreed that she could continue;
but in the main the servant class were decidedly against such
irregular households, no matter how they might commend
themselves to the broadminded.[3]

From time to time the courts were enlivened by actions for
damages in respect of supposed enticement of cooks and housemaids. Enticement was a contravention of the Tenth Com-

[1] Leonard Mosley: *Curzon.*
[2] *Remember and be Glad.*   [3] Reginald Pound: *Arnold Bennett.*

mandment and one of the blackest crimes in the suburban decalogue; but it was not always the easiest offence to prove. For every instance brought to court, there were dozens which merely resulted in ruptured social relations. One bench listened to the grievance of a mistress who knocked on a neighbour's door and was ushered in by her own absentee maid ('You know, Mary, you are engaged to me until the sixteenth?'—'Yes, ma'am'); another heard an allegation that a servant had been kidnapped by car from the house where she worked. To be accused of 'procuring and harbouring' a young woman under a statute of Edward III was an unsettling experience for a householder, but with luck the charge would be reduced to one of harbouring. The usual damages—unless the offence was aggravated by assault, slander or libel—were about £25, of which £4 or so was payable by the guilty maid. At Marylebone County Court in 1930, Judge Woodcock, K.C., laid down the rules for the benefit of householders: 'Every person who employs a servant, who is in the employment of another, is liable to that other if she knows of that employment and she is also liable, though previously ignorant of such other employment, if, after notice of it, she continues to employ that servant.'

A grievance which resulted in a perennial flow of letters to *The Times* between the wars was the 15s. tax on all menservants performing duties of a 'personal, domestic or menial nature.' In 1930 the Earl of Denbigh joined the critics, condemning as evil in principle a levy imposed on persons willing to offer employment to others. *The Times* in a leading article described the tax as 'a foolish and illogical anachronism,' originally intended to limit the numbers of 'house stewards, masters of the horse, grooms of the chambers, clerks to the kitchen, confectioners, *valets de chambre*, park keepers and postillions,' not to punish the householder who gave a workless man a job in his garden. The Earl of Denbigh was encouraged to ventilate his protests in the House of Lords, but he received no satisfaction from the Paymaster-General, Lord Arnold. The tax, said Lord Arnold, could not be regarded as a disincentive to employment, since the yield from it was increasing every year (it brought in more than £140,000). Most menservants, he said, were employed by persons paying super-tax with an average net income of £60 a week. He thought the tax had 'a modest usefulness' to local authorities, whose funds it helped to implement. But three years later *The Times* was still lamenting that the tax had 'a chilling effect on generous impulses.' It quoted Hazlitt as saying: 'Footmen are no part of Christianity; but they are a very necessary appendage to our happy Constitution in Church and State.' What would not literature have lost, asked *The Times*, if Don Quixote could not have afforded to encourage Sancho Panza or if Falstaff had been asked to pay a tax for his page? In 1937 the Chancellor relented and the tax was abolished.

A more endearing feature of *The Times* was its running headline 'Faithful Service.' Under this, it regularly drew attention to announcements on its front page of the deaths of servants who had remained with their employers for very long periods. In February 1939 it reported the death at Grasmere, after eighty years' service with one family, of Miss Elizabeth Hind. Her employer, Miss Roberts, was the grand-daughter of her first employer. She was born in the John Peel village of Caldbeck and was seven years old when the huntsman died. Occasionally an old servant would qualify for an affectionately reminiscent article in *The Times* by an employer. There was one that same year about 'Our Zee,' who 'gave up her share of butter and sugar during the war that we should be properly fed' and who was 'as incapable of forgetting what she believes to be her place as she is of occupying more than the front two inches of any chair in presence of her so-called superiors.'

In the late 'thirties the importation of servant girls from the dictator states created a good deal of controversy. To accept refugees from political tyranny was unexceptionable, but not all German maids were refugees. In 1938 a Member of Parliament alleged, to cries of 'Oh!' that Germany was sending over propagandists in the guise of housekeepers and companions; he was told that the Minister of Labour, who granted labour permits, knew what he was doing. In some quarters fears were expressed that Hitler was sending over, not servant propagandists, but servant spies. A good many of the German maids admitted at this period were destined to be interned in the Isle of Man during the invasion scare of 1940.

Sometimes householders wondered how the Russians had solved the problem of domestic service. Were not the Bolsheviks notoriously against lackeys and slaves? Did every man clean his own shoes and every woman scrub her own floor? Apparently not. In 1938 there were reports that ways had been found of circumventing the nominal ban on servants in Russia. A Soviet woman carrying a suitable load of social or cultural duties could hire up to three servants if she wished, and no one could denounce her for *bourgeois* tendencies. This applied notably to wives of presidents of village soviets, and wives of army officers or of factory owners. As *The Times* said, even a labour leader had the right to employ others to do his drudgery.

XXI

HOME HELPS—AND FOREIGN

IN the Second World War the Government was notoriously
slow to feed women into the war machine, but in due
time nursemaids turned their talents to poisoning rats and
maids of all work rotated the handwheels of anti-aircraft pre-
dictors. The widespread withdrawal of domestic labour, far
more sweeping than in 1914–18, caused much hardship to the
old and infirm, and to mothers of big families. In the spring of
1944 Mr Ernest Bevin, Minister of Labour, appointed Miss
Violet Markham and Miss (later Dame) Florence Hancock to
consider what measures, if any, were needed to organise domestic
service after the war. Should the Government take steps to aug-
ment the supply of workers? If so, should it fix wages and hours?
Should there be a national corporation to regulate, train and
place domestic workers? Should there be a uniformed service?

Miss Markham and Miss Hancock were not concerned to
stimulate a supply of obsequious labour for idle, wealthy
women but to provide trained help for those who had real need
of it. In their report they said: 'Unlike many dull and monotonous processes in industry, domestic work is a skilled craft.'
They pointed out that even the Early Church found it unprofitable for the Apostles to serve tables and that other arrangements
had to be made to carry on daily ministrations. If the home
was not to be threatened, some similar adjustments were
necessary in our complex society. 'Is the home with its many
and varied traditions, its individuality and the flame of ancient
sanctities still alight beneath the surface of a mechanised age,
to give place to the drab uniformity of the apartment house or
the residential hotel?'

Then, on a less rhetorical note, the authors of the report got down to their recommendations. The chief of these was that a national corporation should be set up to supply and train competent domestic workers, and to do everything possible to raise the status of this occupation. The proposal found favour and the year 1946 saw the inauguration of the Government-sponsored National Institute of Houseworkers, 'a company limited by guarantee and not having a share capital.' It undertook to run training centres, to hold examinations and to award diplomas. Henceforth, said the press, there were to be no more servants in Britain, only house workers.

Although it has done much valuable work, the National Institute of Houseworkers is by no means a household name. In its early years it suffered from the effects of cold economic winds, several of its training centres being closed down. Today it has centres at Brentford and Swansea, and a third is operated at Bridge of Allan by the Scottish Association for Homecraft Training. There are eight-months courses for juvenile students, between fifteen and seventeen years of age, followed by up to a year's pre-diploma service in a household; six-months courses for adult students, over seventeen; thirteen-weeks courses for working housekeeper students, over twenty-five; and courses of varying lengths for home helps. Miss Hannah More would note with regret that the students are taught social studies and other liberal subjects. She might also be taken aback to learn that the training fees are from £220 to £250; mostly, these are defrayed by local authorities. The fees are high because the courses are residential.

There is a big demand for the Institute's diploma-holders as resident servants, though many of them prefer to take posts in institutions. In private service, qualified house workers may wear the Institute's uniform—turquoise edged with beige—along with the Institute's badge. The Markham–Hancock Report said there was no reason why Service ribbons should not be worn with this uniform.

In certain parts of the country, the Institute also runs a daily house workers' service, which in 1960–61 was supplying 300,000-odd hours of service to more than a thousand households. The worker is paid a guaranteed weekly wage by the Institute and goes to different households on an hourly basis.

Miss Markham and Miss Hancock made another proposal which fell on fertile ground. It was that all local authorities should be compelled to organise a home helps service for the benefit of the old, the sick and the pregnant (a number of authorities already ran such schemes). When the National Health Service was launched in 1948 there were 11,000 full-time and part-time home helps; by 1960 some 50,000 women were helping in 300,000 homes. In 1961 the president of the Institute of Home Help Organisers expressed the hope that these women would not be dubbed 'Mrs Mopps.' She said: 'I do not for a moment say that a "Mrs Mopp" is not a person of quality, but a home help is so very different. The home help is nearly a miracle worker.'[1]

The years of full employment which followed the angry weaning of the welfare state did nothing to encourage girls to be house workers. Artisan families which in less prosperous times might have put their daughters into service now stuffed their subsidised homes with hire-purchased luxuries, to the loudly expressed envy of the newly penurious middle class who were unable to employ the daughters of artisans even if any had presented themselves. In 1931 nearly 5 per cent of private households in Britain had full-time resident servants; by 1951 the proportion was 1 per cent. There had been a day, before income tax, when a householder with £1500 a year could maintain, feed and pay wages to a housemaid on one-fiftieth of his income. Now, a resident housemaid would account for more like one-fifth of his spendable income. Only by sacrificing car and holidays could he afford the luxury of personal service; he preferred to settle for a daily help one morning a week and a baby-sitter (the new nursemaid-substitute supposedly devised in California) one evening a week.

The more flourishing members of the middle class, notably in the expense account range, began once more to import their maids from Europe. Homing warriors and occupation troops all testified that girls from the defeated countries were vastly more hard-working, accomplished and respectful than the

[1] Mrs R. E. Wales, reported in *Daily Telegraph*, September 21, 1961.

Rewards of Service

native product, and those who did fulfil these expectations often paid the penalty of their qualities. Today labour permits for European house workers are granted at the rate of about 20,000 a year. Mostly the girls come from Germany, Italy, Switzerland, Austria and France.

The '*au pair*' traffic started up again, and any pretence of pairing was soon abandoned. French newspapers ran headlines like 'In Britain 2000 French Girls Live Like Slaves' and the Swedish press cried 'Swedish Girls Exploited—Protests Against Low Wages In England.' Even the British press freely censured the way British families abused *au pair* girls; in the excitement it was sometimes forgotten that British girls on the Continent were also employed, on occasion, as cut-price drudges.

An *au pair* girl was supposed to be treated as a member of the family, to accompany them on their social calls, to be given every opportunity to learn the language, and to receive pocket money of between 30s. and £2 in return for 'light work.' There were tales of girls forced to do housework or act as nursemaids for twelve hours a day, and to wait at table, or to eat their meals in cafés; there were tales of girls drifting home in a state of dudgeon and, sometimes, in a state of pregnancy; there were also tales of girls who considered themselves above housework of any kind and who arrived with trunks of evening clothes. The *au pair* traffic has been swollen by irresponsible agents who leave it to welfare bodies to smooth out any troubles that arise. As these lines are written efforts are being made to control or re-shape the system. Perhaps one day, among the nervous girls who stand with their suitcases on Victoria Station waiting for testy householders to claim them, will be someone capable of writing the adventures of an *au pair* girl as racily and ruthlessly as Monica Dickens described her experiences as a cook in *One Pair of Hands*.

In America, the servant shortage in the 1920s had reached the point where the wives of $10,000-a-year men were having to pick up their own nightdresses from the floor. The very rich could still import their English butlers, and the richest of all had Russian princes as chauffeurs; but in the middle income ranges the shortage of help had never been more humiliating. At the registry interview, the tables were turned; the mistress sat politely in the cubicle and the maid asked her the questions. 'How many have you in the family?' 'Are there likely to be any more?' (with a glance at the mistress's contour). 'Do you live in a lively place?' 'How far are the nearest movies?' 'Have you any pets?' 'Is there a car for the use of the maids?' 'Is there a private bath?' 'Do you send the laundry out?' Like their employers, the maids were eager to go to Newport in the summer, to Palm Beach in the winter, and would-be employers whose dates did not fit in with their plans were rejected out of hand. If the mistress's assurances were not satisfactory, the maid would nonchalantly say that she was not interested. If they seemed satisfactory, she would ask for $75 a month (butlers were now receiving $100 and upwards). Maids who found that their situations did not live up to their expectations sometimes misbehaved flagrantly in order to be sacked summarily with the balance of the month's wages and the fare home.

As in Britain, the depression signally failed to coerce women or men into domestic service. The State was driven to create jobs to preserve the self-respect of the workless, but it could not persuade them to become cooks and handymen. Sons and daughters of families on relief also shied at the notion of going out to do housework; in college towns, however, there were always students willing to do house chores in return for

room and board. Syracuse University drew up a rough code
for students' guidance. It thought twenty-eight hours of work
a week, preferably confined to four hours in any one day, to
be reasonable; and, if desired, the student should stay in
three evenings a week, without work, to give his employer
freedom. He should not be expected to do the family laundry
or heavy cleaning, or be allowed to entertain callers after
eleven o'clock.

The women's magazines were full of articles with titles like
'Servants Are People Too' and 'Put Yourself In Her Place.' In
many cities housewives pledged themselves to observe codes of
hours and wages; a nine-hour day with overtime here, a sixty-
hour week there, a fifty-four-hour week somewhere else. In
desperation, housewives began to employ unmarried mothers
and mental patients. Wide circulation was given to a poem by
Cecily R. Hallack, called *The Divine Office Of The Kitchen*
(1927) which began:

> Lord of the pots and pipkins, since I have no time to be
> A saint by doing lovely things and vigilling with Thee,
> By watching in the twilight dawn, and storming Heaven's
>   gates,
> Make me a saint by getting meals and washing up the
>   plates.

This poem was much admired by John D. Rockefeller, who
thought its sentiments irreproachable. Mistresses wondered
whether they should leave a copy of it lying about where the
hired girl might see it. But somehow the poem failed to light a
torch in the kitchen. The women with Martha hands just did
not have Mary minds.

After the Second World War, American women made wry
little jokes like 'Guess what? I've got a new maid. I only do
the rough work.' The New York Department of Labour
checked on the maids who had found other employment in the
war and found that only one in seventy-three was willing to go
back into service. At this time, servants did not qualify for
industrial compensation in many states; there was limited
unemployment coverage in New York; and there was no old
age or survivors' insurance anywhere. By 1951, however,

domestic workers—even the proud Nannies in Central Park—
had their Social Security cards.

Which brings us to today, when the highest of luxuries—
transcending limousines, electric barbecue wagons and fall-out
shelters—is to have efficient, willing, resident servants; whether
shipped by a Mayfair agency ('Situations in Fabulous
California'), filched from the Cunard Line or brought in, raw,
from the Virgin Islands. The housewife whose husband cannot
afford $200 to $300 a month for a resident help must fawn on
her daily woman, drive her to and from her home, ply her
with cigarettes, make her appetising meals and lend her a fur
coat or a piece of jewellery from time to time.

In all of which, Daniel Defoe might find it difficult to trace
any surviving remnant of the Great Law of Subordination.

NO SHIPS, SO SERVANTS CAN'T COME

A shipping line's decision to cut out passenger ship
calls at the lonely South Atlantic island of St. Helena,
is causing a servant problem in some of Britain's statelier
homes.

For several years the islanders have been coming in scores to
work as maids, cooks, gardeners and chauffeurs at big private
houses.

But when the Union-Castle Line ships cease to call at St.
Helena next year there will be no means of coming to Britain.
Unless something drastic is done soon the islanders will be just
as captive as Napoleon was.

Combing the remote outposts
A 1961 report, *Evening Standard*

INDEX